LAND, SEA AND AIR

Dear Ron
with best wishes
Harry Lempton
25
11
09

Land, Sea and Air

by

Harry Simpson

The Memoir Club

© Harry Simpson 2009

First published in 2009 by
The Memoir Club
Arya House
Langley Park
Durham
DH7 9XE
0191 373 5660

British Library Cataloguing in
Publication Data.
A catalogue record for this book
is available from the
British Library

ISBN: 978-1-84104-196-4

Typeset by TW Typesetting, Plymouth, Devon
Printed by Good News Press, Ongar, Essex CM5 9RX

THE MEMOIR CLUB

invite you to celebrate the publication of

Land, Sea and Air

by

Harry Simpson

on

Wednesday 25th November 2009

at

Exhibition Room, Petersfield Library, 27 The Square, Petersfield, GU32 3HH

from

5.00 p.m. – 6.30 p.m.

RSVP by 16 November 2009 to The Memoir Club, Dartmoor Suite, The Courtyard, Arya House, Langley Park, Durham DH7 9XE   Tel: 0191 3735660   Fax:0191 3739652   Email: memoirclub@email.msn.com

SPERO MELIORA

Dedication

To my wonderful daughters Dianne Gayle whose book *Herbs, Trees & Traditions of Cephalonia* inspired my thoughts, and Julie Jackson with her own daughter, fluent in English and Greek, Rhea now a new teenager training at French School near Athens.

Also to my first wife Lilian Jackson, mentioned in the book *Planter's Bungalow* by P. & W. Jenkins, concerning the Malay peninsula, who much travelled the planet with me. She has throngs of personal basis in my thoughts, and with the family, and we always think of our son Roger.

To Alfred Fleming of Portsmouth who whilst with me in the Royal Air Force at the beginning of World War Two introduced me to his young wife and baby son before he went missing. Also to William Crowe, a Scottish friend in the Royal Air Force who officiated at my wedding in 1943 and afterwards did not return, together with other Royal Air Force personnel who died serving our Queen's country.

To Irving F. Kanner MD, a fine friend in Iceland, who provided food for thought whilst serving in the United States Army Air Force with his infectious hospitality of fifty or more types of whisky, who developed early computer medicine afterwards for the United States of America for a period before departure.

Thanks to John B. Day, a true English gentlemen who kindly provided my Foreword, a devoted friend after school of my son Roger, and loyal friend of mine to this day.

Contents

List of Illustrations

Introduction

I was at the present time perhaps thinking of retirement in my own personal extension of 'Pythagoras', a house belonging to my younger daughter's husband, a Greek Tutor of Mathematics. Although I was introducing myself to my new computer, telephone and facsimile, I had no internet which I required for UK, Europe and other communications, to match my house facility in England, in order to execute the work I was actively engaged in, despite my possible thoughts on retirement.

I have great pleasure in writing my experiences recollected over the nine years of putting together my manuscript, taking so long owing to logging off occasionally for two serious accidents and trying to organise proper essential truthful details of the Banks of UK who were not acting, in my opinion, as they should.

Life has been so interesting to me, and still is, so I trust you will enjoy the experiences recorded. I feel the events should make a possible film. My friend Earl St John of Paramount, if alive today, would explain the need for more people to know these features on film, hopefully to enrich their experiences in living.

Whether it be in business, or on Land, Sea and Air, using the 'Slender Arm of a Restless Wind' of the author helps the programme of my story.

I acknowledge the encouragement of Lynn Davidson at The Memoir Club and Sara Allen, who typed my original manuscript.

I say a generous thank you to all.

Foreword

I first met the author through his son Roger in 1967.

Roger and I were both re-sitting our 'A' Level exams as seventeen-year-olds at a 'crammer' in Surrey that we commonly referred to as Godalming University. He was an utterly charming and charismatic character and we became good friends. Therefore it wasn't long before I had the good fortune to meet the family – and what a group they were!

Harry and his family lived in a substantial home outside Petersfield in Hampshire which was presided over by his beautiful wife Lilian and their two equally lovely daughters. Parties were the order of the day and the house was full of laughter and fun. I had invited myself to 'stay' for nearly two years and virtually became a member of the family. They were halcyon times indeed.

Roger and I shared everything: flats in London, holidays, parties and even girlfriends! We were indeed best mates.

Then one evening in September 1974 everything changed. Roger was killed in a car accident. He had been helping his father build up their highly successful abrasive grinding disc and cutting wheel manufacturing business at the time of his death. We worked and played hard.

Harry had always been a tough and uncompromising business man and he now single handedly set about growing further his abrasive manufacturing company – for a while challenging the giants of that particular industry.

Always one for fun, he still managed to laugh (often at himself) and has led a truly remarkable and fascinating life. From his slightly roguish RAF war days, right up to the present time, he has packed more into a year of his life than most achieve in a lifetime.

Having lost my own father when I was fifteen, Harry taught me so much about life in general and I will always be grateful to him for the opportunities he has given me.

I wish him success with this book – it should make an interesting and amusing read.

John B. Day

CHAPTER 1

Early days

I WAS BORN 16 DECEMBER 1914, the day German airships belligerently invaded the quiet tranquil blue skies of England during World War One. Little did I realise that my life was so soon to include a part in World War Two, and from a small infant, life would always be so interesting throughout: the spirit, the nature of our beautiful planet and the far stars of destiny.

Within my first recollections I can only think of the wonderful way my mother used to thread linen to make clothes for all three of us children, and dress me for the heat of the summer in cotton to be cool and free.

Our school path was over the nearby railway bridge, then down a hill to the horse bridge by the little river Cole in the valley. There was a large lake on the other side feeding a stream into my part of the river, which to this day holds enthralling episodes of the difficulty of taking a minnow on a bent pin, of swinging across on a willow branch to explore my interest in the opposite bank, falling off and running away soaking wet! The path continued through a large wheatfield embraced against the warm breeze until we arrived at school where always our teacher was waiting to welcome us, with enthusiasm for the day's work ahead.

One day on the way to school I saved my brother's life. My younger brother Jim was walking at my side, until we should play hide and seek amongst the tall stems of the rich golden sway of wheat. Suddenly I notice with fear that my brother was in the path of a steam puffing tractor harvester, taking no action at all. I hell bent rushed and pushed him away from the flaming blades of destruction, so very near.

Apart from this incident, I recall little of my early years except that on one beautiful summer's day with the sun loving our presence, so warm, my teacher called me to stand before all to explain how we should all dress coolly and so concentrate easily on work. During this embarrassment I looked below at my attire, thankful for such a thoughtful mother.

Naturally I graduated to senior school and, given a new pedal cycle to manage the longer distance involved, I enjoyed the new route which started along the lane leading from the house to the same river, about three miles further away from the bridge I previously used to cross. It certainly was a part of the river where the running water felt alive, active, rippling over small rocks and stones then slowing to dark pools under the green weeping willows, with the little birds fleeting to and fro on active missions.

After crossing the river with difficulty each time, as I was watching the fish, this sojourn, always so informative, regularly made me have to hurry to make up the time for I did not want to miss the necessity to stop for a bottle of ginger beer at the little shop before the hard long gradient hill which ended at the school grounds. Off my cycle to leave it at the wicket gate near the large cricket pavilion. From the pavilion one was not allowed to cross the immaculate grass of the rugby football and cricket pitches, so I always took the gravel path at the side, which led to the school to join the official entrance main drive, opposite the headmaster's study with its large window, always looking out with menace, then climbed the many steps through the carved stone entrance, to the tall assembly hall in time for prayers. The school was a majestic building dominated by its square tower.

When I was not at school one of my favourite interests was to collect in the morning the family daily milk, so I could swallow generous quantities whilst returning to the house. Sometimes I would replace the space in the jug, if I thought it was hugely noticeable, by adding water. Mother, I felt, would not notice; however later I found out she knew all the time. There was a cotton serviette, held in place by beads along the embroidered edge. The milk float was a light cart, open at the rear, led by a horse and with a lightly dressed milkman, with a white smock, who allowed you to measure into your jug the quantity of milk required from a gleaming silver 10-gallon canister of warm fresh clean milk that had just been taken from the nice warm cow.

I was the middle of three children, my sister Nancy the eldest, who followed my mother as a very bright pupil completing all senior exams before sixteen years; my younger brother Jim followed my sister academically. My father was an inventor; there was no central heating at the time so he invented a self lighting fire for each room. He was a paper manufacturer's representative and created wireless crystal sets. He liked the open sky and country and dreamt of near the sea. I was not so academically gifted. I was enthralled by countryside expansive possibilities of nature and movement of mechanical things, the horse drawn carriages still roamed, as the motor car was very primitive and expensive present models were yet to come.

Another interest of mine was to explore the river Cole between the two bridges, so I came to know every part of the river, its course and flow in the seasons when and where you could swim, bathe or fish in all its moods when dominated by the weather. Thus muddy boots or shoes and wet clothes were always my problem to explain. Sometimes the winter would be so severe the lake feeding the stream would be frozen and we would skate with wooden skates held to our ordinary boots by leather straps, thus you could also skate on the river but this was precarious because there was little still water to support you and even if it did it was liable to shrink with the river base moving. It was the same in the extreme heat of summer with the possibility of drying out the river bed.

My father at the periods of snow and ice would bring out the family sledge, a long wooden platform with thin steel runners and a swivel front piece to which were attached the guiding ropes.In operation the sledge was very fast and exciting but sometimes it went too fast with one of us ending up with cuts and bruises. The seasons were so varied yet the summer was always broken by our long vacation by the sea in Wales where we would just adjust to the variations of the summer throughout July and August

I found school interesting and informative and gained prizes for coming top of my form. One such prize was *The Black Arrow* by Robert Louis Stevenson in a beautiful black crinkly leather edition with gold edged pages. This prize became a part of my life and filled me with adventure, a sort of spirit that has never left me, although later I was due to lose the book to a friend. I had deep regrets and do so to this day.

An art prize was really a geometric exhibition of my work so I did not become attached to it in the same way as to *The Black Arrow* and to me it was just a passing phase to do better design mainly in hard straight lines and angles.

There are obviously many incidents in school life, but one stands out: the day I broke my leg playing rugby football. It happened on a lovely spring day. I was playing wing position on firm ground when my opposite team player tackled me just as I was catching the ball in flight, moving forward. It was a forceful tackle that dropped me to the ground. I looked at the grass to get up then noticed my left foot was pointing in the opposite direction, I instinctively tried to stand but as I moved the foot swung round. I had no firm feeling, but fell back on the turf. Frankly, at the time I felt little, but soon realised the pain and bodily discomfort were not trivial. Naturally, I was eventually tethered to a stretcher and taken off the field to the library hall within the school. The painful odd thing to me was seeing my foot jumping up and down with my leg still, whilst I was being carried off the field and up the school entrance steps.

I was alone on the library floor with schoolmasters checking my situation and comfort while attaching wooden splints. I was waiting for an ambulance for a long time, just looking at the carved architecture of the high wooden ceiling, but at this time I did not consider the beauty so much. The journey to the hospital was painful with my foot again jumping up and down but to a lesser extent with my senses making the leg much more painful than before. Eventually my foot was set and I waited for my father to come and take me home in his car. My journey to and fro, together with the difficulty of entering and leaving the car, caused my leg to always be twisting, so it was necessary to break it again three times to ensure it was set in the right position for the future.

Eventually matters became more stable with a plaster of Paris mould instead of loose wooden splints, and I retired at home for some long weeks. My foot and leg have never been straight but whilst the join is easy to feel out of place I have not felt any problems at all for quite some time. My rest was pulsated by visits by the headmaster and others resulting in an enforced depression concerning my end of term examination possibilities. I quickly returned to play rugby football again, when well enough.

I have mentioned my father's motor-car. This was an exciting fringe of my school life and my early youth. One day my father notified the family he had purchased a motor vehicle and would bring it home very soon. I waited with excitement for the day to arrive then early one evening there was great activity outside to ensure the motor car could be accommodated in the newly built garage, The entrance from the lane was a rising gradient into the garage without any problem to where I was kneeling at the end of the run. On the way in the motor looked massive. I knelt further down to see the round gleaming golden radiator with thermometer on top zooming towards me, a tremendous unearthly creature with its menacing grill front about to devour me into the caves unknown. This wonderful impression never left me.

Of course the motor-car with its rain hood down or up was a new dimension to all the family, touring around the villages nearby: the lovely areas of Shakespeare country, the cherry blossom of Evesham Vale and the common land with its wild strawberries on the hedgerow banks, all with no strangers around, nature so peaceful and silent with the movement of nature's friends, little and intrepid. Sometimes we were cold, but we also enjoyed the warm elegant air to refresh our bodies after the stuffiness of layers of soft wool rugs in such an open car. Naturally I was in the middle of the rear seat so I valued the presence of natural spirits to help me feel free, cool and warm.

Whilst resting my broken leg, I really started to think of my future and made my mind concentrate. It said to me: you remember the day you were lying in the unkempt end of the garden in the very long grass watching the great steam trains hooting past on their journey to the far away west country, and you looked at the sky to see an aeroplane emerging over the horizon and slowly it passed over you to disappear in a straight line from where it started. I said 'yes' to myself and thought through every detail of my life so far and, without further consideration, I had no doubt that to fly was my destiny. I decided to press my father to ensure I could join the Royal Air Force direct from school, to learn to fly.

Unfortunately my destiny became impossible after school for my father decided 'no' to my wish to join the Royal Air Force, although there was general agreement amongst my tutors and school friends about my singlemindedness. My father explained some time later in response to my repeated request for an answer as to why; his answer was simple, brief and precise, saying that under no circumstances was he prepared to have my broken bones and pieces delivered to the house whilst he was in charge with me under the age of consent. Perhaps my broken leg incident prompted this.

On leaving school, a little depressed, I looked for work but this was in no way easy; in fact there was a very serious depression over the country and no amount of writing produced any result so I decided against all advice to walk round the nearest industrial site and call in by knocking on the doors. I polished my pedal cycle and set off full of hope.

For some peculiar reason my spirit thought so too, My first call was no, my second call no, but my third call was yes, in very polite conversation. I felt it was because they admired my spirit in the dreadful circumstances of depression. I started the next day to earn my pocket-money sized salary; I was attached to the telephone exchange to help in waiting time and to pass messages to and fro. I soon became popular with the staff and had no time to blush with my habitual shyness.

One day I answered the front door to check an enquiry. To my horror there was a mob of furious people demanding action of some sort. It was overwhelming but I had no time for distress and said I would pass their message on, if I could understand what they wanted. In answer to my request, I was bulldosed by a horde of impatient ladies swearing, pushing huge cotton sheets at me and seeking revenge for the bright red stains on their white washing that they had hung out to dry in the gardens of their neighbouring houses. At the time, I was nonplussed at the fury. During the stir and noise a senior member of staff came out to help me; he knew what to do to try and settle the anger.

I was congratulated on my effort; however, it was not an uncommon experience for this sort of rage. I was now on the staff of this modern Bakelite production factory that manufactured coloured moulding powders and sometimes with strong winds and ventilation failures all the bright fast colours of the rainbow descended on the nearby lovely white drying washing. Generous compensation was always paid.

In the short term the factory eventually closed and moved into a new very modern premises built on a large site a few miles away and with no houses in the vicinity. Naturally I was pleased to move away from the congested site and moved to the new location with great hope for the future. The chief manager, Mr F.J. Robinson, in charge of the old factory took me aside to inform me he considered me good raw material for a more responsible position within the new site and stated, 'I will see to it, you will experience all the different sections, and if you have any problems at all come to see me; I will decide what to do.' Thus I felt extra enthusiastic to learn and absorb information for my future and do my utmost to satisfy the trust in me. The chief manager was also the director in chief of the new factory, which to me was a vast purpose built factory containing huge machinery and was already well established, expanding rapidly within the depression so harmful to other parts of industry. I was truly thrilled and excited at the prospect and very grateful. The gentleman concerned became my hero and friend for life.

I quickly came to realise the production was unique, patent guarded, with headquarters in the United States of America and operating round our planet. It took some time and hard interesting work and eventually I was given a life contract with the company; but I had a good time too!

I recommenced my life at Bakelite, as soon as the short term factory was closed.

I cycled to the new purpose built factory each day, fine weather or foul. If my bicycle went unserviceable for any reason I caught the train. The distance was about ten miles – say 35 minutes plus. The railway station was by the nearby railway bridge I used to pass on the way to my first school and four stations east I alighted at a station called Tyseley. I opened a bank account nearby to cash my weekly cheque. It seems strange to say I am still with the same bank today, and while life has changed I have not received any privilege at all from the bank to this day: in fact the opposite.

My employment was first located in a section of the drawing office; it was interesting to be at the point of learning about the chemical plant modifications and future design and to participate as assistant to the technical man in charge of this office. Whilst my time was slightly boring, after such an active life, I did learn patience and understanding. Within a short time my chief, Richard Roberts, and I discussed many interesting topics; one was about ladies working within the company, so I introduced my elder sister Nancy. They eventually got married, a great event for all concerned. Soon afterwards my chief was promoted to be technically in charge of the sales section and given a beautiful new Wolseley automobile, so decided to sell his international Norton motorcycle and sidecar. My father purchased the machine for me. He had previously refused me a small motorcycle such as my friends already possessed. The most attractive was a Sunbeam 250cc but I now possessed a 490cc international racing bike; it was very powerful indeed with a racy looking sidecar. It was suggested the sidecar should be removed to enable me to learn solo riding first. Thus I start to understand this powerful machine with twist grip throttle 0 to 100 m.p.h. in about half an inch; I did master the machine but fell off a few times in the process.

I decided to attach the sidecar to take a lady friend, but I only went a short distance to the nearby river bridge at which point the sidecar went inside the bridge wall and I on the machine went over the river stream, the other side of the same wall. Anyway we extracted ourselves and that was the last time I saw this lady friend. Though not seriously injured, she was elected local beauty queen and objected to my kind of treatment, although we were to remain friends.

As soon as I was eighteen, with my gathered information, I went down to Castle Bromwich airfield about ten miles away to see the Royal Air Force: in fact it was 605 Squadron Auxiliary Royal Air Force with Iraq-type aircraft. I met with an officer who explained to me that it was not a flying school but issued an invitation to join; I was pleased to apply and accepted. I went home and was so pleased and for some reason I was happy to be trying to fly as rank AC2. I did not realise what I was doing really, but was very happy to be in the Royal Air Force. My next visit was to be issued with a uniform: puttees, breeches, black tie and blue shirt with an alterative clip top jacket and heavy boots. Naturally I took all this equipment home. Nobody seemed to be interested but I practised trying to easily wear the uniform as required.

To make the puttees smart was a major problem. The boots needed hours of wearing to avoid blisters and brass buttons plus shoe polish were my major occupation for many hours. Eventually I was ready for parade and enjoyed the precision expected. I met some very interesting other AC2s just joined and was commanded by a regular non commissioned officer of the permanent Royal Air Force, very high calibre indeed.

I never saw an aircraft, however, but my initiation to learn engineering was to make an open ended spanner. The result was a great achievement and when I had accomplished this test came immediate promotion to the next grade. All this took a long time plus a lot of my spare time and made me unhappy for I wished to fly. I arranged through my sergeant to work in the aircraft hangar, when flying took place at the weekends of 605 Auxiliary Squadron. The adjutant was a full time regular officer responsible for training all the activities of the officers and men to the standard expected by the permanent Royal Air Force. The Commanding Officer was Auxiliary but of high standing in society. He was Lord Willoughby de Broke. After the Second World War, I came across his name when I joined a very successful country club which publishes a very good country magazine and arranges venues for members. As I am now over ninety, this activity is run by Lord Willoughby de Broke as chairman (it no doubt concerns the son, however we will see).

Often my task was to lean on the tailplane to ensure the aircraft, a Westland Wapiti, would not turn over when the engine was opened to full throttle. Leaning on the tailplane was at first a frightening experience but eventually you got used to the sudden rushing wind, often cold to freezing, through your hindquarters, not knowing when the typhoon velocity would cease. This experience alternated with running holding the wing tips to ensure the pilot was safe to taxi to his direction of take-off position. After a number of these episodes, I was in contact with the flying officers, training or qualified, and received invitations to fly. My fellow friends on the ground declined or accepted according to the known skill of the pilots in their fine puttees or polished leather boots and breeches with black tie and white shirts.

Hence my first flight was in the rear gunner's open cockpit. I recall it with vivid memories of fright with no security beyond thin wire cable attached to the side of the open floor and we took off with my feet wedged in the small channel each side of the no floor below. I did not realise my pilot was a learner and this was the first time he had carried a passenger but others did and had declined the invitation. It was an amazing first flight. I was in the wind of the engine and propeller called the slipstream, and it was so cold, without flying kit. I felt unsafe as we bumped in the turbulent air with just a thin wire cable holding me down. It did feel completely nervously unsafe for I thought the wire too thin to hold my weight especially with both my feet off the little ledge. Various thoughts quickly passed through my mind, mainly that I was not wearing a parachute but only a harness with the attached wire cable to a toggle at the base of my back. Should you fall through the open floor you would dangle some few feet underneath the base of the aircraft in a non recoverable position.

We eventually landed and I was too nervous to utter a thank you. The pilot was Grant Ferris who later became leader of the House of Lords.

Although I enjoyed several more flights, I was more than anxious to fly myself, although some thoughtful pilots did share some flying details with me. I had a squadron summer camp at Manston, a famous Royal Air Force station in Kent, and further hair-raising flying as a passenger, such as flying low over the sea underneath the height of the long steep beach with people sunbathing above me. Sometime later I decided to take leave from 605 Squadron, because I could see no way to learn to fly except by a flying club or privately, so I departed very happily with my experience and looked forward to becoming a pilot somehow.

All this time with 605 was a major part of my spare time and I had chemistry to study at technical college to help me progress with my occupation, and rugby football with old school boys. I started a cricket team for a disabled friend, Philip, of a well known local family, who asked me for help. The family bought a field near my local railway bridge, cut the grass fine and provided the equipment. The cricket was most successful, but unfortunately the disabled friend in our second year died. Hence the cricket folded and I experienced death for the first time. It was very sad.

From now on my life became very active and demanding, Career wise my days were full of practical training, mainly concerning the manufacture of phenol formaldehyde synthetic resins by day with technical chemistry and engineering at night. Weekends were full of sport in the winter months, playing rugby football for a senior club, Moseley RFC, and organising rugby for the company: i.e. a field to play on, training players, creating fixtures with a very enthusiastic atmosphere. Senior staff at Bakelite Ltd. were so helpful from the managing director to all department heads.

In the summer I took part in a friendly club of motorcycle enthusiasts of my age. We visited very many parts of our country, including swimming and walking together sometimes with lovely young ladies. During this time I met my first real girlfriend. She lived in Stratford-upon-Avon, in the lovely Shakespeare country. One of my first questions to answer concerned horses for she possessed many horses for cross-country and hunting. I replied with apologies for I was not such an experienced rider but was willing to ride with her one day, thinking I could learn very soon the rudiments and so meet any possible challenge in the future. I was called by telephone the following week on the Monday to meet her for a local cross-country walk on a very quiet horse starting from her home. I replied thank you and agreed to meet in accordance.

I did not worry too much and went immediately to my work friend who was a Cavalry Officer in the Territorial Army and put my proposition to him: to ride a horse by Saturday next weekend. It was natural to laugh hard at the idea; however I stated it was very serious for me to accomplish my desire to ride as arranged. We then discussed the practical applications necessary to achieve my goal, in a very serious way, so the following arrangements were made. I was told riding a horse was easy but that I needed the right equipment to start so we agreed I should borrow his uniform without the official identifications where possible, as we were roughly the same size. Then it was necessary to take the spurs off his spare finely polished brown leather riding boots, this operation to be done properly by his Army contact next day. We talked concerning how to ride a horse and I was given instructions to mount from the correct side which you could view in relation to where the stirrups were placed; the way the horse was held so I could take control with the reins when the horse was released. I could feel and tell what the horse wanted to do and whether to have a hard grip or soft grip on my instructions to the horse whether with toes, knees or hands. I received several more tips to iron out the wrinkles to be experienced and I was happy with the acquired knowledge.

Thursday came and all I had tried on were the magnificent smooth breeches, needing adjustment of the laces and shoulder braces; the riding boots without spurs had yet to be returned, thus I was left with one more day to check all things including shirts, hat and more. I was about to despair when the riding boots appeared without spurs. They were perfection and really looked the part but it was obvious the spurs' removal had caused a conspicuous repair. Together we accepted the situation as not quite proper but it was the best we could expect. Now with all my equipment I went home to prepare for my appointed date with a horse tomorrow, full of understanding.

Saturday duly arrived; I decided to wear my normal motor-cycle clothes, flying helmet, waders and long waterproof coat plus goggles, gloves and silk scarf. The riding clothes were packed neatly in a large holdall and strapped to the carrier all set. I enjoyed a beautiful journey to Henley-in-Arden some fifteen miles away through a landscape of rolling hills embraced with streaks of sunshine and fluffy white clouds causing vivid shades of green far away. Then on to Shakespeare's town of Stratford-upon-Avon with its theatre just new from the old beautiful black and white timber building burnt to a wreck by fire, both just by the swift flowing Avon with weeping willows so free and the Grammar School nearby, Shakespeare's place of learning. Again the countryside was at its best but still improving towards noon time and my appointment.

I duly arrived at my destination, leant my motorbike against the stable wall by the changing room next to the harness store and changed. In the mirror my reflection was of a true, about to ride, gentleman; the breeches looked splendid, so professional. My girlfriend came along on her horse. We met as I walked a little to ensure an easy fit to my new attire. The smile and hello seemed to confirm the acceptance of my appearance. I was pleased!

We walked together to the stalls where my horse was tethered. The girl of course was with her horse in hand. I noticed the horse for me waiting at a mounting block; we both went over to see it and a few words were exchanged concerning the beautiful weather, the track we would take and of course the normal good behaviour of my much admired horse. OK and we were all set to go, she to her horse, me to mine.

I looked carefully, thought of my theoretical what to do; I mounted quite safely and settled down to take charge; the horse was released and I was ready with the reins in a medium grip. Nothing happened until my companion mounted and walked away, so I followed and was surprised my horse was so obedient to my gentle commands, both hand and knee. Soon I was moving behind my companion at a walking pace, thoroughly happy and thinking it was not so hard after all.

My companion decided to change the pace to a trot. I was not sure of what to do but did make an effort with my knees and the horse responded to the new pace quickly. This was a great ride. Then I noticed a very small bush ahead and thought the horse would not notice so took no action. All looked well, but as we approached very near the bush the horse put his head down and swerved around it, at the same time throwing me off over his head. I hit the grass easily in a flat position, without thinking, and very soon got to my feet and looked for the horse to mount again but it was gone, gently trotting the way home via the track we had previously negotiated.

I immediately felt embarrassed, just like the early school time when I was told to stand in front of the class for all to view my summer clothes. This time, however, I was in the clothes of a splendid riding gentleman for all to see. I slowly took hold of my sad self and walked back following the horse to the stables and after a good wash changed to my normal clothes to await the return of my companion. She came; we laughed and enjoyed a wonderful picnic of green leaves of lettuce with a good piece of bright cool ham and more; we finished with wild strawberries collected from their nest in the thin grass on the bank of the hedge and opened a carton of thick cream. We later enjoyed a wonderful friendship until I went away to fly.

Later in my life I became very involved in horses both in England and in France as owner of first Arab and then thoroughbred stables, breeding and racing; but I never tried to ride a horse again.

CHAPTER 2

Flying training

A T THIS TIME THE government was in a dull mood watching Hitler and the Nazi regime exploiting the power of Germany and it seemed we did not know what to do. It was obvious to all that the rearmament of Germany was for the fanatical reason of wanting power in Europe after the negative situation after World War 1, 'the war to end all wars'. British armed forces were at an all time low and the small part-time forces were like a splendid gentlemen's club, with young officers enjoying the training situation at weekends. In reality the members were the cream of our future society whether in politics, government, medicine, industry or the armed forces: all well educated and keen.

I went to Hendon airfield to see the Air Show each year performed by the City of London Auxiliary Air Force Squadrons 601 and 602; these were the elite of the service, not to be missed, and were a great inspiration to all interested in flying.

The current situation needed more pilots to fly in addition to the very few Auxiliary Air Force squadrons like 601, 602 and 605 that I had enjoyed for a brief period, hence Class F reserve was later to be introduced by the Royal Air Force. I thought my application would be subject to the usual government delays, but no, I was off to an appointment at Adastral House, the Royal Air Force HQ in London, ten days after my application.

Naturally I informed the senior executive at my workplace and the idea was received with open arms. I also explained that if accepted it would mean taking two months off for flying training. I duly caught the train to London and arrived at Adastral House for my 10 a.m. appointment. I was informed that my interview was in many parts and so I progressed through the day starting with education. You needed to pass each section to get to the next part.

I did wonder about lunch but 12 noon came and there was time for a local sandwich after which I was expected to accomplish a medical in two parts. The first was a physical examination and afterwards I passed to a flying amplitude test combined with a physical. This second part was a most impressive test, involving sitting in a special chair, where one was strapped in and accelerated to all angles and speeds, then suddenly stopped for checking, say, blood pressure, eye reaction or mind reaction. Eventually after an hour or so I thought I was finished but there was one more interview to be told, 'You are accepted.' Off I went to catch my train in a dream journey to tell my family I was now a reservist in the Royal Air Force. My father made no comment but I was happy.

At my last interview in London I was told I would be notified about my flying training very soon. After a week or so I received my posting for flying training in Leicestershire: so near this was no adventure for me; there must be better places to learn flying and so I asked for another date and place. My request was granted and soon I was due to go to west Scotland. Prestwick airfield was new then, adjacent to two top golf links and not far from Robert Burns country. The hotel was first class and the situation to operate from so near, that I was about to enjoy what I had always wanted to do from schooldays, and appreciated the company's help but now also felt more committed to the fortunes of my work on the development of synthetic resins.

Many things were happening. I changed my beloved 490cc International Norton motorcycle after a fall off in a country lane owing to a Bentley open tourer pushing me to a fall in the grass on a tight corner, head over heels. There were four girl occupants laughing, and they did not stop to help. I wished for a similar Bentley with cycle mudguards, a true thoroughbred of a motor-car, one day, to retaliate because I was not amused. I bought a Triumph saloon car, a very good automobile.

I packed up playing for my senior Moseley Rugby Football Club, partly because my projected position was taken over by an England international on transfer. The club fixtures were too demanding in my programme of life. However, I still always travelled to London with company executives to watch international rugby matches and enjoyed the modest night life of dinner and meeting people. On one such occasion I enjoyed a meal with Uffa Fox, an international sailor and sailing boat builder; this kindled a desire to sail a boat sometime.

I was now working on a new research using a copper brewing still which is a vessel heated by steam and cooled by water with a propeller shaft of variable speed to facilitate and effect the process of

chemical reaction concerning the raw material combination formulated. In the main, research in a normal production plant vessel
would be prohibitively expensive and dangerous for the operator and
if the reaction was not controllable the plant could blow up, or at
least would boil the contents to a solid mass and ruin the large vessel
for production requirements.

Thus it needed training oneself to use skill, to stay calm, to
standardise research batches to meet production requirements safely
and to develop improvements or new resin combinations. One such
resin was Bakelite R1373, a new concept of chemical formulation,
and I was the only one to be successful in its exact manufacture: an
enviable situation, I thought.

Synthetic thermosetting (STR) resins (Bakelite) were the invention
of Dr Baekland (Dr B.) who was looking for a resin to use on the
strings of his violin. This remarkable man was a Belgian who
invented the flexible film for cameras which he sold to Eastman
Kodak in the United States. With the money he built a chemical
laboratory to do research: hence the start of plastics, the name
eventually acquired by all synthetic resins i.e. resins that go solid and
will not melt. Non STR resins are those that go solid but will melt
again.

I was always visiting the other main sections of the factory
employing resins in some shape or form and I also continued to adapt
the internal and outward situations of the company's business.

At this time I was to prepare for my initial flying training
programme and was due to leave home the next day by train to
Glasgow and thence to Troon on the west coast. It was a pleasant
journey without excitement. All went to plan, and I checked in and
settled in my room at the Orangefield Hotel which had all facilities
and faced towards the dark green humble grass of the airfield. I met
others on the same flying programme and after dinner we enjoyed a
drink and a chat about the notes provided. In the morning the Chief
Flying Instructor called after breakfast to explain our plan for the next
six weeks, and afterwards we all set off to the airfield to start our
technical classroom training. We enjoyed our stop for lunch at the
hotel and in fact we were to take all our meals there. Naturally we
were disappointed not to fly on the first day but from the second day
it was all go. I was appointed an instructor for my flying tuition and
I gathered you could be sent home if you did not pass all stages to

qualification of Class F pilot of the Royal Air Force in the time allotted. Flying solo was the first hurdle. I was fitted out with a heavy insulated flying suit, and a parachute that seemed to hit you at the back of the knees so making it difficult to walk. The soft flying helmet and goggles I discarded for my own black ones with pink rubber lightweight curved goggles with ear phones, thus I felt elite and better dressed. Photographs were taken, both individual and group.

I somehow was able to photograph the Chief Flying Instructor, David MacIntyre, with the Marquess of Douglas and Clydesdale (later the Duke of Hamilton), both ex-Royal Air Force and the school originators, with Lady Houston, who sponsored them for the organised flight over Mount Everest in the Himalayas for the first time in history, in 1933.

Shortly afterwards I walked out with my instructor and climbed into the rear cockpit of the waiting D H Tiger Moth aircraft which looked beautiful in its bluish red paint. My instructor from the front cockpit gave the thumb-up sign and after my return sign, off we went.

We were flying about one hour. I felt the controls and absorbed the verbal instructions like a duck to water. I enjoyed every moment: the freedom of 3D from the planet, the sunshine, clouds chasing each other away from the mist near the land and the magical thought that I was flying at last with this Tiger Moth as my friend.

We also flew in the afternoons and it was rare that bad weather interfered with our training. The aim was to go solo. One day we were in the air bright and early when suddenly the instructor called me to land. We taxied to the HQ and came to a halt. My instructor seemed to be busy repairing something in his cockpit, then he climbed out waving his aircraft control column and said, 'You take the aircraft; report to me back here – I will be waiting.' This I translated to mean to go solo and execute a circuit, so off I departed, full of confidence. I took off, flew the circuit and prepared to come into land. I had time to admire the lovely summer landscape, so peaceful, but felt it looking at me and saying, 'You are too high to land.' I was in the glide with the engine off and near the perimeter fence. I knew I was too high, so I opened the throttle for another circuit which was accomplished without the landscape talking to me, I taxied over to HQ where my instructor was waiting. I apologised for keeping him waiting and he replied, 'You were very good and made the right decision.'

My solo time was 8 hours but unfortunately some pupils departed for they did not make solo time in 10 hours or more.

The course continued with increased pace, with side slipping during the glide into land: a wonderful method of losing height fast; blind flying on instruments underneath a no-see cockpit hood; cross-country flying to other airfields, landing, reporting and then taking off for home; aerobatics of rolls and loops and more to become a precision pilot with my friend the Tiger Moth.

Whilst all this flying was going on we found plenty of time to enjoy the Scottish countryside and visited to the neighbouring towns or villages. One such time we missed the last bus and walked the fourteen miles home and even walked the Troon golf links along the coast to the town. Sometimes I used to walk Prestwick golf links alone to admire the rolling sea and the sand dunes with pieces of fine grass nesting in the shade of the breeze. At this stage I was not into playing golf, but could imagine it was serious fun in lovely fresh bracing air.

However my ultimate thrill was often to travel to Robert Burns's cottage, Alloway, by the little stream and to meditate over his records of such an amazing full short life. For me at the time Robert Burns was more famous than Shakespeare, for you cannot imagine a country on our planet that does not sing the jolly 'Auld Lang Syne' for celebration annually. All this exploration of Scotland was thrilling to me for it was my first time. I recall now my introduction to the haggis, which tasted very good with a little Drambuie.

The visit to Scotland and the flying course ended with a misty farewell to the friends I had learnt to fly with, and to Robert Burns, my hero, together with the rolling surf and dunes. Sadly I departed and made my journey south to home.

My family welcomed me and wanted to know all my experience, my father too! Next day I was at work on my synthetic resins, where all wanted my story and report on flying, I was never quite the old self again.

In the second year I took leave to complete the flying requirement; the Royal Air Force awarded me their coveted Wings for my uniform. However I was still a civilian and the short leave each year to fly a few hours was not interesting enough for me to improve. The service eventually thought the same so a Voluntary Reserve (VR) was introduced to make airfields more available to fly at will, but still as a civilian, for when you had time off work and the few aircraft were available to fly. I passed out on more complicated ex-operational service aircraft such as the Hawker Hart and the Hind version with water cooled 2×12 cylinder Merlin Rolls-Royce engine. My first solo flight in the Hart was interesting. I took off to practise aerobatics and was bound to adjust for the different feel, so different from my old friend the Tiger Moth.

I was executing a loop and lost speed at the top so my aircraft stalled for a moment; the extended cooling radiator fell back into the cockpit area with a thud and sand poured over me whilst upside down. I choked for a short time and thought. I landed and made my report and was informed it was an aircraft without brakes that had been replaced in the desert near the Gulf and brought home for reserve flying.

On another weekend occasion I was landing from just over the telephone wires at the perimeter of the Castle Bromwich airfield and was landing at 70 m.p.h. when I noticed a Tiger Moth taxiing towards my path. With my heavier aircraft without brakes it was necessary to use the rudder to control the aircraft on the ground and you could not do changes of direction without adequate speed; with speed falling off quite rapidly on settling on to the grass and the aircraft landing with no engine it was not manageable unless you increased speed by the use of the engine to use the rudder effectively in the slipstream.

I therefore watched intently for the light aircraft to change course but it became obvious to me that the light aircraft was not looking for me or anybody else and it did not change course at all. I decide to open the engine throttle to obtain mobility.

At this time I was getting near the opposite boundary and decided to avoid hitting the light aircraft by opening the throttle more to change direction. Then I was going too fast to stop at the perimeter and carried on into the timber yard. To me it was spectacular: after going through the fence the aircraft and I hit neatly stacked timber piles, the propeller flung the timber pieces like a fan and just as I hit the second pile the aircraft tail reared over my head to say 'enough' and left me upside down on my straps. Fortunately I fell to the ground on release of the safety straps and no fire started but the smell of petrol was intense. I was pleased to walk away.

On the Monday after this incident I was asked to transfer to London HQ office and represent the company in my technical field of Bakelite resins but I declined for I was happy with my present situation, so full of energetic activity. The offer returned the next year and I was told: 'Harry, you will not receive improvement in your position unless you change attitude and direction when promotion is offered from the top.'

I left all my activities and departed to work in London, staying in quite a good hotel within walking distance of my office near the Houses of Parliament. I did nothing socially, just worked and thought, 'How do I regain my situation, so active in all my pursuits with friends to call on and one lovely friend who was a young lady who had started work at the plant and we were having fun walking, touring the countryside of Warwickshire to find new places, also my family hide-away places, going to sporting places and participating the reality of competition whether as a player or a spectator?'

After a period of nine months, travelling home at weekends to catch up, I decided to change. The company had just moved to very palatial premises near Buckingham Palace. So after much anguish I moved to the village inn, the Plough at Elstree, to start a new era. It was so different because all things seem to move so fast in the London area. I had to learn how to catch up and make friends because they were busy too.

I commenced to fly at the famous De Havilland factory airfield at Hatfield, leased to the Royal Air Force for us reserve civilians. It was good to meet similar flying people and the Hawker Hind, a beautiful bi-plane, became my friend. The reason I say this is because to fly with precision you have to feel you are part of the aircraft, to get action together with it. I also started not to go home so often for I was getting involved with the film actors and actresses who frequented the inn where I was living. I became a close friend of Earl St John, the chief of Paramount Films, who enjoyed life, living in a wonderful house called 'The Fortunes' with a carved wishing well in the drawing room and a grand piano on an elevated stage. His wife, the lead singer of a top ladies' group, also stayed nearby when she could for they were very busy. His car was a long cream Cadillac tourer with a pink hood and pink upholstery inside, plus a chauffeur dressed to match. I was able just to call in as I pleased. I was introduced to all the famous people in the film business at the time and then suddenly I thought all things were going to change fast.

We were having dinner in 1938 at an exotic Road House nearby when the radio announced that all Royal Air Force reservists must go home and wait for instruction. At this time the Prime Minister, Neville Chamberlain, was in Germany trying to make a deal with Hitler for war seemed evident. I departed and drove home but by the time of my arrival the radio message had been cancelled for the PM returned from Germany waving a piece of paper indicating a truce with Hitler. It was obvious nobody thought the piece of paper worth a dot, but things were nervously normal again though my business activity continued on at an increased pace and I introduced bulk tanker deliveries of liquid resin for the first time for making fibre and wood chipboard. Nevertheless the company staff were safely reserved as a strategic necessity for the war machine except for me and one other Army reservist who had a life contract like me and was committed to serve.

The country knew war was on its way and quietly the Government pushed reluctantly to increase armament production. In 1939 Germany invaded Poland and we declared war on Germany so the society I had newly acquired was left behind with my work and I returned home to wait posting to serve my country in the Royal Air Force.

After the declaration of war all was quiet as we waited for something to happen. There were some minor incidents but I was still at home waiting for my call, so I attended to my friends in the company and met often the girlfriend I mentioned before going to London. I gradually settled down to a brisk life of activity that seemed to want to go on for ever. I changed my car for I was suddenly in the position of needing to carry my girlfriend's mother on all visits no matter what I wanted to do, so I changed to a two-seat sports car. Unfortunately this change was misunderstood so I lost my girlfriend and never met her again.

My chief executive, Mr F.J. Robinson, introduced me to his daughter who was just leaving college. Although she had the desire to know me and was very good looking, I avoided the situation because I felt committed to practical things or sport, particularly with my future as a participant in the current war situation waiting for posting.

The Royal Air Force quickly found out, just as in World War One, that we reservists were not expendable to throw into action without further flying hours and no experience in tactical warfare with planes being very scarce, so they decided to assemble all reservists at secret locations to sort out the problem of selection of what to do for the best with the few aircraft available and the war front quiet.

I was eventually posted to the south coast to a fine hotel without any furniture to live with a hundred fellow selected reservists that had not done any flying, who were just as fed up as me. However, there were three with wings and with four others we soon became good friends for a party. We stayed doing very little official work apart from occasional drill formation initiated by ourselves so as to look tidy walking about the sea front and town. I was in charge of our squad of friends and so we walked around as a tidy eight. Entertainment was the local theatre and a few bars and under the conditions we experienced a little fun. In our eight were twin brothers who came from Yorkshire and seemed very experienced at attracting ladies and who knew the night life in London; another came from Portsmouth, and was just married, the son of the owner of a very high class antique business, parts of whose family were quite highly ranked in the Royal Air Force; the others I had yet to know. We toured the inns nearby and visited frequently the two super smallish hotels and the historical ruins. Nearby was the site of the Battle of Hastings where we faced William the Conqueror in 1066.

One evening we visited a bar in the town where we were always made very welcome and one of the brothers talked to a girl who was with her friend. I was introduced, made conversation and arranged to meet her next morning for coffee, for she had a date with another friend. I was captivated by her beautiful friend Lilian and we clicked immediately and a very strong relationship developed. I was no longer fed up with nothing to do and her family was very kind and generous. A few years later this friend and I were wed.

Suddenly I was posted to flying school and went off by train with just my squad of friends to Redhill airfield for a refresher flying course on Magisters, a small monoplane. Although it seemed a makeshift decision resulting from pressure from us, it was a start to do something useful in the Royal Air Force. We arrived and we were happy and all went well, but it was strange to be doing another initial type of flying course. I had to remember that part of my initial squad were new to flying and three did not survive the challenge. On passing out of Redhill we were posted to a twin-engine training school at South Cernery airfield in the lovely part of England associated with chalk stream fishing in gin-clear water, Cotswold stone coloured houses and Roman roads. The airfield was a permanent station which accommodated a beautiful manicured grass airfield and proper control tower, all so different from the civilian airfields that seemed so private and personal to oneself.

We lived in bell tents on the edge of the airfield and rose in the morning to ablutions in open cold water bowls. I admired one of my friends who stayed in bed longer as he could shave there with an electric battery razor, a present from the United States of America. I thought this was a great idea and tried to buy one but could not find one, and set my mind on course to copy the method as soon as possible. Eventually at my next posting I did find such a razor but could not shave in bed, and after waking I found the practice of electric shaving an easy lazy way of operation, normally so tedious to perform in the bathroom after washing one's face.

The flying was serious. We were in pairs, I with my Portsmouth friend Alfred Fleming, and after brief tuition were flying solo by alternating as pilot and passenger. The aircraft was an Airspeed Oxford, a monoplane with an enclosed cockpit for two side by side developed by the aviation author Nevil Shute from Australia, who was a very serious modern designer and manufacturer of aircraft before the current war. It was very useful for our purpose, with a retractable undercarriage for the wheels, and full instrumentation for night flying. Instead of wearing the thick flying suit to keep out the cold air in the open cockpit, we purchased a black lightweight cotton type overall. The training was intensive and thorough: however we enjoyed time away from the station although the war situation was getting active and serious. The Battle of Britain was not yet in sight and the tranquil blue skies over England were still free for all to see and feel.

My situation with the move to twin engine aircraft was obvious, as I had not gone to single engine fighter command so it was a different strategic war operation. The fight of the Battle of Britain was not yet expected. We expected possible invasion from over the Channel, so all available aircraft were in use to strafe all directions from Germany to the Channel with bombs or machine guns, and the twin engined Blenheims were the aircraft involved. We hurried to an airfield near Oxford called Kidlington to practise night flying. It was exhausting work every night with no time off for days, then we returned to South Cernery for the final passing out to an active service operational squadron. I was detailed to join Coastal Command. For this it was necessary to do a reconnaissance fourteen-day course for flying over the sea to include navigation and search tactics. By the time I finished the course, my close friend from Portsmouth who had joined a Blenheim squadron was almost immediately killed strafing an armament train moving towards the Channel in France, I was informed by his wife and this was confirmed by his squadron commander.

My next posting was to Operational Squadron No. 224 in Leuchers, east Scotland near St Andrews. They were flying over Norway each day, and the casualties were really bad from the guns of Germans waiting for them. I did only a few sorties as second pilot before I went to regroup in Northern Ireland, at Limavady airfield, but I stayed for a week to do a conversion course at Silloth airfield adjacent to the pure swift flowing Solway Firth on the west coast of the Scottish borders. The task was to convert the new operational twin-engine Hudson for service at Limavady. The programmes were hectic with bad weather interfering with both daytime and night-time flying, landing and take-off. We lost an aircraft on the nearby Scottish hills the other side of the Firth. The aircraft was not easy to fly for it was the latest service version of the American Lockheed: fourteen passenger planes that needed very experienced pilots who could handle the faults in the design. We were however very short of aircraft so we should not complain. It had a good engine manufactured by Wright Cyclone of the USA.

Limavady airfield was next to the village with one inn, which seemed to be the head office of all activity on this side of Loch Foyle leading to Londonderry town. The outlet to the Atlantic was near Inistrahul Island, a conspicuous focal point in good weather for all seamen and airmen. The airfield enjoyed a concrete runway directly pointed at a large hill or mountain that seemed to intimidate anyone within its distance. At this time there were only two in the squadron qualified to fly by night so I either had to do the night take-offs or those in the early morning, so there was not much to negotiate.

The first time I took a new Hudson off to test its reliability after a service was a special experience. It was fitted with four fuel tanks. The inner tanks were used for take-off as was normal, but after take-off it was usual to change to the tank wings, to conserve the internal tanks for landing so the wing tanks could be used to jettison fuel until empty. Take-off was normal at about 500 feet but when into the circuit the bright red fuel light came on saying no fuel. OK, we could hand pump more fuel, but quickly the red light came on for good which signalled no more fuel. So you look ahead to see where to land as at 500 feet there is not enough room as you are horizontal to the airfield. I had therefore to consider dropping down in front below regardless of the conditions ahead. Ok: we started action to force land regardless of the terrain. Below were just trees so there was no choice to do anything if the engines packed up. Suddenly in this tense situation I thought to change the tanks from wing to inner tanks, as this opposite action had been the only alteration after taking off to fly. The aircraft responded immediately, and we eventually landed as normal. What a fortunate result!

Examination later proved that the mechanics servicing the aircraft had reassembled the tank linking spindle control the wrong way round.

At this time we had two aircraft each with personnel responsible for assuring us as pilots that an operational aircraft was always available. The situation changed quickly to only one aircraft per operation and so our friendship with our mechanics disappeared. Apart from the Irish pleasantries we were welcome and various families liked to entertain us away from duty. I enjoyed playing tennis and dry and wet fly fishing in a quite swift flowing river, the Roe, but with flying all different hours we appreciated the patience and understanding of our neighbours who were never sure if we would turn up on time to participate in their sometimes well organised parties. I was also friendly with a local naval base that possessed submarine and frigate warships; in fact unofficially we exchanged situations of importance to us both. I took a few Naval Officers flying on our operation sorties and I sailed once in their submarine, but I must say that whilst our interest was an operational exchange in our spare time, I disliked going submerged even for a little while.

Without warning my next operational patrol was to fly an engine modified aircraft. The current well experienced reliable Curtis Wright Cyclone engines had become my friends as with all Hudson crews. We thought it was unnecessary to change engines to Pratt and Whitney. After an initial surprise, I plotted the course with my second pilot and set off to meet the convoy of ships coming in from the west coast of the United States. It always made me think when I met ships coming into our range, that they had been at sea for very many days, sleeping and working on board in sometimes severe weather, heavy swells and through U-boat infested Atlantic waters. Yet they were so cheerful when they acknowledged our arrival by returning our signals. My main thought was how lucky I was because after a few hours always I could be at home in the Officers' Mess having a meal and drinks and a little later would be in a comfortable bed on firm ground.

We were into our flight about one hour when I changed seats in the cockpit to allow my second pilot to obtain experience of control of the aircraft, whilst I worked on the navigation. After another hour suddenly the red flashing light showed shortage of fuel to the port engine. We immediately hand pumped the emergency fuel and although the flashing light went out momentarily it was flashing again and the port engine was dying, so I opened the starboard engine to maintain height and shut down the port engine for good. The second pilot was nervously trying to close the extra throttle and despite my insistence to leave things alone, he would not, so I ordered him to leave the controls and I would take over. He looked nervously pleased. It was difficult to change because the cockpit is small under these circumstances so I partly wrenched him out and struggled underneath then humped my back to lift him and get his legs out of the way of the controls. Of course I immediately opened the starboard engine to stop trying to hit the sea for the loss of height was so rapid. Anyway I got control of the aircraft with the good engine flat out and as height was regained I felt we had touched the spray of the white foam into the wind of the sea. My crew thought so too!

I turned for home for I did not know what was going to happen to the good engine, sent a 'May Day' signal to base and started to climb on the one engine that was flat out and set course, After nearly three hours we arrived over base at 10,000 feet and on the way home I was thinking how far a glide would take me if the good engine failed. To manoeuvre an aircraft with a lost engine you are trained to fly against the good engine. Thus we landed; the crew were happy too and I asked whether we had hit the sea. They all agreed we did, and we taxied over to the HQ. On arrival and after the crew left the aircraft I decided to check the bad engine, and started it up. All of the engine-modified aircraft were grounded on the basis of my report awaiting a full investigation.

Eventually the report came from the makers of the engine and the Royal Air Force engineers which simply stated that in the redesign of the engine there was a slight difference in the radial fins that caused slightly more heat to the carburettor which was sufficient to vaporise the fuel, thus the pressure increased to reduce the fuel until the engine stopped. My action to fully open up the good engine enriched the fuel supply so it cooled the carburetor and avoided shut-down. All the aircraft had to be modified by simply drilling a hole in the carburettor chamber to avoid fuel compression. The aircraft so modified were safe to fly again.

Later I had two incidents on the ground, one after landing from an early sortie, when I was taxiing along the perimeter track in the direction of HQ to report, Suddenly the aircraft felt as if it was going to disappear in the ground, for the Irish workmen doing a repair had dug a large trench and left to take their lunch without marking the hole in any way. In consequence my wheels disappeared into the hole I did not see. There was a suggestion that I might have been going too fast or that a member of the crew was not paying attention, however it was ruled that all holes to be made in the future be properly marked to avoid the problem.

On another occasion I decide to let the second pilot take off, not for the first time. However on taking off with my help we were about to get airborne when he veered off course to the left and could not control direction. I immediately reached across to shut down both engines and the aircraft continued to spin off the runway until it eventually stopped, facing the way we had come. I stayed with the aircraft until it had stopped to switch off everything. By this time all the crew had left in case of fire and I was alone ensuring the safety of the aircraft.

I walked back to the aircraft maintenance unit to take my second aircraft, with permission of course, and we were airborne in less than thirty-five minutes, only a minute or so late to start my U-boat patrol for the next convoy.

CHAPTER 3

Bismarck and Canada

NEXT TIME, AFTER EARLY morning operations, I was attending a
well organised tennis party and was in the first set when I was
called to hear I was wanted on the telephone by the Base
Commander. So with apologies I went to answer and was told to
return immediately to base to be briefed on a secret mission; a staff
car was on its way to pick me up. I changed from my white tennis
clothes into my uniform just in time to welcome my lift back to base.
A Flight Commander and I were detailed to take our two aircraft to
meet Hitler's mission of twenty-seven Heinkel 111 aircraft that were
ordered to bomb our support ships to the battle of the *Bismarck* by
the Royal Navy.

As I was being briefed for my second flight, all hands were engaged
to stabilise in some sort of order the information being sent in by
HQ. First they were trying to find my crew members who were with
me in the morning operations and the search produced all but one,
so the Base Commander stated he would take the place of the missing
internal air gunner whose position was to operate a 330 mm machine
gun from the open passenger mid window, moving with the gun
from port to starboard as the occasion demanded. Next the route was
detailed by Group Commanders in HQ Liverpool. We were
scheduled to cross over neutral Ireland and permission had been
granted to fly just above 5,000 feet as the Irish would need to fire
their anti-aircraft guns to a limited height of 5,000 feet. From the
Irish coast the course would be the same with a slightly different
course for the Flight Commander in the other aircraft.

The rendezvous was with some Royal Naval destroyers who
needed us for protection. We both set off together and it was strange
to see anti-aircraft shells bursting just underneath our aircraft, hoping
the Irish understood their orders for our secret mission which of
course was not known to them.

After leaving the Irish coast the journey was uneventful for about
an hour and then I stumbled on a German Heinkel 111 aircraft armed
with 20 mm cannons on a converging course and I decided to attack.

The Hudson was a slower aircraft, not built as a war machine, with no armour plate at all for protection so to catch him I considered the best approach was to gain superior height and dive down to attack. I flew into the sun like Biggles in the First World War and took some twenty minutes or more to reach enough height to attack. I also thought perhaps he did not see me.

I started to dive and the crew settled in their position. I had my two 303 mm guns on top of the control column to fire through the nose of the aircraft; they were cocked at the ready and members of my crew had their gun amidships also cocked ready for the Base Commander who was on the lookout with his head in the astro-dome. The dive was quite steep with engines nearly flat out. We had been,watching the Heinkel all the time since we met and now I was manoeuvring my direction to intercept, with my thumb at the ready on the trigger of both my guns. The Heinkel turned as we got near, still out of range for my guns, so we followed when I could see the rear gunner fire. Immediately a bullet went through the astro-dome and took off the Base Commander's hat, so he came down to the amidships to man the machine-gun. At this time the Heinkel jettisoned his load of bombs, six in all, and turned towards the cloud cover now near. The rear gunner kept firing at us as we were coming into range. I commenced to fire my 303 and I could even see the features of the rear Heinkel gunner. There was a clatter of cannon missiles inside our aircraft, but the damage was not noticed at the time for my 303 was pumping into the rear gunner's position. The position went silent. At this point I had to avoid colliding into the Heinkel so turned away to assess damage to the aircraft and myself for one of the cannons had shot my left foot which was on the rudder foot control. I turned to follow the Heinkel, making for the cloud, with both ending up unable to see each other; so I broke cloud cover to see if my crew were OK and to assess the damage. My foot hurt. I felt the air rushing through the hole in my left foot, making me wonder for a moment if we could get home.

There were several entries of cannon shells; apart from the Base Commander's hat, cannon hit the oil connection system of the hydraulics and leaked heavily so that one thought of landing without wheels; others in the main aircraft seemed relatively free from damage.

My foot was troubling me and I thought I must do something, but could not reach my foot on the control bar but I could not see blood anywhere so I waited and decided to return home. The sea was empty and I set course. It was very difficult with all the air rushing through my foot so I had to change position to get down to feel it. On reaching it I pressed the hole in my flying boot and it felt dry so I assumed it was not a through hole.

I sent a May Day signal to base and proceeded to handle the aircraft OK, waiting to see what would happen. We crossed the Irish coast at 2,000 feet on the reciprocal course of entry and expected 'Bang, Bang' but nothing happened at all. On arrival at Limavady airfield it was just getting dark and I worked the hydraulics for landing but did not know whether the undercarriage would work so decided to do an extra circuit to check things out. I got visual clearance from the control tower and landed without incident. As soon as I stopped safe on the runway, the Base Commander, Wing Commander Gurnow, jumped outside and ran away to telephone his report to Group HQ in Liverpool, screaming, 'We have very many cannon holes in the aircraft and it all was very dangerous in battle.' Next day the aircraft engineering section reported after examination we had received nine cannon entries! The hole full of rushing cold air in my foot was a figment of my imagination but the skin had been split by the ricocheting cannon off the rudder bar and my heavy bruise was the result.

I still have my holed flying boots in my wardrobe to this day. The Base Commander felt hurt because his beautiful royal deep blue Australian uniform had been holed but after all it was his first operational flight which proved exciting. The rest of my crew just needed a rest; after all this had been their second long operation in one day.

The Royal Navy history of this battle and the sinking of the *Bismarck* has always reduced the part played by the Royal Air Force to bring success after a bundle of Royal Naval problems.

The exciting tour of Northern Ireland operations was about to finish for I was requested to complete a Specialist Navigation course in Canada. The Royal Air Force was technically operated by officer pilots as they were promoted, so needed to become specialists in whatever branch of the service was required.

My transfer to Canada, and ultimately the United States of America, was a very big step for I had to rethink my life contract with Bakelite and my original school desire to make a career with the Royal Air Force for life. Now I was faced with a decision for my future regardless of the war excitement, so I decided after much thought to stay with Bakelite for the Royal Air Force no longer attracted me enough to become the top senior officer i.e. the Air Chief Marshal, because I was not a permanent officer trained through Cranwell; those I met from Cranwell College were the ones destined. So I intended to avoid the permanent commission, but appreciated the opportunity to say no if offered.

I received fourteen days notice of my departure from the UK for Canada to be stationed at Godderich on Lake Huron near Toronto. I hastened to tell my Bakelite seniors, for being an American company there were obvious possibilities of meeting the staff of Bakelite in the United States and Canada to exchange confidential information in a war time situation.

Apart from giving good advice the Chairman, Mr H.V. Potter, and Managing Director, Mr F.J. Robinson, were most helpful in seeing me socially installed into the top members of the USA plant, with Dr Baekland's son in New York and Dr Redman in the Niagara Falls area. This was a great honour as there were only two of our staff away at war. In this way I was equipped with the Bakelite mission to the United States. One piece of advice I received was very important to me: 'Harry, you are going to meet daughters of very important people so please do not get carried away to try to get married or have some other kind of romance, and spoil the trust I give you.'

I made my goodbyes to the family and friends and set sail from Liverpool aboard an armed merchant cruiser. It was an interesting ship and accommodated seven other officers in a separate wardroom within the main one and in the blacked-out ship we set sail for Halifax, Nova Scotia, with a feeling that it was not just an ordinary sail but with the expectation of tackling any situation that came within fighting range. We were to be alone for the whole route across the Atlantic Ocean. It was difficult to settle down as we had nothing to do in our position whilst it was quite different for the crew who were busy as beavers, plotting and counter plotting all likely eventualities to engage the enemy with only two guns fitted to the deck fore and aft.

After a few days someone suggested we run a lottery on what day and time we would enter the harbour at Halifax. It was strange as nobody including the Captain had any idea when we would arrive.

The situation appeared to be that we would stay at sea until our fuel ran out, for we were destined to take action as required against whatever was in store.

We did meet odd ships as we progressed. One was a large Greek fishing boat on a calm day and as we hove to the members of the crew were in their lifeboats frantically waving. The Captain of our unnamed merchant cruiser decided the boat was harmless and departed.

The next day there was a German battleship coming into range after sinking various naval ships and we thought the Captain was going into battle if he could, but in the end our futile armament was not required so we arrived in Halifax and I won the lottery with the exact time and date.

The following day we caught the over two nights train into Toronto. It was a wonderful journey, the landscape so interesting. The train was heavenly with Pullman coaches and dining cars with so much space just for seven of us, so different from the crowded situation in England that we had got used to. Sometimes we stopped for water or to pick up mail. We slept in pull-down bunks of generous size and eventually arrived in Toronto station. To great admiration as great war heroes, we were met by a Christian organisation that showered us with goodies and offers to show us the sights for we were due to stay at their best hotel for the weekend. So on Saturday and Sunday we were free to be escorted to Niagara Falls, local historical forts, good eating places and the local yacht clubs, and so on until Monday when we caught the train to near Goderich and lifted to our base for work on Tuesday morning.

This Specialist Navigation school, the only one in the Royal Air Force, was evacuated complete from St Athens, Wales, into an old airfield of the Canadian Air Force, and naturally was small because of the extremely high qualified staff in mathematics, weather, geology, astrology, meteorology, flight capability and world navigation. It was a hectic course to cover six months, for the specialists were urgently required to teach in England and man the rapidly expanding Royal Air Force operational and station requirements to be more effective overall.

Lake Huron was very near; often we walked by the lake, along the shore and felt the magnificent open space in all its moods; for the weather was dominated by the effect of all the Great Lakes which added many local variations to a relatively stable climate system.

Sometimes we all visited Toronto University to study the night sky through a large telescope. On the first occasion one or two officers thought it was a good idea to retract the telescope to review the girls' dormitory windows, hoping to see a more interesting vista, for they had quickly learnt from staff of the possibilities on our introduction to the manipulation of the telescope equipment. At the time I was learning about the cosmos with our professor, and he paused for a moment and turned to show me the planet Saturn with its wonderful coloured gas rings. He immediately noticed the angle of the telescope and loudly said, 'You cannot find anything at that angle.' Naturally after renewed proper observation and study of the heavenly details, the professor departed and the telescope was once more retracted to the previous level of the girls' windows, while raucous laughter and sighs soon drew all our attention, but basically we saw nil for the outside lights ruined the view. I enjoyed the professor's information on the universe, its role not only in the navigation of aircraft but in the navigation of the planet Earth, the solar system and beyond from the Big Bang to now and the future.

The station possessed a few Anson aircraft. I had previously flown this type of aircraft and considered it very safe for it was light, laborious, but did float for a few hours if you had to land on water. I enjoyed the hours of night flying taking star and moon positions with a new type of sextant to support the dead reckoning of normal navigation from maps and charts. It was amazing how near one could position oneself using night sextant shot angles of the quick moving moon some 240,000 miles away and combining them with those taken of stars very many more millions of miles distant. I also enjoyed using the sun by day, 93 million miles away, by using the simple horizon sextant the Royal Navy used with complicated mathematical workings, or getting bearings using a sun compass or other landscape shots from a still position. I have mentioned sextants: the Royal Navy type of working out was complicated with time consuming hours, special nautical logarithms and trigonometrical mathematical tables to estabish latitude and longitude positions.

The Royal Air Force used reduction tables for air navigation per latitudes; it was much less complicated and they were in the process of producing simple abbreviated tables of four volumes for the whole planet Earth. Life was however still mathematical for you were taking moving objects from a moving machine as on a moving earth in various declinations needing corrections.

I see the earth orbiting the sun at 18,000 m.p.h. spinning once in 24 hours, and endorsing the seasons by being at an angle of 66.33 degrees. It contains an atmosphere travelling with us and the inside is molten at 3,000 degrees Centigrade, with us people walking or sitting on the crust, floating as countries or swimming in H_2O, the sea. It is difficult for me to understand why we are fighting each other in such delicate circumstances.

I remember learning that the sun is a gas nuclear explosion of four parts hydrogen making one part helium in 18,000 degrees Centigrade which also releases the surplus energy to make us warm, and gravity to keep Earth in line with the other planets.

My mnemonic to set the planets in order round the sun is: 'Some Men Very Easily Marry All Jane's So Up Nations Population' representing Sun, Mercury, Venus, Earth, Mars, Asteroids, Jupiter, Saturn, Uranus, Neptune, Pluto. Sometime I must find their distance apart, the orbit speed and more.

The load of work seemed to be increasing and apart from helping each other, some of us spent many evenings after dinner sitting at our desks plodding through our subjects. For instance Meteorology was a dry subject influenced by a few weather ships spaced across the Atlantic. Forecasting the weather was in its infancy and was limited to draughtsmen mathematicians drawing up pressure systems from weather equipment observations.

All came to an end and those successful were awarded the symbol 'N' by the Air Ministry to indicate we were competent specialists in navigation, rather like a degree from University. During the time on the course I did spend some weekends away in the USA, with the Dr Redman family for instance. I spent time at nearby Niagara Falls from all angles and occasionally got very wet with spray both from the American falls and the Canadian side. I would not say the frontier guards were always friendly.

I enjoyed several social parties in Canada and survived occasionally with no buttons or fewer buttons on my uniform jacket because the young friendly girls wanted them and cut them off as souvenirs in appreciation of the Royal Air Force service. One day I obtained from a freak gambling machine fifty packets of 200 Lucky Strike cigarettes, and had good fun disposing of them to grateful people.

I also enjoyed a few weekends in the United States with the occasional dinner or luncheon in a gentlemen's club or well known restaurant. I visited the Bakelite plant for a discussion or two, and on one such occasion I was asked to lecture about the Second World War in Europe from my own experience.

The British government and the Royal Air Force had answered the US people's call to keep them informed. The US policy was against joining in the war but to set up lease–lend to buy war equipment. Naturally UK thought to send the current heroes, and did so, but it was a disaster for public relations as looking at wounded or disfigured personnel had the opposite effect and did deter the interest to do more as the people considered their own families.

My large strong audience saw me as one of them and were basically interested to know how the war was going in Europe. They understood the references and compared them with their media situation, Towards the end of my story the situation became a little less formal. I was asked personal questions, such as what was it like to meet a German in the air. I replied that nothing came to mind except it was either him or me. I gently told them of my experience of being shot causing a hole in my foot which I could feel the cold air streaming through, but which turned out to be only a bruise and cut skin caused by a ricocheted cannon shell off my rudder bar whilst flying towards the sinking position of the German battleship *Bismarck* in the Atlantic Ocean in May that year.

I answered several other questions and could see the silent audience spellbound and anxious to help Europe in any way they thought was possible. Afterwards I met Dr Baekland's son and enjoyed oysters and beef. On another occasion I exchanged technical information related to synthetic thermosetting resins and I eventually brought the information home for digestion by the Bakelite executive UK.

I met some very interesting people, mainly civilian but the ordinary Canadian Royal Air Force service staff controlled the non specialist activity. Apart from the interesting work all day and often part of the night I did find time to contact my future Bakelite friends. One was Dr Redman who invented thermosetting lacquer and who had left the USA plant to retire in the Niagara Falls area. His daughter I once met touring the English Tyseley plant. They invited me to spend Christmas at their beautiful house and I was pleased to accept. As the Christmas holiday approached I prepared to leave and of course we all were discussing the holiday ahead. One officer was on his way home, not having passed the qualification requirements, and it so happened he caught the same train to Toronto as me. I was met by Dr Redman's daughter and she asked me where my friend was going for Christmas; without more todo he was invited to spend Christmas Day with me at her home.

Together we did enjoy a riotous time before Christmas Day, visiting all the friends of the daughter, Alice, and her brother in deep snow conditions. Christmas Day we all stayed quietly in the house and I enjoyed having conversation with the doctor, although he had lapses due to a past illness. Next day, Boxing Day, in the USA, Canada and elsewhere, it had long been the custom to wear compulsory uniform in England though not in North America. I was due to go to the United States to meet Bakelite friends so I was lifted to Toronto airfield to board an aircraft to fly to Philadelphia and so to the Army v Navy traditional annual football game. The aircraft was sent privately by my future friends. I felt very important sitting alone talking to the hostess and sometimes the pilot in my uniform, now necessary.

We landed and were met by a private limousine with the driver under instructions to take me to the correct grandstand entrance to find my seat and meet my friends. I was about thirty minutes late. I duly negotiated the correct entrance and was walking down the steps to meet them, when the game suddenly caused a roar of delight. In consequence I decided to sit down on the steps until things quietened down. A big black male attendant came to me and said, 'Look, mister, you cannot sit down there,' so up I stood again. The crowd were roaring and standing up and I could not move up or down or sit and this caused my own commotion with the attendant, such that my friends nearby looked and pulled me towards my seat. I was so thankful to sit down and to feel safe.

It was a great game and afterwards as a party we left to have cocktails with the Navy in their hotel. In the elevator on the way up to the top were several girls, and half way up one said to me in quite a loud voice, 'Say, buddy, what airline are you working for?' It was an interesting way to start understanding the American way of life.

After Boxing Day I went back to Toronto the same way I had come, but I needed to pay my own taxi to the Redmans' house. When I arrived I noticed the drawing room was dark, though it was normal to have twenty-six lights shining plus a four foot log fire burning. Anyway I was late and let myself in with my borrowed key. I put the lights on as I entered the drawing room to see if there was a message for me and to my horror stumbled on the daughter with my officer friend, who should have caught the train on Boxing Day as arranged. I thought immediately of my Bakelite superior's advice whilst I dealt with the situation.

I said goodbye to my friends and departed to Dorval, the Royal Canadian Air Force Base at Montreal, for the staff were being informed by the Air Ministry of our likely posting to UK and to make arrangements accordingly. I arrived there with several of my course and we waited for an aircraft to fly us home through the USA lend lease scheme. Suddenly however the US government declared war, so all aircraft were grounded and consolidated to await sanction before the operational requirements of the US were met.

I was staying at the best Montreal hotel and was starting to wonder where my pay was coming from for I only had limited funds and for the US government to provide an aircraft seemed doubtful in the immediate future. Even so, some of us did a little shopping for the new nylon stockings plus make-up to take home, and we ate out for each meal. So we were getting short and could not find out from the RCAF when the Royal Air Force overdue payments and current payments would arrive.

One night a few of us visited the Samovar Night Club and received a great welcome from all the staff which included the chorus girls entertaining us at the table with a drink or so. A jolly lively evening was in progress but we knew we were not flush with money. When the interval came we thought of going back to our hotel, but the girls had the idea we could stay longer if we would participate in the show with the chorus at midnight. We considered this a jolly good idea for we were having fun. Midnight came; we were admitted to the chorus without rehearsal and each lined up with a girl. Each Russian song was rendered with some kind of dance routine and a good funny time was had by all.

The next morning we departed to HQ Dorval airfield for we were getting broke. I was met by a seventeen-year-old girl who was most sympathetic but said there was nothing she could do for the problem was with the Air Ministry in London and she thought it would take at least fourteen days before action would take place.

I discussed the possibilities and frankly said, 'What would you do if you were in our position?' She without hesitation said, 'Go and ski in the Laurentian Mountains; they are not far away. You could get there today by bus.' I said, 'Ok, but how does one fix it all?' She said, 'Leave it to me, I will do it all. Check out of your hotel and come back in one hour and I will have everything ready. You will be in your mountain hotel by 5 p.m. today.'

I enjoyed a most interesting journey by bus to some departure point by a frozen lake where fishermen were trying to catch fish through a hole in the ice. I did not see a great deal of success for I quickly caught an arranged private car to the Laurentian mountains and on to the Laurentide Inn where I was going to stay. The owner was told my pay problem and arrangements were made to deliver my salary every fourteen days to him to dispense as required, with the balance coming to me when the Air Ministry woke up to the situation of contacting me via Dorval RCAF.

On the way my driver did some fur trapping in deep frozen snow near our destination and although I was scarcely equipped in clothing, I learned part of the art and helped, but never did actually carry out the operation afterwards.

At the inn I received a great reception from the owner and staff and settled warmly in to what was to be a most interesting time. I made a telephone call to the girl at Dorval to express my appreciation for the excellent arrangements made so efficiently and confirmed this with a thank you letter first class the next day.

My first morning was like a magical dream. I woke up early to see outside the window the sun shining on pure white glistening snow everywhere, yet I was beautifully warm just in my nightshirt and thought what a stunning view. There were no visible footmarks anywhere, and such tranquil silence to make my dream so heavenly real. After all, it was positively real. I decided I had much to do so I quickly got dressed and looked for breakfast. Hungrily I ate my fill. Soon I was dressed in outside clothes and marvelled at the fantastic scene with my ear muffs on to prevent frost bite. My hands were warm in thick fur gloves and my feet enclosed in fur boots.

I had the feeling I was in paradise. Too soon I observed a dark distant figure coming towards me from just over the brow of the nearest low crest of the Laurentians. As it approached I could see it was a skier with a cloud of glistening powder of snow flowing behind in the path of descent with the clear sun in the distant horizon. The figure came on and with a ski manoeuvre stopped within an arm's length of my position, dowsing me in the shining powder snow. I brushed my goggles and recognised with surprise one of my friends from the course I had recently completed. Immediately he smiled and said, 'I thought it would be you because the young girl telephoned from Dorval to tell me you would arrive yesterday nightfall.'

We went into the inn and settled down to talk. I was amused to hear that the young girl at Dorval had sent him and apparently was sending four more friends tomorrow; what a wonderful person to so look after our needs. Afterwards we discussed the likely situation of our future as experienced serving officers of the Royal Air Force having an unexpected holiday. After a glass of Canadian whiskey we went into lunch, still really wondering at our good fortune but also wondering what was happening to the war without us.

In the evening I was informed by the owner of the hotel that some fourteen or fifteen models were coming in from New York for a relaxing time before being photographed for an exhibition starting in three weeks' time. This news was accepted as most interesting and we hungry fellows decided we should do something to arrange a welcome.

Next day we commenced to build an ice igloo and have cocktails within before dinner at night. With certain members of the staff we built it in two days, with large pieces of ice, to me too heavy to carry. It was a great success and would accommodate fifteen to twenty persons. Hence of course we had a very good venue for having fun ourselves: refreshing drinks after our morning ski exercise, which was so demanding because of our lack of skill. We tried to progress to crossing to the local village which took approximately four hours uphill and down; and practised standing up and moving without real control to stop many metres further on than intended. Our wooden skis needed lots of butter grease on the bottom to slide but once they did go it was difficult to stop and our only way was to fall over. However, we became quite proficient after a few days and were considered ready to receive our New York guests.

We enjoyed the igloo, obviously, and after a few days our guests arrived. By this time we were five in number and ready. What followed was amazing fun, in fact hilarious, because we all had so much to do and had little time to do our own thing. It was so friendly. All the models, full of beauty, were slightly chaperoned by the team managers but the igloo was a great focal point before dinner. It was so warm and friendly and welcoming with candles on a dark night.

We played very hard: snowballing; skiing; fur trapping for some; you could do little else in such an isolated wilderness. True to promise, our RAF service back pay and current pay was delivered after fourteen days and after the owner took his share for the first time we possessed money and toasted the young girl at Dorval who arranged the delivery each fourteen days thereafter.

I felt we were forgotten men living in a paradise world and it would go on forever. In a month or so, however, the young girl from Dorval called our attention and issued us with Air Ministry instructions to report for duty at Dorval to receive first hand our postings back to England. Aircraft from the USA were still scarce, and there were two possible: one in Bermuda and one in Jamaica. I tossed up for the option but lost so was detailed to go home via a troopship from Halifax so with my spare collection of baggage, full of nylon stockings, ladies' toiletries and make up, tobacco and other luxuries not obtainable in England I trained to Halifax, Nova Scotia, homeward bound with no regrets at all.

CHAPTER 4

Back to England, and Iceland

O N ARRIVAL AT HALIFAX I was lifted to a service base camp for all personnel likely to be going to England. It was raining and everywhere was wet and damp but the mess accommodation was dry, sparsely furnished but light and cheerful with various newspapers and the radio. My first detail next day was a medical, for I was bound to join a troop ship in the harbour. I was relieved to know that all the embarking troops would be medically examined to avoid any disease breaking out on the passage. I waited and waited and enquired when I would depart, only to be told they did not know but the ship was from mothball vacation in the United States, and was getting shipshape ready in the harbour.

Naturally I went off to find the ship to enquire the status and departure date, but nobody seemed to know, for the ship had been loading with coal for fourteen days. It expected to fill in a day or so. So I returned to the damp wet town to find something to occupy my mind, but everybody seemed to be engaged on war supplies and had no time for anything else. A very good situation and commendable, but I was bored waiting around in such a dismal situation.

The day arrived to sail and on embarkation I was received by the Captain who explained his position: that he was getting the old ship ready for passage by loading the coal for the furnaces and boilers, that he expected a thousand or so troops to board now and hoped to sail that night. He was a splendid fellow with a lot to do; he told me I was required to look after the Army officers on board particularly to ensure they had a restful passage. I was in fact the officer in charge for the Army officers, and their duty was to look after the well-being of the crowded troops on board who had very tight accommodation.

The voyage was uneventful at a very good speed, alone through the German U-boats infested within the Atlantic Ocean. I arranged cocktail parties for the officers at different times for some were always on duty and the Captain was entertaining too, even considering his difficult position with an old coal burning vessel, and very busy with

41

items that kept going wrong or needing attention throughout the twenty-four hours.

We eventually disembarked at Liverpool. I caught a train home to my family and took a few days off and toured the lovely tranquil English countryside with a friend's car and a full tank of petrol. It was so rewarding for me. My stories of my adventures in North America were thought interesting, but the chief interest were my ladies' nylon stockings and toiletries at a time when so many nice things had disappeared owing to our war. I had taken the hint from the pilots who crossed the Atlantic to deliver aircraft for us, for I was eager to have the latest information on such developments to delight the ladies back home, particularly my girlfriend Lilian for we were getting serious, in love.

At home I had received a notice to report to the Air Ministry, London, so off I went by train and taxis and reported in uniform for my posting. To my surprise I was interviewed by a young civilian girl who was very similar in age to the one at Dorval. She was very interesting and wanted to know my view concerning my visit to North America. Afterwards I asked if she had my posting. She replied, 'Yes, you have a choice of Malta or Wick in north Scotland.' My thoughts told me, You have just come from overseas, why go again and miss your girlfriend who is thinking seriously of marriage, and your own family? So I considered Wick, the home of 612 Squadron flying Whitleys with twin Rolls-Royce engines. We agreed on 612 squadron and she disappeared to check on details with the Wing Commander in charge of postings. After approximately fifteen minutes my informant returned to say 612 Squadron were on the move to Iceland, would I be happy to join them there? For some obscure reason I replied, 'Yes,' followed by 'Have you any alternatives?', but in vain!

I asked for arrangements to be made to fly me to Iceland, but she replied quite kindly that it was up to her officer in charge and I would need to talk to him. I went to meet the man who seemed to be working out my programme, so I sat down. Later he asked me why I had made my request. Although the officer was senior to me, I said, 'Sir, I am a senior pilot and often I have given lifts to other service personnel who are in a hurry. I expect the same for me, please.' He stood to address me and said, 'Even though you are a Squadron Leader, dear fellow, I inform you we do not have spare aircraft waiting for people to carry around chaps like you; you will need to travel the normal way by train or ship.'

I replied, 'Sir, no doubt 612 Squadron have aircraft on passage between Iceland and the mainland so near, so why can we not ask them?'

He then tried to grow even taller with his chest out. 'I work for the Senior Air Marshal and do not intend to waste his time or mine, so please conform to normal procedure, so may I say goodbye, sir, for I am busy'

I departed feeling hard done by and went to the Tube to lunch in Shepherds (a famous inn where service officers met when on leave in London) and walked down the steps to the platform. The whole area was full of children with their family and relatives and on seeing me they burst out cheering for they could see my uniform showing my wings in pale yellow. I had to pass the people ready to sleep the night there to miss the German bombers' nightly raid. It was a heartrending sight and I thought I was unworthy to receive such admiration for I was only doing my duty.

I had witnessed before such scenes on travelling through London when on leave and once I was on the surface to have my cap blown off and be knocked down by the blast of an explosion. You could see the civilian teams of helpers of all types with service assistance, regardless of danger, carrying out their duties to the injured and those trapped by fallen debris. I quickly forgot my posting problem.

All this time I was finding out how much the Royal Air Force had changed in so many ways. For instance, I was not used to ladies in the WAAF doing so many tasks as plotters, doing batman duties in the sleeping quarters and the mess. Pilot training had changed to include navigators with half wings and more half wings as wireless operators, armament operators and more, only trained for the job in hand. Thus they managed to meet the commitments of replacing casualties and providing aircraft to fly more operations with diversity.

I eventually caught the train to Liverpool and stayed some time in an assembly base, while waiting for an Iceland ship to be ready. Here I met several interesting future companions, although the waiting was boring and the weather full of misty rain and fog. At least we discussed what it was that made this part of England famous and set out to explore, but as usual when we were busy finding good food for lunch and dinner the call came to go aboard a small vessel to

Iceland. The passengers in the main were Royal Air Force personnel and as my new friend and I were the senior officers we were detailed to look after the welfare of the contingent. We had a full time duty on hand. The ship's quarters for the first night had the occupants trying to sleep in hammocks, one hammock touching another; it was just so overcrowded that nobody could really move to go to the toilet without waking up all about. We did all we could by getting ship personnel to rework the crowded hammock positions and to investigate other sources of complaint before we could settle into our own cabins for the night.

The passage took three nights and four days at about 5 knots. We arrived at Reykjavik by midday and lifted to the airfield in an atmosphere of damp drizzle and silence everywhere for at this time of day there had been a serious accident with a 612 squadron aircraft coming to land after operational convoy patrol. With my new friend who was posted to be the new Flight Commander, we hurried to the scene of the accident to meet the Squadron Commander and to see what we could do to help.

The accident area was a scene of utter devastation with not one recognisable piece except for the engines scattered far apart. As we got near I picked up a flying boot and felt queasy when I found a foot inside. We could not help and the Squadron Commander was too busy and sad to talk, so we returned to our quarters for a solemn evening and a drink goodbye. This was not the first time friends of mine had been killed in an accident from operations or because they did not return from operations, but it was always a sad time until you realised it could have been you; hence a toast goodbye with a determination to carry on come what may.

I settled to my new duties with no means of carrying them out so without instructions from Headquarters in London, I arranged with the Squadron Commander to do operational flying with his Squadron 612, and originate my navigational requirement at the same time.

Life in Iceland was lively, so different, apart from operational flying which I will describe a little later. Iceland is positioned at 63 degrees north. It is partly a new non-active volcanic island, but is near other active zones on the continental plates or crust.

The climate of Iceland is affected by its latitude which is where the frontal systems originate, the cold dry air circulation of the North Pole hitting the warm air from across the Atlantic, thus the variable weather of the British Isles is formulated. Icelandic weather is either cold, very cold or wet and dampish and medium cold although it has plenty of ice as glaciers.

Because Iceland was composed of volcanic fresh, hard, bubbly, aerated lava the air was very abrasive, and dusty, so with a strong gusty wind blowing, the lava contact destroyed the fabric on the peak of our hats, so you could tell the experienced personnel by the absence of hat fabric on the peak.

Iceland was made dry of alcoholic drink to avoid fraternisation with the service personnel invasion. With its oldest democratic parliament in the world it also created a law that permitted male and female to live together without the need to marry for six months with no regrets if at the end of the time one departed.

Iceland could live on fish which was plentiful in the lovely soft clear fiord waters around and the fresh internal gin-clear rivers from the melting snows meeting the sea. Salmon was a special feature; there was wonderful plentiful salmon fishing available for service personnel controlled by an HQ accountant officer of the Royal Air Force. Later he was found to have commandeered the fishing personally and after the services departed he sold the rights for his own gain. He was however dismissed the service and the fishing was returned to its rightful owners.

The low areas had lamb farming and even that tasted of fish, but there was no difficulty eating meat because pony steaks could be found in the good eating places.

I was asked to take over the Officers' Club in place of the officer posted back to England. As Iceland was dry of alcohol and the only sale was surgical spirit at chemists for medical purposes, which was well and tightly controlled, there was an interest in being a guest at the Officers' Club for a drink with a member. The club on the whole was a bit of a dirty place with chippy paint and NAAFI food and drinks. I felt it not worthy to receive anyone so I organised the Nissan hut layout to be painted to look more inviting, and introduced many changes for it needed to be more adaptable to members' relaxation including HQ senior officers. With a changed committee of young officers to help me we were keen to make a good atmosphere for all who entered. The club was limited to small quantities of bottled beer, and gin with various additives such as Martini vermouth and juices.

One day Intelligence indicated that a Norwegian ship with a large consignment of Scotch whisky was approaching Iceland to drop off a case or two for the small Norwegian contingent flying light seaplanes, and afterwards was off to Norway. I was detailed to intercept the ship and commandeer all the whisky. The situation called for RAF police to provide a guard immediately as I intercepted the ship. She docked at Reykjavik before unloading a small consignment, but I was handed the whole whisky consignment. It was unloaded and transferred to our appointed place on the quay. Immediately the forty or so cases of this most needed whisky were stacked very neatly to await the promised transport to base. It was covered with a very large tarpaulin and a guard of two was placed, one at each end of the stack.

All Iceland however seemed to have knowledge of our consignment sitting on the quay, despite our secret operation and the confirmed Intelligence message received. I stayed a short time on board for little refreshment with the Captain, then emerged into falling snow and some rain causing cold damp conditions. I saw very few people around the two guards standing at their posts protecting our pile just about covered in snow. We needed to wait some hour or so for the transport to arrive, and in my discussion with the guard I understood that more than one person had approached our stack of cases, interested to see its contents, whilst the guards were helping the two shipmates finish the stack.

The transport arrived and the cases were transferred on to the open truck. I noted we were short of quite a number of bottles, which I assumed had been 'vanished' by onlookers whilst we were loading the stack with the guards busy helping to keep order. Eventually we got to base to unload them into a special secure Nissan hut. I counted the cases in to find about two missing, some twenty-four bottles, but I was relieved and happy to be home at base with the knowledge that thirty-eight cases were safe.

Next day I settled down to distribute part of the consignment of whisky to people including officers who were awaiting supplies requisitioned but not delivered for some time, hence I was busy with two guards going to the Officers' Club, to grateful officers at HQ, at the mess base and a few others including one to each guard; and so I now had a stock of twenty-five cases and was relieved all was well.

Next day it quickly came to my ears that the whisky situation was known to just about everyone on the island, including service men and civilians. Later I checked the Nissan hut to see if all was well, and to my horror I counted more cases, gone and the lock broken. Panic stations to restore safety! Next day I arranged duplicate deliveries to the original applicants to be sure of arranging some control over the special Nissan hut with the whisky balance now locked again safe inside at nineteen cases.

The next day after my duties (for this whisky affair was always taken in my spare time), I was getting restless with the offenders not getting caught or seen. I checked before bedtime and all looked well. I again checked next day after breakfast before duty, and was shocked to see further cases gone and a little debris.

The guards examined the position and found entry was from underneath the floor at night. I then posted a guard to cover the night hours and thought, There cannot be another way into the whisky stock, but the next day I checked after breakfast and found there was only one case left with only seven full bottles of whisky. How the last consignment was stolen I do not know, but my guess was that it was civilians with inside information, for the amount taken was nine or ten cases. At least I now could give up the situation, and thought the whole thing was a good laugh. It reminded me of the *Whisky Galore* consignment that had floated ashore in the Hebrides off the west coast of Scotland some little time before. The seven bottles I gave my service friends so then I was clean and could get on with my duties without further whisky problems.

Some time later I decided to go to the Officers' Club after duty, and obtained a lift from the Transport Commander in a service vehicle, En route he told me it was necessary for him to collect two lady friends to take them to dinner at the Officers' Club, so into the town of Reykjavik we went. It was dark in the black-out and we had difficulty in finding the exact house. Because of our manoeuvring, we somehow alerted an Army Redcap police car, but took little notice of this event. I knew that owing to the rule of no fraternisation, no service vehicle was allowed to give vehicle assistance to the civilian population; anyway, we found the right house, called and immediately took on board the two ladies and set off for the Officers' Club.

On the way I looked over my shoulder to talk to the ladies and noticed the Redcap police car following, making signals for us to stop. Naturally I expected my friend to slow down or stop, in this situation and as Commander in charge of our station transport but he startled me by going faster, saying, 'Please look after the two ladies; I am racing the car following to the Officers' Club and there I will drop you all off. I will then race back to my depot and book the car in.' It was very exciting going so fast and pulling away from the following car, and running through the club entrance hall.

My friend booked his car in to his depot and waited for the police to telephone, which they did. He answered by saying, 'You must be mistaken for the car you thought you saw is here lying idle.' After a period of time he took another car and met us at the club. He explained his conversation and frankly thought nothing of his exploit at all. I thought how could you; whilst it was thrilling and exciting with danger to me, it seemed reckless for a Royal Air Force Officer to be so involved.

Whilst these episodes seem important they were not really so, for they were only incidents away from duty, which was operational flying and setting up as a Station Navigation Officer, being accomplished in matters needing urgent attention and indications from the Chief Navigation Officer at the Air Ministry of problems to solve for Iceland.

The United States Air Force had arrived at Keflavik, nearby our operational flying station at Reykjavik, and I was naturally in touch with regard to navigation and the weather for operational flying. We were however not always in agreement for sometimes the US weather man prevented US flying and we had to fly instead. The flying was always subject to the weather which in the main was snow, rain or a mixture of both, with seas very cold or rough and so often flying was hazardous. The water was so cold that should you have to force land on the sea your survival time was less than two minutes and this was also the same for the convoys going across the North Atlantic or taking the route via Bear Island to northern Russia (Murmansk). Apart from that, we had problems of patrol with the Royal Navy to protect convoys by chasing U-boats, hoping to prevent attack.

Unfortunately from all points of view our patrol operation flying left an area in the middle of the Atlantic uncovered and we only went with the convoys to Russia as far as Bear Island, because the limited flying range of our aircraft made the unprotected areas free for massive German U-boat attacks with considerable destruction of ships, and loss of life and supplies. In addition the Russian aircraft would make matters worse, feeling free to do nothing to prevent U-boat and aircraft attack from Bear Island onwards to Murmansk, and such supplies just lay with not a care to deteriorate with the cold weather.

As the majority of merchant ships and naval vessels assembled in the fiords of Iceland, Vaal Fiord in particular, not very distant from Reykjavik, we at our nearby base welcomed visitors to our mess and there were many tales of heroism. I recall one occasion when a Royal Naval Admiral came in his finest gold trimmed uniform to see for himself the failure of convoys to get through with supplies, the Russian convoys in particular, who was due to report to the Prime Minister, Winston Churchill. He decided to board the senior naval ship in charge of the convoy setting course for Murmansk.

The convoy set sail and was roughly on a satisfactory course as far as Bear Island and as soon as it was unprotected all hell broke loose. The German attack was the heaviest so far, and approximately half the supply ships were sunk. The destroyer with the Admiral was hit and sank, throwing the Admiral into the sea. He, stripped of his clothing, dragged himself aboard another naval ship only to be hit again; however he made another naval ship and apart from seeing distant Murmansk, he later arrived back in Iceland and turned up in the mess wanting to telephone the Prime Minister to say there was great difficulty with supplies to Russia and we should wait until we had the equipment to provide protection all the way. The Admiral was dressed in an ill-fitting ordinary naval uniform borrowed without rank but with a borrowed ordinary hat with 'Admiral' painted on with the paint nearest approaching yellow. It was an extraordinary escape from such a cold rough sea where you could only survive for a couple of minutes.

It was confirmed that no Russian aircraft ever appeared to help; it was felt the essential supplies were not needed because we understood that if ships got through the supplies took ages to unload and remained on the quayside for many months in insecure protection in all kinds of Arctic weather.

I took it that the Admiral's message got through, for soon we had Liberator aircraft to fill the two gaps with no protection which were extremely successful against the U-boats which were massing in packs to tackle convoys. Soon it was nearly goodbye to their attacks owing to the success in our combat causing enemy casualties.

The limited normal range for our squadron aircraft did not influence our patrol duties which carried on regardless. The few long range Liberator aircraft were only used to fill the two gaps and could land in Canada or Gibraltar but were a huge success in controlling the German submarine warfare from Iceland and elsewhere.

On two occasions I passed near the German reconnaissance Condor aircraft patrolling the north of Iceland to check weather and movements of any change the British were making below and in the clear ice-frozen north you could see individuals in the long range Condor aircraft, but as we were both far from home we both took no action to fight but tended to wave goodbye for the Condor was much faster and veered away from my course. None of these aircraft were shot down, for we had no fighter aircraft available.

I settled down to complete my navigation assignment of two major items.

The first was to find out why lease-lend aircraft flying USA to UK missed the mark and why many just disappeared. The second was to do a survey of Iceland to find out why the first was happening. I borrowed a Humber shooting brake from the station transport section from my friend with full authority for me to convert the vehicle as I wished, to suit my task of checking the Iceland magnetic field for strength and any peculiarities that might affect aircraft navigation which in the main was now by gyro compass on long flights.

The modifications I carried on to my shooting brake were to put a Perspex astrodome through the roof to take star measurements and to fit a sun compass to check measurements without magnetic field influence It had a drawing board made into a desk with accommodation for my air almanac, mathematical navigation tables with corresponding nautical almanac and tables, together with bearing arms for checking the true bearings of the land situation.

The situation was not easy for I also needed sufficient accommodation to live and sleep in all weathers. All was eventually completed, and I practised my programme before setting off the next day after a glorious night of aurora borealis with such a marvellous display of bright delicate colours and moving shapes and sizes.

My first day was interesting for my motor progress was slow owing to wet ice and appalling road conditions; however, I practised some shots of sun and stars. My route lay through desolate terrain with snowdrifts, sulphur hills, glaciers nearby and occasionally green

1 *The author in the centre (in the white shirt) – learning to fly*

2 The author at the controls of the twin engine Oxford

3 The author in the middle with the wings

4 The author with 612 Squadron at Iceland/Wick

5 The author with Magister

6 The author, centre right, on a secret mission, East Fortune

7 The shooting lodge which was the officers' mess as at Alness, now a private house

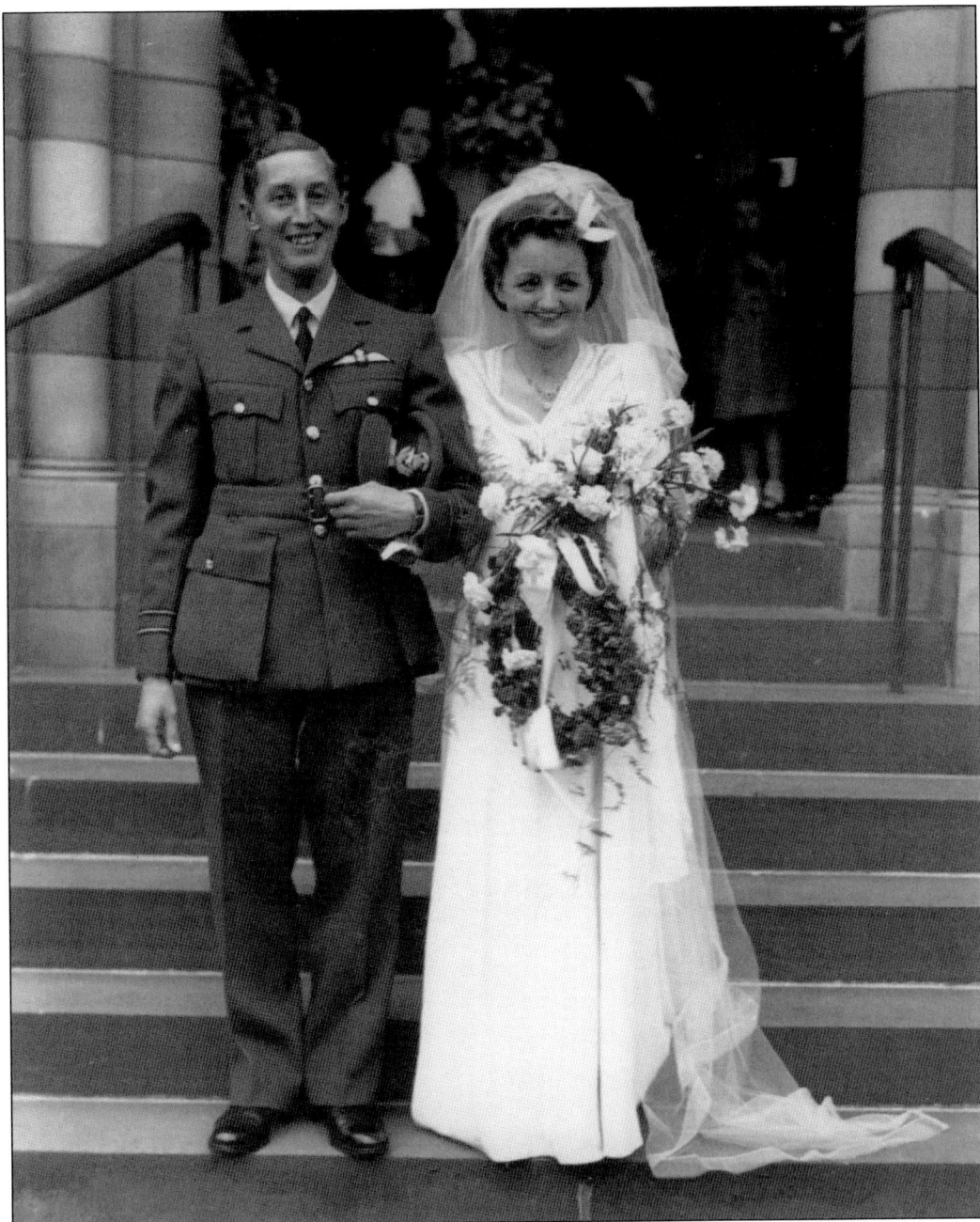

8 Marriage to Lilian in 1943

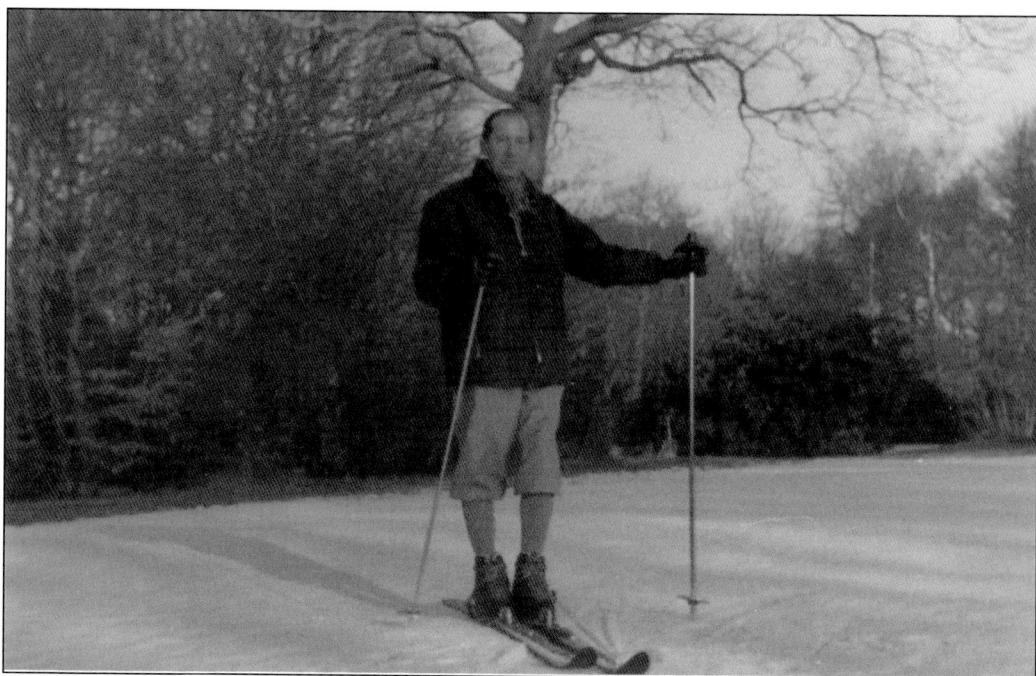

9 The author skiing at Durford Wood

10 The family skiing at Gstaad

11 *My Rolls-Range for business. The White XJS belonged to my wife Lilian*

12 *Full Member's Badge of the Royal Automobile Club often caused official salute through Whitehall*

13 In the Bentley meeting Roger from Marlborough College 1963

14 Sailing again

grazing lowland for sheep with knee-high planted forests. The appalling weather conditions varied between Arctic snow conditions and lowland rain.

I set off from my motor route to Akureyri, just south of the Arctic Circle, for experience of the remote northern part of Iceland and the sea areas. Then I rejoined my shooting brake and set course for Reykjavik.

Eventually from my analysis I decided I had taken sufficient measurements to satisfy myself enough to work out much useful information. I came back to report to my HQ in London after going through the details at base. My main observation referred to aircraft built and tested in California, USA, where the magnetic force was weak compared with Iceland near the magnetic pole. Thus any pilot correcting his gyro compass course by the magnetic heading compass was in danger of misreading the situation and could get lost.

The Royal Air Force padre at base was a new fellow, but he inherited the good kind generous intentions of England in the supply of warm socks, stockings and woollen headgear to distribute, so welcomed by all in the cold winter Arctic weather. There were so many pieces that there was always a large quantity in reserve and he did not know where they should go. I decided to help and brought along my friends to take whatever they wished. Of course I greedily helped myself and I still have sufficient to keep the winter weather at bay to this day.

One day I said, 'Dear Padre, I would like to take you nearer God by flying over the Arctic Circle because you have not yet taken to the air.' I really thought my suggestion was very cheeky, but the nice padre said, 'Yes, I would like to experience flying for I need to know,' and we did so fly together within the week. He felt so pleased and we came very good friends in such an inclement climate. Unfortunately a month or so later he was posted to Gibraltar and was killed flying on the way. I was very sad for he was such a good friend to all.

The Base Commander normally possessed some type of light aircraft for communications purposes. On one occasion he instructed his pilot who had not flown a Tiger Moth before and who felt his task impossible because he was only used to heavy aircraft. The instruction was to execute a compass swing, for the aircraft compass was out of date and had last been checked in England. The situation came to me and I saw no difficulty although I had not flown a Tiger Moth for a long period. I decided to take the aircraft to Keflavik, the next door United States base, for they possessed a suitable landing site. I obtained permission for a compass swing the next day. To ensure the correct alignment takes a long time, particularly so in preventing aircraft missing their rightful destination.

We met in the morning, and the weather was OK so we set off with the originally intended pilot as passenger, taking off in turbulent air and setting course for the United States base which was so very near that one had little time to feel the aircraft characteristics before coming into land on a very large runway. I had not time to consider alternatives and just put the aircraft into a glide landing position for touchdown. The wind decided to blow multiple tabulating gusts so my light aircraft was difficult to adjust. Anyway, I pushed the aircraft down and landed with the wind direction diagonally across the wide concrete runway with hardly any run afterwards.

The laborious compass swing in all directions was accomplished and we landed back at our base without speaking to anyone and pleased to have accomplished the task.

After a few days I took a powerful Air Sea Rescue launch to Vaal Fiord to board a United States battleship as a guest for drinks in view of the helpful work they had done. Although the US vessels were dry, a little refreshment was enjoyed whilst meeting many officers, including the actor Douglas Fairbanks Junior. After a brief conversation I departed for the ship was due to sail and my Air Sea Rescue launch was waiting. Strangely, some time later after the war I again met Douglas Fairbanks Jnr on a railway station whilst travelling to a distant destination.

At one time my friend the Squadron Flight Commander, John Wilson (who accompanied me to the posting to Iceland), and I decided to take the weekend off and departed to the wildlife reserve. We used the squadron shooting brake and started to enjoy the utterly tranquil scene of the bird sanctuary with only the sea and the light sky with us, walking along a non existent path close to meagre vegetation of green bushes and the sea. Suddenly we were startled by close rifle fire and turned to see some American servicemen shooting swans. Of course we immediately called loudly; it was illegal to shoot anything in this bird sanctuary, but to no avail. The servicemen were approached by us and so an argument developed whilst they were still shooting. The scene was hideous for they were shooting at the body of the wild swans and the heads and necks were twisting out of control whilst the gunners laughed at the poor swans' antics. Eventually we suppressed the action and the servicemen left the scene and promised to pack up shooting and behave. It was all a most awesome sight and such a cruel episode that we found it difficult to comprehend and spoilt completely our sojourn so tranquil before. After a sandwich of bully beef and biscuits we returned to our base to forget.

Our flying operations created engine difficulties that needed emergency action but unfortunately we had few or no engine spares; in consequence arrangements were made to collect reconditioned engines from a Rolls-Royce factory in Glasgow, Scotland. I felt the situation was a bit stupid for the reconditioned engines were made I thought from Fighter Command throw-outs, tired engines that had been employed from 0 to 40,000 feet in a quick burst, whereas our employment was for long periods at low altitude over the sea. I considered the expansion of the engines under heat was different; hence whilst going to Scotland was interesting for a break, it did not solve the real problem.

The Squadron made numerous trips to Glasgow and I was always willing to volunteer and did so enjoy my flight. Apart from collecting an engine I could collect kippers and green cabbages for the mess, for we only ate bully beef and Cheddar cheese with a daily ascorbic acid pill to take the place of greens. I was also anxious to meet with my serious girlfriend, now evacuated with her family from the south coast of England to quite near Perth, Scotland, and working for the fire service in Glasgow. Sometimes I would eat in the city hotel restaurant with my aircraft crew where so often I was not allowed to pay owing to the kindness of appreciative local business men wishing to host us for a meal. I was always pleased to see my beautiful betrothed girlfriend but often she would be on duty, so sometimes we missed each other. On one occasion I gave a lift to a senior officer who wanted to fly as pilot and on the way without knowledge gently touched the sand dunes on the approach to land at Stornoway in the Hebrides where we had planned to land for further business. I also wanted to take the opportunity to load with exquisite fresh kippers that would only last a day for breakfast in the mess at Reykjavik. Still, it was very worth while, and we appreciated a delightful change from the monotonous repetition of strange stale bread and some kind of very salted bacon plus our ascorbic acid pill.

Flying from Iceland in the slow Whitley aircraft without adequate radio contact with base caused us to fly with two homing pigeons in case we needed to force land in the sea or disappeared without trace. The pigeons would fly back to base and the commander of pigeons could warn the operations staff the fate of our aircraft failure to fly and return; also, should we have a last message, providing we had enough time they would be able to read a written message that was tied to the pigeon's leg.

You may feel this pigeon method was a little old fashioned but to us flying it was very helpful at the time. We had however to be careful about the pigeons' part of the operation, so we practised the pigeons' capability on the way home. Unless the right instructions were obeyed and a crew member action was right it was easily possible to throw the pigeon the wrong way and the poor friendly heroic pigeon would immediately lose all his feathers because of the wrong entry speed of the slipstream of the aircraft.

Fortunately my dear lovely pigeons were much revered, although I did not know their names and the communication language in chirps was not understood by either of us.

In Iceland we threw a Burns Night of celebration and invited the British Consul for 25 January, the birthday of Robert Burns. I had previously studied his poems and verses whilst at Prestwick and had spent many happy hours at his cottage nearby. I considered Robert Burns far more important than William Shakespeare, for although Shakespeare was a prolific writer and playwright I am sure Robert Burns was more famous. For instance, there is not a country on this planet Earth that does not sing 'Auld Lang Syne'. I have many editions of Robert Burns' books and enjoy Burns night celebrations with the Scottish bagpipes welcoming the haggis. With haggis I prefer a little Scottish Drambuie; the taste is quite exquisite and refreshing. I apologise if I have mentioned this before.

Before I get carried away I must say the mess party was very good; the whisky flowed into us all including the Consul wearing his clan kilt. After a little singing it was time to stop, as when I had collected him his wife had said to me, 'Be careful, the Consul likes the whisky but not too much, please.' I decide to take the Consul home about midnight as he seemed to be enjoying himself and I remembered his wife's warning, hence with a little assistance we set off. We arrived at his home and I helped the Consul through the door to be confronted with his wife brandishing her arms at me. I felt, what had I done to deserve this? and I said so, but to no avail. I was stuck, the Consul was quiet and because he was not so physically fit, I offered to help but he was quickly taken over by his wife, I did not enjoy whisky so was quite sober. I felt a little hurt when I arrived at my quarters, but the next day I received a courier letter thanking the Squadron Commander and me for a wonderful Burns night and my assistance to and fro in the wind and snow, signed by the Consul with a thank you from his wife in addition.

On another occasion I somehow got lava dust on my cheek and felt slightly uncomfortable at night, for it was pretty primitive in our Nissan huts. I had a cast iron stove for heating which was always flat out and very hot or possessed no real fuel at all and was impossibly cold; however, the cold situation rarely happened. It was the same with the water, either hot from a jug on the stove or you could not touch the ice cold liquid in its temporary canvas wash basin stand. The best form of bath was to take the lovely warm waters of the geysers nearby. The male batman was always apologetic and worked hard to try and keep things even, but on occasion it was too hot for sleeping properly and I scratched my lava dust patch which eventually turned into impetigo that I could not control.

I booked into the Royal Air Force Hospital and went to bed. The RAF nursing sisters looked supreme and so attentive; they painted my cheek with a deep purple antiseptic and offered me a glass of beer when I woke up at lunchtime; but the time then was 7 o'clock in the evening and lunchtime seemed ages away. I had been in hospital before when I caught a cold while exhausted from flying more than normal long hours over the Atlantic Ocean from Ireland, when I slept for five days, only waking for food and the toilet; strange to say now I did not wake to claim my beer, but I did have a cup of tea at 5 o'clock the next day.

With more applications of the hideous purple antiseptic the impetigo soon started to depart and in five days I departed too. The RAF nursing sisters were to me very dear friends in their bright blue and white uniforms and so appreciative to the needs of the erstwhile flying officers broken to the extent of wondering whether they would fly again or even be able to walk again. It is now well known that doctors and nurses provide the initative to the patient, 'Please get better; we are here at your side to help you do just that.'

I was so well protected that I wondered what to do next to pay my respects for so much help in mending my body, so important to me. I had been given three bottles of Drambuie and immediately gave one to the nursing sisters. They were so grateful to receive something in the dry alcoholic climate of Icelandic hospitality that they could dilute to share between themselves.

The other two bottles I kept for the occasion of the completion of my posting to Iceland for I was near my twelve months completion of operations and I was due to marry my girlfriend very soon as I hoped with all my heart.

So I eventually gave up my converted shooting brake, finished my navigational obligations and departed to my new unspecified posting, to be known after my return.

I set off with a lift to Aberdeen after landing at Dyce to drop off a member for entry to the Royal household, then flew on south to say goodbye to the crew and find my own way home to my family, feeling quite sad.

CHAPTER 5

Marriage

NATURALLY I WAS ON leave from duty until notified, and the big operation was to be married to my dear betrothed girlfriend Lilian MacDonald. The darling had given me an ultimatum: 'Either you do or I am leaving, for I am not going to be in love with someone who keeps disappearing.' I replied, 'Darling, in view of a likely non return from operations I felt it only fair that you should not be encumbered with such a situation.' Privately I was thinking of my father's statement to me, not allowing me to join the Royal Air Force from school, and the Royal Air Force etiquette of officers not being able to marry before thirty years old.

We had multitudes to accomplish before the great event. Naturally we were to marry in Glasgow for her operational fire service requirements needed to be met and the aunt she was staying with felt it was her position to organise the whole event, which she did beautifully with perfect efficiency, so with all arrangements made for our marriage within the Church of England I was pleased to accept the kind respect for my domain and felt so very Scottish honoured.

The reception was going to take place in the city Grosvenor Hotel that I had come to be so familiar with on my trips from Iceland and although food and drink were in unbelievably short supply and rationed we entertained fifty guests and had much champagne, after a wonderful ceremony within the church. After the reception of hilarious and jolly give and take my wife and I settled into the express overnight train to London with two bottles of Drambuie from Iceland. I must say that whilst the journey was a little rough but uneventful, we arrived tired out at the hotel-cum-apartment in the west end of London without taking a drop of Drambuie.

The staggering change in situation for my wife and me was the lack of being told what was right or proper or possible, so we immediately seem to change. For instance, during our courtship we were very conscious of not offending each other's respect and dignity and here I was wondering what to do without restraint. I was holding a bottle of Drambuie when I was called to the bathroom. After I had knocked on the door my wife said, 'Please come in,' and lo and behold I was so embarrassed, I could not speak, for there was this beautiful lady with no clothes on circulating the bath water and then lying still. I offered a glass of Drambuie which was eagerly taken by both of us. Thus the situation changed, but so delightful and thrilling this episode was to create a lovely marriage to be.

Afterwards I did recall my earlier bachelor leaves in London and the occasional visit to the famous continuous show at the Windmill Theatre (that never closed) which did sometimes produce a lady nude but only as a statue standing remarkably still in a far corner of the stage. It was always full of people but various gentlemen on seeing someone leave their seat nearer the stage jumped the seats in front in order to race other people to the better nearer seat.

Apart from trying to shop with very little choice, for luxury goods were in short supply, we visited theatre shows also in short supply before dinner. Always for eating we ventured out to the best famous restaurants and we thoroughly enjoyed ourselves.

Naturally when we came home we enjoyed talking about our day's experience over a glass of Drambuie before retiring. After about seven days we departed from London to my home and to my new posting, which was Long Kesh, Northern Ireland, and arrangements were made to take over a country house nearby, some twenty minutes on a service bicycle away from base. My wife, who had never owned a bicycle and wished she had, slightly complained so I purchased a second hand lady's machine with cover guards for the chain and so on. To settle down to our new mode of transport we made interesting practice runs to collect eggs and other farm produce such as lettuce and vegetables.

The house stood in about fourteen acres with fields around it, with a garden at the end of the avenue leading to a handsome white imposing front door. The house was unique with no running water anywhere; there was no electricity and the dry toilet was outside. The heating system was one large fireplace in a very large downstairs room which possessed an adjoining kitchen where the fuel was paraffin and the equipment three portable burners and no oven. The situation did call for restraint which we exercised without undue forbidding hardship; for my part daily or when applicable I took the dry toilet apart and proceeded to walk to the bottom of the field at the side of the house to dispose of the contents in my newly dug trench. To ensure the minimum of work we made a chalk line on the toilet wall so that I knew when to operate.

For a bath, I was lucky for I could get a nice shower at the base. My wife was more unfortunate for she had to use an old large tin bath in the spacious drawing room and it seemed impossible to do this bath operation without someone to help. The system was first to light the fire to a roaring state to provide sufficient room heat, second to boil water in three large saucepans on the little paraffin burners. You then estimated the volume of cold water required that would correspond to the amount of boiling water in motion, as it needed to be obtained from the village pump, the only one around for miles. Now you started to fill up the bath with cold water and then added hot water to a reasonable temperature for your entry. It quite quickly went colder, but then you had a friend, me in this case, to supply boiling water whilst you held the soap and whatever. I found this assistance exhausting and very technical to avoid damage to the bather. My wife was very patient and did not complain unduly. The whole primitive arrangement was difficult and so on the odd occasion I kept guard outside the men's shower at the base to provide some respite so well deserved.

One night after dark we held a cocktail party. Guests included the base commanding officer with fellow officers and various local country folk, and it was a jolly occasion with various drinks with canapés on and around the handsome massive table in the centre of the room. At 20.30 hours the young Wing Commander was stretching across the table to obtain a bite to eat when suddenly the table and all the contents collapsed to the floor. We were all were shocked when looking at the debris with no part of the table standing. I with the Commander examined the wreck and it became obvious that the heat of the fire had caused the table to shrink and collapse on itself.

A little later the many candles on the mantlepiece started to dwindle in brightness, so my wife hurriedly produced new larger candles. Suddenly there was a very large bang from the huge ornate mirror above the fireplace which decided to crack right across the largest part owing to the candle heat. With this situation in hand all our guests happily departed, After the last guest had left and we had finished the clearing up we decided to eat our prepared dinner which was lying in the pantry.

The reheat on the paraffin burner was completed so we sat down to eat our minced meat pie, We hungrily ate it all and on finishing I remarked, 'Did you notice the taste of paraffin?' My wife replied an indefinite no, but we both burst out laughing for our first paraffin pie initiation. It seemed that in the morning whilst preparing the cooking of the pie the burner ran out of fuel. Paraffin was added but much spillage occurred and in the renewed preparation in the confined place the hands contaminated the handles of fork, mixer etc.

For all three episodes to happen in one day or night was exceptional, maybe on the lines of disasters coming in threes.

When I first arrived at Long Kesh I reported for duty next day and was ushered to the Wing Commander's office. I knocked and entered to find the Commander playing cards. Immediately as I bent over to shake his hand he told me to take a card and said, 'Do not tell me the card; sit down.' I thought this a little odd but to me he was a young officer so well decorated with wings and medal ribbons; I thought there must be some explanation.

At once the Commander explained, 'I only get the cards out when I meet new and visiting HQ officers because it shows I am bored about being not able to fly, I expect you will be too!' We thus talked over our experiences. Apparently the base was an emergency airfield kept open for emergency landings day and night and we were to share night duty. Hopefully the Air Ministry would provide an operational posting soon, for this posting was rest from operations and later they would allocate us proper jobs again.

However the Commander did have a light aircraft and said, 'I do not use it much and you are welcome to fly it when you need to.'

I found my duties annoyingly simple and appreciated my new friend the Wing Commander for we discussed propositions for the future and how we would obtain them whilst waiting and chasing the Air Ministry for action. It all reminded me of the time I was waiting at Dorval airfield in Canada where I was happy or lucky to experience the snow and ice of the Laurentian Mountains. Here I was newly married and learning about the primitive Irish country life, waiting as before.

My wife and I found my night duty tedious, and frightening for my wife as our home was so isolated; we needed to do something. One night we enjoyed a lovely roast chicken for dinner and eventually went to bed. At around 3.30 in the morning my wife woke up, shook me and stated; 'Do you hear that strange noise downstairs?' I listened and I must admit I thought it would be better to deal with the problem upstairs for here we had a torch. I replied, 'Please go to sleep, I will deal with it in the morning.' This was not a good enough reply, but I took no action and eventually we both got to sleep again.

After going down the stairs in the morning for breakfast, my wife visited the pantry to find the chicken missing from the position that it had been left after dinner the night before; in fact there was no sign of the chicken at all and the pantry window was wide open. I thought a fox had opened the window and gone off with the chicken and caused the noise, but my wife said, 'No, it was a big rat not a fox,' because she had seen one hanging about previously. The dish holding the chicken was on the ground outside under the open window.

Enough said; my wife decided not to stay alone in the house when I was on night duty, so we arranged for her to stay at the nearby friendly farm where we purchased our eggs, salad, vegetables and chicken. On our visit to confirm the arrangement I saw one or two rats in the farmyard but my wife did not mind for she was with friends, the farmer and his wife, and we were in cycling distance of each other.

I did take up the offer to fly the Wing Commander's aircraft to meet an appointment with HQ seniors in navigation, and set off with little effort to adapt to the controls and instrumentation by day to Speke, near Liverpool and returned late afternoon. Naturally one refuelled the aircraft on one's return so it was always ready to fly again.

On this occasion I landed and taxied towards the refuelling bowser near the fuelling station complex. You were always aware you had to be careful not to do this with speed, so a slow approach was always the order of the day. Although I stopped before the petrol bowser the mechanics waved for me to come closer, so with a burst of the throttle I moved but failed to stop within a few inches of the gap, hence the propeller touched the bowser fuel stand. Feeling sorry for myself I reported to the Wing Commander concerning the slight damage, but he was not at all put out and said bad luck, a propeller change was not important.

I felt relieved for after all the Wing Commander was responsible for the aircraft. Later he told me, 'If you need the aircraft again it will be ready in a day or so, just tell me,' but I felt a little foolish and decided not to do the same thing again.

Soon the Wing Commander was posted and just vanished without a goodbye or a message. A day or so afterwards my posting came through to go to Patrivie Castle, the group HQ in Edinburgh, Scotland, for Coastal Command.

My wife and I did have time to settle the disposal of our house which frankly we had become quite fond of, in primitive kind of way. We realised we were going to miss the fresh food, our cycle rides, the friendly farm and the pure delight of living in such unspoilt deep green countryside, despite the weather with the possible delight of four seasons in one day.

The arrival in England seemed strange, for the living conditions seemed much more severe than when we had departed after our small honeymoon, but we were fortunate enough to borrow a car and have a allocation of petrol again to explore the nearby country delights of calling in at the inns we knew and hearing the stories of the pro's and con's of the sombre progress of the war with a beer or so.

I proceeded with my wife to Edinburgh HQ after being briefed concerning the situation of why apparently the Air Officer Commanding had lost his favourite Navigation Officer who advised the strategy of the total aircraft available in the north-east of England and Scotland: our performance if we invaded the continent or received an invasion from the North Sea. It was emphasised the Air Marshal only required answers in yes or no language, like a school teacher questioning a small boy on whether or not he knew something he should know. His surname was the same as mine and nobody knew what his reaction would be.

I arrived at HQ Patrivie Castle and did not attempt to meet the Air Marshal but enquired concerning accommodation for my wife and me. I booked into the advised hotel and invited my wife to stay while we found somewhere to live. After a while we were together again but disliked the grim situation, so squally and dark with misty wet rain everywhere, particularly when I was away all day.

I had now met my new chief who to me was a slightly pompous Air Marshal who welcomed me, to say I am sorry to see you but you need to fill the role of my fellow Navigation Officer who suddenly went down with a serious illness. To me this needed no reply so I waited. After a few moments I was asked what my name was. I replied and at that he rose to a standing position, I thought to blow his nose, but no, he nearly collapsed with fright at hearing my name was the same as his. After a few moments I was told, 'I am sorry you have been posted to fill in whilst my Navigation Officer is away ill; when he returns then I will not require you.' I replied, 'Thank you, sir,' and departed. I reported to my London HQ and asked concerning the length of the illness. On my desk at HQ there were the details of the research the ill Navigation Officer left behind, so my duties were established to provide the answer to a very complex subject as defined by my superior navigation specialists at Command HQ, London.

The Royal Air Force was divided into Commands: Fighter, Bomber, Coastal and others. Coastal Command included all the groups that were employed to attack German submarines or ships plus hostile aircraft operating in the Atlantic Ocean, North Sea, the Channel, and through the Bay of Biscay to Gibraltar and back to the Baltic off Germany, plus of course the coastal waters and harbours of Great Britain. It was a huge task with a shortage of aircraft and equipment. In the Atlantic, however, though the loss of supply ships was devastating we were near to suppressing U-boat attacks with a few new long range aircraft equipped with radar to close the gaps.

My seniors at Command HQ, London, were two; the senior was South African and by far the youngest Group Captain in the Royal Air Force. His second in command was Neville Stack (later to become Air Chief Marshal Sir Neville Stack), a Wing Commander, son of a famous lady who was head of beauty exercises in England. They were both very hardworking and their superb technical navigation skills made life for me very rewarding and later we became great friends.

I commenced my duties by visiting a number of air stations holding squadrons of operational aircraft to judge air worthiness and the useful role with what equipment was carried, particularly radar instrumentation.

The up to date radar instrumentation was most valuable to extend the usefulness of each aircraft in search, attack and safety of landing in bad weather after the sortie, hence I assembled my information to judge what action could be taken in the event of moving south to help with any invasion or an invasion from the North Sea, and assembled my report.

The research notes of my predecessor I discarded as inadequate for a true assessment of strategic action that would be required to cover the information given. I completed my report within the four weeks allotted by the Air Marshal and called for my presentation. On entering his office, I quickly said before he asked any questions, 'Sir, may I explain the present situation and so the group's position to date.' He listened intently to my explanation in conjunction with the papers of my report and said, 'Harry, I thank you for giving me such an excellent way ahead; the question is do we want to win or lose? The answer is obvious so I will immediately put your explained action into being; please monitor and follow through for me.'

Afterwards we became quite friendly, he calling me by my Christian name instead of the surname, and soon he told me, 'I want you to stay.' HQ London confirmed, but shortly his fellow returned after being not so ill so there was nothing he could do about my continuing appointment and I departed to a new temporary posting at East Fortune airfield not so far away, near North Berwick on the Firth of Forth, but not the Air Marshal's command.

My wife had worked very hard finding accommodation after she had joined me and at the time of my posting we lived in a superb ground floor spacious apartment in Aberdour next to the sea on the northern coast of the Firth of Forth. After the dismal hotel in Edinburgh, it was perfect and so beautiful with red skies at night on the going down of the sun. We walked much along the shore and looked across the Firth from our bedroom. The weather seemed kinder too, but it all ended so soon.

To arrange the move we took a few days off to locate accommodation in North Berwick and jointly insisted on another seaside situation, for the East Fortune airfield was only about thirty minutes away. We did find another seaside apartment, not so large but on the third floor alongside the sea with an angled view of the Bass Rock. Often the wind made life a little difficult for walking; nevertheless we were happy.

I was not due to stay very long at the base for it was a temporary situation awaiting a more permanent appointment so had little to do. There were six of us in the same boat comprising three experienced pilots and three experienced navigators, also two of us were specialist 'N' navigation officers, so we expected an assignment of a secret nature, some daring raid perhaps! We ensured our fitness by physical exercise but my work was hush-hush even to my wife. A few weeks passed with no action, and inevitably we were restless so we put pressure every day on the adjutant to find out what was happening. Very soon I was posted to Alness, Scotland, on the Cromarty Firth just below Invergordon, the location of the historical Royal Navy mutiny.

My wife and I were very pleased and we enjoyed a little leave in Crieff with her family before departure. We climbed the local Knock, a small mountain full of purple heather dispersed between small blueberry bushes. We ate so many blueberries our mouths became very stained; we walked alongside the lovely Earn river in the shade underneath the overhanging tree leaves, which runs from the Grampians through Loch Earn, with its swift flowing stream tumbling over the wet rocks that caused a lovely bright white foam. All seemed so exciting to my wife and me, and our minds receded from thoughts like, I wonder whether the next accommodation will be hard to find, how pleasant will it be? – rather like expecting your first day at school.

I purchased a second hand light saloon car, an Austin seven with a little 4-cylinder side-valve engine to journey to Alness, our new posting, After an interesting ride past the dignity of the mountains interspersed with wonderful pine forest we arrived to stay in the village inn in the high street. There we met two other officers and wives who seemed to have the two best rooms, not that any particular bedroom was more than just a sparse simple room with a bed and wash basin plus a jug of cold water, but the ones already booked were slightly larger. We all however did have one stark electric bulb centre light with a switch by the door and as there was no heating it was a cold dark run for the last one into bed.

We all shared the same table for meals in a room which also doubled for the drawing room and radio. The only heating was one small fire, so you can imagine the rush of six people trying to finish eating in order to establish a warm seat there. The three wives occupied their time searching for a house to let as accommodation and the pleasure of leaving the austere inn. I felt I should not complain for there were only a few inhabitants in the area, the war was on and the lack of heating and the very plain food were due to our UK wise rationing programme.

I settled into the Officers' Mess for the first few days which was in an evacuated wonderful shooting lodge with steeple roofing over a very ornately built large house with a huge hall, I shared a spacious well equipped room with another Squadron Leader which was extremely helpful for the knowledge I could glean, so to understand my surroundings more quickly. The Base Commander was a New Zealander and a fine sporting fellow. The base was an operational Sunderland Flying Boat Squadron and maintenance unit for servicing the aircraft that were mostly on sea mooring buoys in the Cromarty Firth just a few yards from the base building and our mess.

It was a most interesting departure for me, so far only understanding land aircraft. The Wing Commander in charge of the Squadron was immediately seen as a most polite, efficient person who joined the Royal Air Force from school through Cranwell Officer College and I suspected he would one day be the Air Chief Marshal of the Royal Air Force.

The Wing Commander and I made several flights to Edinburgh group HQ with the Base land aircraft and occasionally were forced to stay because of bad weather or HQ duty. Some nights in a hotel near the airfield, we shared the same room and I was amused on the first occasion for as we departed for bed I said, 'Excuse me, may I have the shower first?' He replied, 'You can, for I go to bed dirty and start the day clean, so goodnight!'

Within one week after I left Alness the Wing Commander was killed flying the Base aircraft alone to the airfield near Edinburgh HQ when extremely bad weather plus low visibility forced him down to hit an unseen mountain.

As in all situations the Army was about, and we did not take any notice for they did not disturb us. Here in Alness it was different. Through intelligence we understood that the local Army camp were in quarters that within provided hospitality alongside a huge fireplace burning six feet long logs plus a little Scotch whisky for comfort. One very cold night my wife and I decided we should investigate after dinner.

Off we walked with pieces of frozen snow falling in front of our faces and whilst we were very well wrapped up we did feel very cold by the time we arrived at the Army camp. We were immediately welcomed and seated adjacent to the fireplace with a very good measure of whisky for comfort and just beyond the scorching heat. The thrill was fantastic; it was as though we had entered another magic world away from all forms of inhospitable weather now threatening our everyday life.

The explanation of this six-foot log hospitality was that the Army post was guarding the local distillery who needed to cut many pine trees and the Army willing obliged in this austere time of war curtailment.

An interesting true recent history concerning the shooting lodge before it became the Officers' Mess follows:

The shooting lodge held many fine lavish parties to celebrate successful shoots or other activities and apart from the guests staying the night with all their finery and a change of clothes there was a very attentive butler on hand to help. One day after the guests had settled in to their respective chambers and were meeting in the hall for drinks, teas or whatever, the butler collected all the jewels from each guest's chamber together with the lodge silver and valuable ornaments, put all into a bag and disappeared.

Before dinner, there was much consternation amongst the host and guests but eventually all appeared to dinner. At this point a large serious fire started to burn the lodge. The butler by this time was burying his haul of valuables in a prepared trench in the large wood adjacent. The story does not end for the valuables and the butler were never discovered.

I felt the valuables had not been found so I and a fellow officer started to search the woods with spade and fork and after several attempts found no clues to make any progress. On the other hand we did not have sufficient time to establish a thorough all-out search, so I feel all is still in the woods to this day.

My wife found a delightful property nearby which belonged to a nurse now stationed in another town so we moved in. The base was very near so we spent many hours meeting our friends in the Officers' Mess. The bed however was a single wire mattress that had stretched beyond its normal life and so had become a sort of hammock. It was interesting and impossible to sleep two without rolling over each other all night long.

We also possessed a large fat rat that ran between the house kitchen and the wooden shed outside. In Ireland I had learned how to tackle rats from the farmer where my wife stayed when I was on night duty, so I took the opportunity to use my skill one day when the rat had nearly knocked me down with fright. It stopped to look at me hard so without thinking I kicked the rat high in the air and, blow me down, we never saw the rat again; my wife gave me full marks.

At the weekend we often held a mess party or dance on the Saturday night. A good time was had by all. On this one occasion my wife and I joined in and held conversation with our Canadian friend Squadron Leader, flying Sunderlands, with his wife an English WAAF officer. All seemed quite normal, with ladies in long dresses and all enjoying themselves. As the evening matured I took more notice of what was going on. The bar area floor was swimming in spilt beer and possibly barrel leaks. I noticed one lady in a beautiful white long dress; now the dress had a foot or so of liquid beer stains from the very wet floor and mentally I envisaged that the beer soon would be up to her waist. I must say the dance party ended soon afterwards, so my thoughts ceased.

The Sunderland flying boats were moored nearby and to crew one needed to prepare three hours in advance of flying to accommodate the necessity of boarding the aircraft by boat to settle all things, the mooring ready for take-off area at sea and to wave off mechanics with spanners and wrenches tied to their hands for fear of dropping them off into the wet cold sea beneath the aircraft from a wobbly dinghy held on by their feet. Against this backdrop we climbed on board with good food to cook whilst on patrol or flying elsewhere. We always enjoyed flying to other flying boat stations, Pembroke dock on the coast of South Wales, or Oban a little nearer, for good reasons, as a training exercise or for checking in spare parts basically for recreation and making our plans.

I was not a qualified Sunderland aircraft pilot and so I without proper training could not be captain of an aircraft. I did fly as much as possible, took the controls and loved the situation of landing on water, being met by a pinnace or boat, taxiing or making way to pick up the mooring buoy into wind and being immediately successful. It was an art in itself, so satisfying to execute without giving oneself a black mark.

My main duty was to enable pupil navigators to become qualified navigators, capable of telling the pilot the technical place to land or where to drop the depth charges or bomb, or sea rescue possibilities. Needless to say I enjoyed being part of a special team in strange weather and sea conditions.

At this time my wife surprised me by saying she was happily pregnant with a child to be born in the spring of the following year. Our programme did not change except for me to feel the necessity to act responsibly for the likelihood of becoming a father so thrilled me. I wanted to make things more comfortable for my wife, for really I had no idea how to adapt to the technical details of what I was expected to do and how to be responsible for problems I knew nothing about.

At this stage we both smoked, my wife a cigarette or two after dinner and I puffed a pipe as often as I could. My pipes were magnificent ones of famous brands, made from heather type plants that blew with the wind of the desert, made into briar balls with a circular core from which the pipe was made. I only smoked a special tobacco titled Balkan Sobranie from an air-tight tin; it was the finest tobacco in the world taken from the rarest and topmost leaves of the Yenidje plant which was blended with the richest leaf of Old Virginia in London. I am sorry to say that later I ended my smoking days with a deep curved pipe, when my wife and I decided smoking was wrong. I still have my pipes as antique items of a bygone age.

The invasion of Europe had commenced and all at the base thought it was a splendid event that would last until Europe was safe, but all were sorry not to be part of it. Shortly, however, I was posted to the southern group HQ at Mount Wise, Plymouth, Devon as group specialist navigation officer. The Air Marshal commanding was a very experienced Chief but I was still in Alness.

CHAPTER 6

A new baby and a new career

AT THIS TIME MY WIFE was ready to expect the birth in about three months or so. After saying goodbye to our friends and the lovely atmosphere of elite understanding, we decided to pack up and fill our little Austin seven and set off next day, breaking the journey into five sections. Dawn broke and we prepared to set off, but we were just settling into the car when I realised there was insufficient room for my wife between the windscreen and the rear of her seat to get in. Naturally I was frightened to advise, out of respect for the unknown medical requirement so obvious to see. We tried again after taking out anything and everything to arrive at the maximum width concerning the fixed seat details. After this exercise my wife tried again and after a little time just fitted in with no real room to spare.

I gently set off for the first stage with the slowest speed to make progress, apprehensive whenever I came near a hole or dip in the road surface. After about one hour we came to the conclusion that all was possible so we speeded a little and decided not to take lunch, so as time elapsed we were hungry but making progress. Just before dark I booked in for the night, and after dinner of haggis with mashed potato the hunger dispersed. Just before bed we did wonder what our position would be in the morning but we both hoped for the best of whatever might be.

Next morning it was raining and cold but the fitting of my wife was much improved and so we set off full of good spirit to the next stage. The roads were bad and narrow with no signposts, for the directions had been removed to frustrate the possible enemy. In the car I had fitted an automotive heater but had taken it out to achieve the maximum seat space at the start of our journey.

So now, wrapped up in our warmest clothes, we featured a tight situation but it was acceptable until we became cold with no lunch. We arrived at our destination just before black-out which would have caused us to stop, as headlights were not very effective in the dark. Again after dinner we went straight to bed to catch up as we were exhausted.

Next day plus another day, we arrived at my home and took a few days off. In fact it was quite hectic for many people seemed to know of our arrival, so it was advisable to stay, to work out the way to cope with the situation of a tremendous welcome.

My wife had the same problem of sorting out her messages and decided it was foolish to attempt to concede to the demands of a different way to welcome our arrival; she enjoyed the relief from the tight pregnant journey! Thus we decided to do nothing to hinder our progress south, so we opened house for a day and night and met many friends and eventually disappeared to bed to dream about the next part of our journey to be safely accomplished.

We again set off after solving the tight problem of space by having no breakfast. The weather next morning was full of sunshine, causing a super warm feeling to start our early morning journey and with the better roads we made very good progress. We naturally felt the pangs of hunger when we crossed the hills before the large town of Exeter and so stopped on a high ridge with a wonderful sun-drenched landscape, so green and shades of grass with darker woods on both sides, and silently thought for a while.

After our recent experience of Scotland's winter weather and the rain and winds of the Midlands of England we felt this silent situation to be heaven. Then of course we shambled around to find our picnic luncheon that had been so carefully made and packed somewhere with our total on-board luggage. We were prepared to believe we forgotten to bring it with us, but lo and behold, I lifted the front fixed seat on its forward hinge, and there was our neat package underneath. After our exhausting time and being ravenous we just rifled the contents feeling as if we had only just eaten breakfast and we were still hungry for lunch, which of course changed on the enjoyment of a flask of milky tea.

We set off once more down the road from our little piece of heaven with lunch and breakfast eaten, without the engine to save on fuel which as you know was rationed, with the thought that we were doing the country a great service by our economy.

Eventually we arrived in Plymouth and motored about to see what accommodation was available before dark. I arrived at the Hoe, where Francis Drake played and finished his game of bowls before sailing to meet the Spanish Armada in 1588. It all looked the same to me for the weather had closed down. After a little time I booked into the main hotel and reported for duty next morning and enquired where I could stay, but this was not in the same hotel. My new assistant Navigation Officer indicated that he was in a house far too large for him and his wife and would I like to share, so the deal was accepted for us to take the ground floor accommodation.

Our destination was Newton Ferrers on the river Yealm, not far from my new base at Plymouth. We happily moved in, and the snow came down, deep snow the like of which had never been seen before. It was deep, almost four feet, and there were strong wind drifts that stopped everything, but never the services on duty. Next day I made my way to base HQ somehow; it was a perilous journey, but as we were two officers with a shovel and spade we made the short journey and I reported to my senior officer.

Disruption of all activity was intense owing to heavy freezing temperatures that set in for weeks. It seemed the ice age was back forever; eventually the three weeks of weather improved to bright spring sunshine, but the great freeze up made the record books.

At this time my wife and I were concerned over the future birth. My wife through the recommendation of a friend fixed up a nursing home at Looe in Cornwall for the delivery. However this important event had problems because from our house it was not possible to get there after 11 o'clock at night, as the ferry across the Tamar river closed down. Sometimes the closure was earlier if no passengers or cars were around to cross, so Cornwall was isolated by time, river and distance. I needed to do something very soon.

I had reported the situation to my Senior Air Staff Officer. My office was a good palatial light place with desk, chart tables, and book shelves at each section plus telephones to HQ operations. It was near the Air Marshal, the Air Officer commanding the base group HQ and the Senior Air Staff Officer (SASO) who worked mainly in the operations room.

Just after arrival and introduction I was called to the Air Commodore SASO in the operations room to confirm my day's plan of operational aircraft operating through the English Channel off the coast of France. Later I was required to confirm the plan for the next day and so on for each day. I possessed two assistants, one an experienced Flight Lieutenant who proved to be very good at chart work and calculations concerning the coastal shipping, aircraft sweeps and searches for German U-boats which were likely from the west coast of France, where they were based at the concrete bomb-proof pens near La Rochelle. I was required in the operations room to advise on operational tactics each morning and worked with SASO. The ritual made me also also late for lunch for the programme was required to organise the next day detail.

The SASO always asked me to join him for late lunch in the mess. The first time I wondered what hit me for before sitting down I asked to have a drink. On the first occasion the SASO enjoyed a half tumbler of what appeared to me all gin. My request for a gin and tonic water was also served in a half tumbler but frankly, on tasting it during 'cheers' it seemed to lack the tonic water. With half our drinks consumed we sat down for lunch taking our glasses with us and were served some sort of meat with many vegetables. The SASO was then presented with a large bowl of lemons and cut up six or more and poured the juice over the vegetables and then did precisely the same for me. After we had lustily eaten we enjoyed a large piece of cheese with oatcake biscuits.

This form of lunch was the same each day. However I did arrange with the mess orderly to ensure I received a tumbler full of tonic water with only a small measure of gin on top but funnily I was converted to lemons and thought one day I would like my own lemon tree to ensure a good quality supply for they did vary in the mess in juice content. Today at 93 years old I now have my own lemon tree in Greece, outside my apartment, which happily provides lemons all year round.

The SASO, Air Commodore Webster, was a short, interesting, hard hitting fellow who flew as pilot in the last Seaplane Schneider Trophy International race, which was always a great thrill for all, the action taking place over Southampton Water, Naturally we became quite friendly when I was in the Officers' Mess and strange to tell when the SASO was due to retire from the Royal Air Force he left to become a vicar of the Church of England.

The base did possess a lovely light Mew Gull aircraft on station at the nearby airfield, Yelverton, and I did borrow it on a number of occasions to fly to Command HQ, Northwood, near London, to see my Senior Specialist Navigation Officers and if possible connect to my Bakelite friends in London, thanks to the SASO.

The problem of setting up a house over the ferry in Cornwall did take a large part of my leisure time with my wife. We called often to check up on the progress of the great day of birth to be and toured the whole seashore between Plymouth and Looe. My little Austin seven seemed to be suffering from the mileage with not the best of rationed petrol, but we found a good fellow at our local garage who would recondition the engine. It was accomplished in two whole days by taking everything apart and regrinding everything taken back together again, so it was in good form for the task of our search and many miles afterwards.

To make things safe Lilian and I settled into the only hotel, situated on the corner of the headland and quay overlooking the estuary of the river Looe and the sea, because we were getting near to the day of the birth and it would be simple for my wife just to journey across the river to the small nursing home with the charming white haired Matron, clear faced with an engaging smile.

The day of the birth came and went without result, so for some days my wife was advised to go to the nearby small beach and sort out suitable pebbles, for exercise. However after a short time, a different task was advised to make the exercise a little more strenuous by walking from the beach with one foot on the kerbstone of the footpath and the other on the side of the road. Strange to say, when my wife just took a preliminary try to see what it was like, she felt the need for assistance and called the matron and gave birth to a lovely baby girl, Dianne Gayle, the next day. We were very happy and thrilled all was well.

In the meantime I had taken seven days' leave to sort out where to live. I was just becoming successful but still living in our hotel, with a smaller hotel booked for the next week. I then received a message about a house on the cliffs of Downderry, so put a deposit down with the agent for fear, in the shortage of accommodation, I would lose the house before I had time to see it. I was also living in the Officers' Mess as well as the hotel because the distance to travel was too great to reach when duty was tough.

Now apart from visiting my wife and child, I called on the Downderry house and thought it perfect so decided to move in to await the return of my family from Looe, with luck. I booked out of my other obligations without fuss, so spent the last three days of my leave sorting out our possessions plus the beautiful traditional used perambulator and baby food which I had received directions about. I was now ready to collect and welcome my family home with champagne and the beautiful deep yellow daffodils I had gathered from the prolific stunning yellow garden landscape about the house.

At this time, although I was much occupied with my duty the following day, this was my last day of leave. The thrill of this new chapter of family responsibility was the most important episode of my life; it was just marvellous!

We settled in. My wife looked and felt around, and decided the things to do for the benefit of the baby, including a place to sleep. All was organised that night; by the morning the baby was placed in the perambulator and went to sleep underneath the large tree in full view of our profusion of deep yellow daffodils, which set the course for the future.

I did need to welcome my Command HQ Specialist Officers so after we finished our deliberations they accepted my invitation to stay at our house in Downderry. The weather was sunshine spring and we all enjoyed the slight diversion from the profound necessities of family life and the HQ strategy was going well at this time so the defeat of Germany looked possible.

Incidentally, at this time the Royal Navy submarines and sometimes other Naval Captains had learnt of our easier navigation tables for calculating position, so I set up the opportunity for them to learn in my office. There was also an Australian flying boat squadron just nearby so they enjoyed the help too!

I found out – obviously, you could not help it – that my Senior Assistant was a devout communist and thought the war would convert the whole country to one loaf of bread for all; whether you liked bread or not you had to eat it. He was very efficient but now I did not like his attitude. My conversations with him became stupid so I did not recommend him for promotion but for early discharge.

The Air Marshal was to retire from the Royal Air Force and we provided a very good merry house dinner to celebrate his long service. His reply was one of regret and he cried on departure from the table. The Royal Air Force had been his life, via Cranwell after school.

I was asked by HQ Command to apply for a permanent commission which they would approve, but I said no! Having been present at the goodbye dinner for the Air Marshal it was clear to me I could not progress to top rank for I did not join from school and go through Cranwell College. I was happy to be able to leave at the earliest opportunity and encouraged all to help me for the war was progressing well.

My flights to London also played a part, for the welcome was terrific from my friends. I could not think what I would do to make heaven for my future family. Mind you, in this deep conversation with myself, I did think I was lucky to survive when so many of my friends in the Royal Air Force had been killed.

To confirm my resolve, I thought of my last flight in the Mew Gull from Yelverton airfield to Leavesdon airfield near London at this time. I was alone, of course, and landed at the small airfield that was home for a division of Rolls-Royce. After landing I checked in with a young person in a small office, stated where I had arrived from and said that I expected a service car to meet me to take me to Command HQ and would return at 5 o'clock p.m. I went off in my service car, did my HQ business, and lunched with my Bakelite friends, without drinks for I never drank any type of alcohol for three days before flying. I left the lunch to arrive back to my aircraft at my promised time. I unlocked it, reported to the young fellow, and took off back home to Cornwall.

This was not my last flight before discharge but it was remarkable for I seemed to have a long time to think. After taking off I set course on the compass south to meet the coast near Southampton. I arrived within visible distance and the sea shivered as a silver mirror of light with many patchy menacing dark rainclouds overhead that turned parts of the sea dark silver. I turned away to the west and kept the coast in view but it was always dark clouds over the mirror sea. I momentarily thought about the past ages and events which the mirror sea demanded; it was though my life was unfolding without time.

I did without doubt recall my lost friends and saw the future in the sombre dark haze passing to port, then all thought disappeared for I was on my way, checking my position. Later I left all to land in the late evening light which suddenly faded with a feeling I knew my destiny but did not know where. I taxied to the hangar and handed the aircraft over to the waiting mechanics, saying, 'Thank you, this Mew Gull is a beautiful aircraft, you look after it so well, thank you, good night all.'

I arrived home to find my wife feeding and soothing the baby for now it was fully dark. I was looking for dinner too!

Our house situation was supreme; the very wide lawn swept down to the top of the cliff with our own sand-filled wooden steps down to the beach, with the rolling surf beyond; then I thought, Where do you wish to go?

The neighbours lived in a delightful house that was their seaside hideaway for a delightful family living in mid England; they only visited it twice a year. The gardener and housekeeper seemed to do little work and spent their leisure hours sitting in the sun each day, as much as the sun would allow. They were good to us, providing assistance and local information. They helped my wife with shopping and domestic chores; for me the cutting of our large lawn was handled with efficient care with the trees, palms and shrubs well manicured.

At times I wistfully thought, over a drink or so, that I perhaps should consider asking if we could take over their situation when eventually I left the Royal Air Force. When the family came down for their recess we always enjoyed their company and half bottles of champagne or half whatever in the evening preceding dinner.

Our child was much admired but was never in a mood to forget the soothing daffodils now fading away for a while and the love of the bright blue sea with the splendid noise of its breaking surf so near always, providing relaxation day and night.

Adjacent to my HQ base was the Australian flying boat squadron, who apart from their dark royal blue uniforms, looked as stimulating as I remembered during my time in Limavady, Ireland. I happily still gave assistance in parts of navigation they required to know but now living more outside the mess I seldom met them socially for I tended to scurry away to get the last ferry across the River Tamar to get home.

The Royal Navy and their submarines also still called in frequently to see our easier new sight navigation tables and wanted to know more when they were free or off duty. I was still pleased to assist and took pride in relation to the requests from our Senior Service. The war was going well, in fact exceptionally so, and soon the base received a call of surrender from the German Commander of the Channel Islands which was duly taken over the telephone as firm and notified to HQ Command near London.

Shortly, Squadron Leader Harry A. Simpson, AE specialist 'N', would resign and be due to leave the Royal Air Force; my decision was too strong for HQ to resist, although I was to be placed on the Reserve list for recall if and when needed.

Germany had as last surrendered, and my life contract with Bakelite was pressing me. I needed to settle down to married life with a family and felt my work in the Royal Air Force was done. I had survived and wished to develop my career. I was granted an early discharge and we, my wife and family, closed down the lovely Downderry home and again departed in my faithful little side valve Austin seven with no problem concerning my wife's space. However we were full of major possessions plus our daughter and her own possessions; other trappings would go by railway.

We took some time to say a misty goodbye to all our friends in the Service. Some we would meet again, including the lovely white haired, clear faced matron who was interested in our daughter's future.

I was on leave, bound to wear my uniform for a further fourteen days, then to pick up a pair of trousers with a jacket from the Royal Air Force discharge post at Uxbridge, Middlesex, where all personal records were available, so it was easy and possible to check your deficiency of service property. After clearance one could head for one's last home leave.

In the meantime, we had enjoyed an uneventful journey from Cornwall to the south coast of England, where my wife's family had returned to live, after moving from their safe house in Scotland. I had precisely conformed to service procedure, to enjoy a few days before reporting to my Bakelite company headquarters that had moved back to London from Brackley. I eventually received a great welcome to resume the modern interpretation of my life contract, acting from London HQ. We were not sure where to live, but my wife's aunt living in Baker Street near Regent's Park had offered a spare mews house nearby. We accepted that as our first option.

I commenced full time duties, and for a short time commuted the journey each day from the south coast by catching the very early morning train to Brighton, then the express to Victoria Station. The reverse journey at night brought me to my destination, after the family had eaten their dinner, with my little daughter already in bed and sound asleep.

I certainly was not made of permanent commuter material, quite apart from cleaning my hands of many newspapers' printers ink. I decided to make time for a refresher at our Midlands factory and update myself on the manufacture of the company products plus the current chemical laboratory work in progress affecting future development.

Thus after a week or so, I packed up the daily London journey performance and set course for my own family to stay awhile. The social commitments were the same, apart from being minus the necessity to play golf with my wife's family, all very low handicap players. I knew I would enjoy my sojourn in the factory, meeting old friends. It was superb, comfortable, yet so different from the experience of World War II, with its own necessity to be engaged in such exciting events of drama with the dice thrown in your favour to return or never to return, so it was natural to feel for those who never had the chance to serve their Queen and country. I noticed there were signs of discomfort in their manner of speech. The odds seemed to overwhelm any real conversation but the thoughts remained with them for I felt so confident and free.

I spent nearly four weeks in the plant laboratory which was working on the development of resins for surface grinding and cutting wheels in relation to metal and masonry industries. Many other items did also work on flexible abrasives but this programme was cut short for the raw materials were still in very short supply and strictly under difficult USA licence ration regulations.

Apart from technical work I exchanged information material gathered in my USA visit, which was much appreciated for no one was now allowed visits because of security regulations operating at the time. With my visit over I returned to my wife's family house on the south coast to make arrangements for them to move to the mews house offered, in two weeks' time.

Whilst this programme was under way I played golf with my father-in-law and sometimes with his two sons. My partner allowed me the freedom of the course, which stretches out behind large shivering sand dunes alongside the sea, adjacent to real marshland, where snipe play and hunt between the quivering reeds and where bullrushes grow.

Sometimes I played golf in the real summer heat whereby the fine cut sea grass was beside large crevices made from the drying marshland and thought, What happens should my ball fall into the crevice and disappear? I had no need to worry for at this time my partner's father-in-law suddenly said, 'Look, Harry, please pay attention, you are playing like a London cab driver!' I did realise what he meant for as we were approaching the 18th green I had already lost nine balls and had no time to look for them for it seemed that good golfers do not stray into the unknown. Even if they did nobody would know and certainly would not look for lost balls.

Sometimes the family would meet other Cooden golf club members in the bar lounge, a pleasant place without golf shoes; however on one occasion I was introduced as the reigning British amateur champion and everyone stood to cheer as I was saying, 'Sorry it is not true,' with deep embarrassment to face and limb. The difficulty was that the two sons were scratch handicap players and expected everyone else should be too!

Sometimes we would go shrimping from our beach pavilion and come in with wet feet to boil our catch, which would be eaten before our feet could dry. We also visited many splendid places of history concerning highwaymen or smugglers along the coast and would try good eating places around, whether inn or hotel. However, with little regret the family intended to move into the charming mews house adjacent to the country solitude of Regent's Park.

My wife and I decided to take over the mews offered by her aunt, so we set off full of hope for the future and looking forward to commence our family prospects. The house was situated through an archway into a completely cobbled mews with the entrance to our house the first on the left. All houses seemed steeped in privacy and silent to the hub of city life.

Through the entrance was a walk to the bathroom separated from the stairs, and a garage. On the first floor were two bedrooms, a drawing room and a shower room next to the kitchen. It was all so romantic with climbing ivy keeping us warm externally and apart from a little central heating there was a log fire in the drawing room. Very nearby was Regent's Park with a very good inn on the way. Our little daughter enjoyed many happy hours sitting or lying in her perambulator with our aunt a short distance away from the mews.

We were naturally a target for our friends, on their visits to London. They enjoyed the free life of tasting the many restaurants, theatres and hotels, though the war time rationing of many food products and the stiff regulations of war were still in force.

Often we met our local friends in the park, to gossip on the faults of government, and perhaps on Sunday mornings to scatter the ducks walking on the footpath edge of the lake. All this activity was interesting and most rewarding to come back to; my office HQ was nearby, I had settled in to be happy to work as the technical manager of sales concerning synthetic resins and their applications. The fellow indoor sales person who was taken on instead of me twelve months before the war had been in the same dull office position ever since. Looking back,I decided I was right to refuse at the time, for my career was a tremendous lot more interesting.

Some customers I had serviced before the war; for one in particular I had inaugurated a first tanker supply for 'Celotex' insulated construction board, the first tanker supply for Bakelite.

Various episodes took place from my factory visit. I was introduced to a new detergent titled 'Teepol' at a time when detergents were new and could replace soap, and more easily clean all types of stain. I had brought some home and decided to try it as a shampoo. I ran the bath water and enjoyed reading the latest news. Afterwards I massaged my hair with 'Teepol' and with shower water rinsed it off and was amazed to find my hair coming out in great chunks. You can guess my disappointment, and I abandoned detergents for ever more. When people asked me what had happened concerning my wider parting, I beamed, 'Wearing a flying helmet!'

On occasions the opposite mews house revelled in activity. The owner was an artist and lived a very private life working in a studio away from the mews, but sometimes he brought his models to his mews house and if we had not drawn our curtains at the failing light we would witness hectic parties with all clothes barred. It was amusing entertainment for a while but one soon found the show rather tame and uninteresting to the point that we did complain because of the disturbance to the peace of our mews in general.

My wife then gave birth to a beautiful baby boy, Roger, and thus we became thoroughly domesticated and immersed in the progress of family life. We received two visits, one from the Icelandic Squadron Leader, John Wilson who was just being discharged from the Royal Air Force after finishing his time. I was friends with him during my tour in Iceland. My wife's brother Robert also came, who was just being discharged from the Army after much battle in the landings and throughout Italy. They had no idea what to do for a living and discussed different possible objectives and then we hit on the idea of starting them off in a business on their own to manufacture abrasive sanding discs used in the motor car industry.

I knew sanding discs were not easy to make, but the current discs, mainly supplied from the USA, were not using synthetic resin, and although there was some attempt during the war to use cold set synthetic resin, it was not considered satisfactory. My idea was to use hot set synthetic resin and be the first. The raw materials needed licence for importation from the USA except for the resin I felt should be developed for the purpose. This idea agreed, my two friends set off to convince the government departments that they were serious and obtained the necessary licence. I designed the plant necessary to augment a central hot oven and the partnership was born using the three letters of each surname Macwilson. I kept all the records of expenditure and details of the manufacturing programme for laboratory work. I used the kitchen of my home to develop the right mix of ingredients. My wife and children were wonderful not to complain too much and the enthusiasm by all was magnificent.

It quickly became apparent when production commenced that my two friends could not cope for they were not technical minded but were good company, so I consulted Lilian and suggested to her that it was necessary for me to join the partnership otherwise it would quickly grind to a halt. I also felt to carry on was not fair to my life contract to Bakelite to do more than the initial idea I had inspired, hence I felt I should leave Bakelite with all its security for the future. My wife and I discussed my suggestion and agreed, if I wanted to leave Bakelite for the partnership it was all right by her, for her own father had done the same to become a notable rubber planter in Malaya after working in the office at Golspie for the Duke of Sutherland of Dunrobin Castle.

Obtaining permission to leave Bakelite was not easy. All levels thought I was mad to consider such a thing, for nobody had done such a thing before. They did their best to persuade me to stay but my mind was made up to trust my new dream to a successful conclusion despite being short of cash. I had considered my father's 'no' to the Royal Air Force into my decision to stay with Bakelite.

Thus I moved to work into our production premises underneath a railway arch near Marylebone station a few minutes walk from my mews. I naturally parted with my motor car, which was a new car design for the majority of vehicles were still the same as before the war so I was walking, with no thought of purchasing a new vehicle until success said so, for my time was spent meeting many government departments as the details were so consuming.

The company was hard to get off the ground, literally lifting heavy sacks of abrasive grain up steep wooden stairs to stores, with large rolls of vulcanised fibre heavy and difficult to handle, liquid synthetic resin in drums that sounded like a Caribbean party when empty; however we were all keen to move forward and did so with ease.

The family situation did not change. The park was near to accommodate our fresh air need and the inn on the way to and fro gave us much pleasure to meet and talk. It was mainly on Sundays for me, I was working all hours to ensure a satisfactory product of high quality to sell, from our own homemade machinery and restriction of production space.

On the way each time to our archway premises I passed a silversmith's shop and sold items I felt we could do without. Curiously we became good friends. I was able to purchase lovely silver bowls made in India at a very good price for they were not considered suitable by his main customers.

After several months we were ready to try to obtain orders for our product. Again I insisted we go the hard way, so we went to the Ford motor company who appeared very happy with their USA suppliers of sanding discs which were used to take away the welding seams and to polish bumpers and general faults in the bodywork before painting. Little interest was given on Friday, but on the Monday they telephoned and wanted to know a price and in reply quoted a price similar to what they were buying at. All was quiet until Tuesday when they asked to see us immediately, so I sent John Wilson, the safe one of our partners, to meet their request.

Our product was nine times better than what they were using from the USA and they wanted thousands immediately. Unfortunately we could only supply our production capacity and settled a supply routine. The Americans were surprised and bitter concerning the situation and did pressurise our licence authority and suppliers. At this time the big three USA companies were a cartel, so difficult to fight, but luck you have to have at times of hard work and concentration: surely this came with the USA government banning the cartel thus making the fight more fair, although the fight was on between the giants and the ant who did a first.

CHAPTER 7

New moves

IALWAYS NEED TO REMEMBER my time with Bakelite and Dr
Baekeland's advice, perhaps others also need to do so. I say, 'Harry,
look, you need to do at least two things in life, three or more if
possible, I did, you can also,' and today I pass on his advice to anyone
not sure what to do next.

I have needed to remind myself when times seemed to become
difficult that there are always four ways to travel through life's
problems, so to think them out. I add, 'The key to success is the fear
of failure,' plus 'You do not get what you deserve, you only get what
you negotiate yourself,' so you need to choose the right path by
consideration of your circumstances; it always works without fail.

Now my working time always considers the possibility to ensure
you make the right decision from the facts that emerge.

Life for my wife and growing family was full of expectations: we
could make plans as my business was going well. In fact quite quickly
we increased production by working three shifts, one early, the
second after lunch to late evening, the other through the night, the
three of us taking it in turns and alternating at the end of every six
days of production, thus having Sunday off only if all was tidy and
ready to start on Monday without fail.

The major part was the technical period of oven baking,
understanding how the synthetic Bakelite resin behaved during its
temperature cycle, like a good housewife cooking a succulent roast
joint of beef to just exactly how you like it. The procedure allowed
time beforehand for the acceptance of checked raw materials, the
mixing with coating, and time to do the finishing: the oven bake,
product test, label and package, ready for the customer.

A commercial delivery van was purchased to deliver once per
week, proudly painted black with the company name Macwilson and
'Abrasives' in bright startling red.

Life was a little lonely for all because of the hours on duty; free
time was not available to really meet each other, and it was all
rewarding by achievement.

However, I now needed to revise the situation, at the same time doubling the production. We decided to find larger premises, which was not hard. They were located in Hayes, near Slough, Middlesex, and consisted of 6000 sq ft on the third floor of a large commercial block, near the railway station, useful for receipt of our heavy raw materials.

At the same time my wife and I decided we needed to move away from our small charming mews house to a more convenient living situation because the children needed space to live and play. We felt lucky for the opportunity to move into a spacious apartment located in rural Epsom, Surrey. The movement of the family was interesting, I borrowed my partner's large vintage open two seat Armstrong Siddeley motor car, which accommodated us all plus most of our belongings.

My business partner with whom I had served in the Royal Air Force, Iceland, now a very firm friend, used his small boot Bentley saloon to help with the rest of our chattels and followed me in his latest classic acquisition of scarce motor cars. All except the motor cars looked a little sparse in our new abode; however as a family we were all very happy.

The journey to the Marylebone production plant was made by a convenient Express Green Coach daily boarding at 7 to 7.30 a.m.; arriving home depended on the availability of a return programme as my time of shift often finished very late. After a while I purchased a good old secondhand Standard motor car to be ready for the new move to Hayes.

Although life was hectic for a while the pace of business was steady, so did not cause too much disruption. In fact I had purchased new specialised ovens and a copy or two of our individual plant to precede our move to the Hayes premises, so we were able to replace our current limited production for an expansion, to a possible ten times the output of product. It was decided to seek more commercial outlets, for a more reliable sales turnover.

The necessity to employ people caused me to create standard working specifications for each operation to follow strictly and to consider again the market we were in, by collecting information on our competitors; I intended to meet to monitor the foe to judge their likely influence on our future, thereby ensuring our expansion of sales in the market concerned.

The new living situation was thrilling. We started to increase furniture from various sources. A belated Christmas present from my wife's father provided the fitted carpet throughout, and her younger brother Robert, now working for me, built a long book casement when not on shift working. My next door neighbour introduced me to a prestigious RAC country club with the main headquarters in Pall Mall, London, so my golf was easily possible again, if I could spare the time. With a social life hand made, my wife easily made new friends. Incidentally I am still a member today of the Royal Automobile Club, which now I think the best gentlemen's club in all Europe, or the planet.

Apart from my business progressing steadily, all was well. My young son Roger, just able to walk, borrowed my Royal Air Force jacket and to my horror started to wear it for walks with the side pockets touching the ground. I understood he was finding the jacket most days, so I dismantled all evidence of wings and rank, then gave away possession of it.

My son also commenced to collect fodder from the kitchen, some fresh, some otherwise, to meet the gardener of our delightful estate for a snack or lunch. This situation became a daily occurrence to exchange views of the day. Eventually meetings became less frequent because Roger commenced his first school, but the friendship remained, to be rekindled over the holiday times. I felt sure this situation was a godsend for the future business fortune.

Dianne Gayle, going to school each day, seemed very happy under my wife's care. She enjoyed a passion for dancing and demonstrated her skill to us all at appropriate times outside, when the sun's heat sponsored the weather, filling the need for floating movements of nature, so heavenly to us all, possibly including our friends, within the beautiful green grounds of our landscape of flowering bushes and lush green grass.

Of course I was away most of the time keeping up with our business, which apart from the rich reward was progressing well, to the extent that the government's licence monetary control department sent written a appreciation for the success of our product gaining ground over imported products from strong currency countries.

My wife was born in Sittiawan, Malaya, and since our marriage had always had a tendency to suffer from hay fever, particularly in times of a high pollen count. Suddenly she became ill with the common form of TB; she was quickly placed in quarantine until we could establish a suitable hospital for cure. Not a huge distance away was a very good centre that specialised in the cure of TB, at Midhurst, West Sussex. My wife's name was accepted, but there was over a three month waiting list, so I looked for an alternative.

I consulted with my GP and our dear friend Robert Wheeler, who was a surgeon in a London hospital, but both could do little to find a solution. I then approached my lawyer, who looked after my business interests; the result was entry in a week or so to a convent that also specialised in the cure of TB and had a relationship with my lawyer's friend, who was the head doctor of a West Country hospital and he would supervise the progress. The only other course was a Switzerland mountain cure which seemed impossible to comprehend at the time.

My sister Nancy, who had married my Bakelite friend Richard Roberts, who lived nearby on the Epson Downs anxiously took my two children into her care, so as to leave my wife in quarantine in our spare single room to await the move.

Very soon I was able to take my wife, with very little allowed personal baggage, to the Nunnery, with its solid dark stone entrance and a very cold interior, to a bed in a dormitory of six persons, with all windows wide open to the cold atmosphere. I departed with no hopeful good wishes, in fact without having been able to speak to anyone in authority, and went home full of apprehension and sadness for such an odd situation.

After a period of visiting and listening to the uncomfortable news of the spartan daily routine, and the freezing conditions without any sign of a doctor or Mother Superior, I informed our West Country doctor and arrangements were made to take my wife into his hospital where she received what I thought was normal humane treatment. My wife responded to the medication and after a few months came home cured of the disease but in a very tender shape.

My wife was away for nearly a year, and during this time the children, although visited by me regularly, were getting a little restless. My wife needed to regain her strength so the children were transferred to her dear friend Betty, living in the charming village of Upwey north of Weymouth, not exactly on the way to Dorchester, Dorset.

Betty's husband was a wholesale merchant of fruit and vegetable, with his HQ shop in Weymouth. I had been introduced to Mike by my wife's friend at the beginning of World War II, when he was a Major in the County Regiment, and had participated through the frantic battles of Arnhem and Nijmegen, Holland including crossing the river with the enemy on both banks. The children enjoyed their stay. Roger was baptised by the kind vicar of Upwey, a little late perhaps but a wonderful thought and I much enjoyed very good golf with Mike on my occasional visits.

Gradually things returned to normal. I engaged a housekeeper to take charge, and the children returned to be looked after by my wife's younger sister Cecilia for a while at home. Naturally I was busy with business through all this mayhem and fortunately never missed a beat; progress with our unique sanding disc was taking more of the market share and we were supplying more outlets so were always moving away from the danger of only just one customer.

The USA giants of the abrasive industry were always a threat with their method of coating vulcanised fibre rolls against my method of coating single fibre discs. This was always on my mind. I was winning at present though always considering the roll coating method but this was expensive; combining with an electrostatic application of abrasive grain could be more consistent for wear life, except for the coarse grades not really used by the motor car industry. We extended our factory space to include a ground floor administrative office alongside a sales office, and the staff increased overall to nineteen within an export programme taking shape with a good distributor agent in Holland and Cyprus, but it was all early days.

My wife's younger brother Robert who started with me at Marylebone decided to marry the wealthy daughter of a famous company chairman and left to take to the country life as a gentleman; he was extremely useful and very good with the gun. He in fact bought me a 12 bore double barrel, side lock shotgun ex Cogswell & Harrison. My time was too precious to participate in the shooting season full time, but we enjoyed the game received.

In West Germany I commenced a friendship with a well informed owner of an old abrasive company; it had been heavily damaged in the war but was now recovering with modern thought and equipment. The owner had suffered from the Gestapo, escaped execution and seemed to be in some difficulty with the present authorities over money required to go overseas for some strange reason I did not understand. However I provided him with a ticket and a small amount of cash to quickly escape to the USA.

Following my introduction I received access to his factory and their ideas for the future. It was all quite friendly, except for two staff who suffered from our troops disturbing their little Nazi habit and routine, these fellows I avoided, but they were opaque to the truth and not important.

The production was of all types of bonded flexible and rigid abrasives and with access to his new building I took an interest in his installation of a modern USA type of plant. Before the owner's departure, I had negotiated a flexible licence which created a close bond to the advantage of both our companies, although it did cost money. One interesting product was a tough flexible wet and dry fine abrasive paper for the motor car industry, employing rubberised backing. Wet and dry was the general term used to eliminate scratches and imperfections of the metal coachwork before finishing painting the motor car.

One Wednesday, quite suddenly without warning, the Ford Motor Company called to say, 'We are getting a stock of wet and dry from the USA.' This was not my supply but I was asked, 'Can you help? We will have to shut down on Monday next for we run out on Friday.' I replied, 'I will let you know in ten to fifteen minutes and will call you back.'

After checking through to the plant in Germany to see if they could supply, I telephoned the buyer and said, 'Yes, I will meet your challenge.'

I called my wife and said we were off to Germany that afternoon; I would be home very soon.

I set course for Germany with Lilian. The weather was bad on arrival at Dieppe; the town was flooded, with sewage floating in the streets, and the houses, shops, banks and offices under water. I did find a bank on high ground which had only the basement flooded, to change money; anyway they changed my cash for some dried out money and advised that we would be wise not to stay in the town to sleep, so we left the town with its disgusting smell for high ground, and spent the night dozing off in the car.

After a few hours we set off for Germany. En route it was snowing, very large soft flakes with wet roads. The windscreen wipers found the heavy snow laborious and started to falter, so we rested for food morning and evening.

As we approached the turning point from the main road for our destination, Siegen, with some eighty miles to go, partly over low mountains, things started to freeze. The road became slippery, the wipers packed up for good, and as I could not see I tried to stop the car but it lurched forward to slide until stopping just before a large pine tree at the side of the unmarked snow covered road.

The moist vapour inside the car and outside created an eerie atmosphere. We waved our breath through open windows to see again. I found some string, tied it to each wiper blade then brought back the string through each front window so my wife could oscillate the wiper blades to clear the snow to see ahead, All worked well, but it was very cold for both of us owing to the snow and cold air coming through the part open front windows. However despite the tedious, almost impossible, task for my wife, the windscreen clearing expert, we eventually made our destination and went very tired to a warm bed.

In the morning the snowstorm had departed. We filled the car with wet and dry abrasive paper, filling all the spare seat space and the boot, and the beautiful glistening snow in bright sunlight stayed for our return as far as Belgium. We circumnavigated flooded Dieppe for the boat to England, where Ford were waiting for us to beat the clock. On arrival they appreciated our endeavour so the supply crisis was now passed with flying colours.

At this time the pressure of the abrasive giants, both UK and USA, was obvious in price and the total supply of all types, with pressure to eliminate our type of sanding disc which was still supreme. I considered more factory space and came to the conclusion that we needed our own purpose built factory with plant to achieve smoother production facilities and bring down the cost of manufacture.

It was considered a good idea to move to the coast to obtain a moist atmosphere to help mature naturally our fibre sanding discs with other development products, so we scoured the coastal towns between Kent and Devon and settled on Portsmouth, whose officials welcomed us so convincingly and plans were made accordingly.

From a family point of view, I mainly fixed my continental visits to Germany, Holland and Italy and elsewhere to coincide with the UK holidays for I had decided to teach the family to ski, so off we would go by road to resolve my business, then finish near our chosen destination.

On one of our very first occasions, the destination was a small mountain hotel at Gstaad, Switzerland, for Christmas time to celebrate by the family learning to ski. My last business call was Germany and before running into town, we stopped on the high ground, to get tidied up for my appointment, by a frozen small pond. My two children jumped out of the car to skate in their leather shoes on the cracking ice. It was all so slippery and trying to stand up was not possible, as the cracked ice with attendant powder ice bent to dry the small pool out. It was good fun for their first initiation of arriving in the enchanting drift snow conditions to come.

After leaving Germany and driving through Liechtenstein we arrived to Swiss drift snow then took the ash gravel snow roads to our destination where we garaged the car and took a horse sleigh to our small charming hotel, much more like a timber country inn shining its warm glowing light over the whispering feathery snowdrifts just outside the entrance of kindly welcome. It was a heartfelt Yule time glorification for Christmas Eve, to warm our family reception to a very special lofty height.

With all kitted out in ski hire equipment, on Christmas Day we set off to a thick snow covered hill adjacent to the side of our hotel. I commenced to teach them in a very simple way how to run and stop; the result was chaos, nobody could even stand up let alone move to any extent, without falling down with everything crossed. Hence I decided I was not a family ski instructor.

So all the family joined me with a guide ski instructor, to learn to ski the proper way. My son could hardly control his enthusiasm for fun, and often fell down to roll over head over heels down the steeper slopes. My daughter was much more cautious and kept to the rules. My wife was very good and soon skied like me.

It was a fantastic holiday and we all were enthusiastic to repeat it.

At home I set up a laboratory chemist to oversee the high quality standards as laid down by my specifications but without any power to alter formulations without my written word. I also commenced a home technical sales staff indoor, and outdoor, to see that our technical properties always got through, to the sales staff and the valued customer.

I was anxious to develop business relations with the manufacturers of electric, pneumatic and other hand working power tools that could use our products, so as to control the safety of operators and adjacent personnel at home and overseas. This was an important feature of our development programme. Much work needed to be done to ensure safety of 7 and 9 inch diameter wheels or discs that could be used by hand held portable power tools at 60 or 100 miles per hour for work, in all kinds of good to bad atmospheres and conditions of physical working.

My company was still working well to plan, I started to travel extensively to look for better supplies of raw materials, export agents, collaborators either way to back our future expansion of sales, who would keep their word, for there were many wiry slippery rascals who would not, and I wanted to set out to be moderately friendly with our competitors to avoid misunderstandings, overseas, in Europe and at home.

On my regular visits to the continent I was surprised on one visit to Siegen, Germany by my close friend Klingspor; I was always welcome in his lovely castle-like house on the side of the mountain overlooking the town with his factory in the distance. We were having a drink before dinner when I noticed a large picture of German soldiers welcoming British troops in World War One. It was not the same as previously observed, and as we were going into dinner I noticed my host turning over the picture from showing the Germans trying to shoot the British troops; nevertheless dinner was good and of the usual high standard.

I returned to the UK through the Low Countries and prepared for my next visit to the USA. Air travel or any kind of travel was still very restricted and cash limited to very small amounts, but I boarded a Boeing Clipper Stratocruiser to fly to the United Sates. The aircraft was the latest in air travel with four petrol engines and two decks; the lower deck one could walk to, via stairs, to have a cocktail or two then return to one's seat with overhead beds, one up the other down according to your seat of two abreast; then there was a gangway and further seats the other side. The range was limited with the necessity to refuel in Ireland and Canada before touching down in the USA at Idlewild airfield. Being on business with limited cash one was extremely careful to avoid being swindled by offers of a better exchange rate with prices so new to calculate.

Shortly afterwards I decide to trim my hair before commencing my appointments and called in at the nearest barber's shop cum hairdresser. The operator was just finishing a gentleman's head, and he departed quite pleased with his short haircut.

I was called to sit in front of the large mirror with a friendly, 'Hello, what can I do for you?'

I replied, 'I would like a very light trim to my hair around my ears and neck so it looks nice and clean.'

My man with large scissors in hand said in a loud voice, 'Look, mister, you've come to have a hair cut and I only do hair cuts, so you will have to have one, that's that, mister.'

The gentlemen now waiting smiled, so the mirror told me. 'I am happy to pay for a hair cut but I only want a light trim.'

The large scissor operator waved them at me a little menacingly. 'OK, you have a hair cut.'

I looked in the mirror a little doubtfully, as the man cut away, but in the end it looked a gentle cut. I was pleased with his efforts but thought I was lucky not to have received a skinhead cut; no doubt the price was the real consideration.

I set off by bus to visit my major raw materials supplier in the south and three companies adjacent to New York City and one in New England, plus of course a Bakelite friend or so. It was a thrilling visit with much achieved and I returned home the same way.

I like doing business in the USA for they are always willing to listen and base their response without looking through the past prejudice. This visit consolidated my thoughts about the future so I set about to complete the programme of work necessary and to arrange the finance with plans to move to Portsmouth as soon as possible. At this time we made a few changes, especially of staff. Our spearhead on technical sales departed to set up his own tool business but remained a valuable customer. My wife's elder brother Ian, who was a high pressure salesman with a soap washing powder company, was invited to join and take over the outside sales. The laboratory chemist was too academically minded to completely follow his brief and departed. It took a little time to find a replacement for it needed someone trained in synthetic resins. Our bank, Royal Bank of Scotland, was in New Bond Street, London, and was getting inconvenient as was our solicitor, though the latter was moving to Sussex soon. The factory staff were well trained and one in particular was heading to become a good works manager in charge.

The next year I was back in the USA and Canada with my wife and accomplished a great deal particularly with Alice, the daughter of Dr Redman, to assist her in driving her large new Oldsmobile to meet appointments and to assist in the tight financial restrictions for a while. To relieve the tight situation at home, an agent was appointed for Canada and further sources for raw material were discovered.

My Canadian friend Alice was used to frequently crossing the border at Niagara Falls but on this occasion she breezed to a standstill saying, 'Hello, I am here,' and expected to pass into Canada on the wave of her hand through the window. Unfortunately for some reason the customs official took exception to this and she was called into the office, muttering something like 'silly little people' and the strange thing was that I and my wife were completely ignored. The officials started a complete full search of our friend to the extent of stripping her and then completed a thorough examination of the car after she dressed. The car was taken apart by three officials in some places to the bare chassis. For my wife and me it was very embarrassing, waiting unable to do anything to help for over an hour and half while this performance took place. Thus we were late for our dinner appointment and our friend Alice was still bubbling with fury from the border incident.

Just after returning home and checking our progress and sorting some outstanding paper work on registration of trademarks and difficulty with a sales application or so, I started to look at our forward programme from an analysis of recent visits that caused me to feel we must prepare for much increased competition from the US giants who still seemed to be exchanging information on how to meet any threat. We needed to put a spurt on quickly, to prepare to meet the challenge.

For a while, we were thinking of buying a house. Epsom was a splendid place within the downs and such beautiful countryside, with friends around. Our apartment suited our needs, but it was inconvenient for going to and from the company premises and we thought of independence for the future. Thus I decided to purchase a house in Camberley; the price, I believe, was £6,000. We needed to withdraw gently my son's friendliness with the gardener whom I respected too! He had to leave his little private kindergarten school, with my daughter moving to the ballet school that was quite famous in Camberley to continue her dancing.

In my negotiations, I was advised by the current owner, a gentleman and chairman of some committee for the Olympic games, that he wanted the money paid in cash. Frankly I could not imagine myself counting out the money in cash but was told this was the way he did business and he had no difficulty with Olympic cash. I suggested he could check my payment through my solicitors to a named bank for counting the notes. This seemed OK and the deal was done.

The house was situated 250 feet above sea level on a rise as one of fourteen on the perimeter of a private estate. The main house was a large one that was used by a religious sect. It was so quiet one did not notice it was there and it did not influence the private road at all.

The house possessed a stunning white wood carved entrance door with a white porch leading via an inner hall to a large room the width of the house, which we used as a reception drawing room, leading to stairs and the dining room. The rear of the house was a flagstone courtyard dropping to a terrace of rock plants leading to a large lawn and a very old large pine tree standing almost on a small outbreak of steep rock. Beyond this was a thick pine woodland and at the side a handsome cultivated rose garden; to the other side garages dropped down to a house just being built for an artist. The first floor was the master bedroom with a balcony facing the rear with my dressing cum bedroom next with two further bedrooms, then through the corridor to lead on to the old servant quarters of three rooms and a staircase to the kitchen quarters and so on. Whilst the ceilings were very much lower the house was still a beautiful quality purchase.

We fitted the house well with lemon coloured fitted carpets except for my dressing room where we fitted a new special handmade Scottish tartan related to the distant clan of my mother and father. All was well: Roger joined his prep school with the same apprehension as we all do on our first break with home; Dianne Gayle joined her ballet school, seemingly similarly without difficulty; however I was not present at the time. Our faithful housekeeper Mrs Wright made the transition without any doubts; my wife was happy and I was happy too for the smooth journey to my work.

To finance a major part of the move to the proposed new factory: special requirements, built premises, the installation of new plant which was becoming more sophisticated as the production increased to maintain our lead in high quality products, a loan was negotiated with a company called 3i formed by a consortium of banks for the purpose of assisting industry to expand in the difficult circumstances of the government economic recovery programme. The negotiation was successful, aided by my selling a small part in special shares in addition to the reasonable loan at 17.5 per cent interest.

Two pieces of land of approximately two and half acres were to be leased for 100 years from the council. The architect received instructions to proceed with one unit of special designed building to manufacture by roll, not singly as now. The plant was ordered from overseas with the help of my German friend so all was to happen soon. At this period we saw no reason to prevent further increases in our current production of single discs.

Owing to our need for new machinery, we found a very important new and well informed source that also supplied the giants, when not manufacturing in the USA. I was also looking for plant to be made in Italy, near Verona.

I am a hands-on kind of business man and whilst I am not very clever with my hands except in sports and things like flying, whilst I do not interfere with production staff and colleagues I like to be present or informed should there be a difficulty or a mistake so I can advise and see in my mind the likely result and check it. For instance, from my experience I feel for the synthetic resin as a living thing and know how it feels in the process of application and how resins react under heat. I can almost see it and talk to it. This may sound odd to many people but it came from the skill learnt in making resins in my early days at Bakelite. I try to apply the same feel to all types of application whether it is machinery or method concerning the manufacture of the finished product and how it is used safely.

The company at that moment was just experiencing a market downturn; this was the second – the previous occasion was approximately two years earlier.

CHAPTER 8

India and Malaya

HERE IN THE UK WE HAVE 'The Abrasive Industries Association' and it comprises the home based traditional abrasive companies whether from the USA, the UK or elsewhere, manufacturers or distributors, primarily to exchange information for the benefit of the industry related to home and export trade. Naturally my company's trade progress was a major topic of interest, for nobody new had entered the market for decades. Their interest was heightened for my company was modern using only synthetic thermosetting resins, which means that resin applied would set to an irreversible solid state via my heating process, while the industry as a whole was using animal glue and non synthetic resin applications.

The Association had sent out feelers for me to join, but I viewed this action as a means to control my price and effort, hence I checked my suspicion out by visiting various companies in the UK to discuss the position of joining and decided not to accede to the offer. I did however develop a friendship with the Chief of a northern English abrasives company to discuss the industry and the Association from time to time.

The travelling pressure was getting very strong and I felt I was likely to miss out on some important issue, hence I employed a chauffeur, so that I could work from the rear seat. Whilst the situation worked well, the car was cramped with all my papers around, consequently I asked Lilian to assist in the purchase of a more suitable vehicle for I understood my local garage was now the agent for the new Armstrong Siddeley 'Sapphire', by arranging a test drive.

The next morning the car was waiting. I confirmed my purchase after testing the working space and awaited one more improvement, the addition of a telephone. The company financial decline now reversed, so all was well. Our sales progress was back on track with a budget and business plan with North American export additions.

Eventually I did not fit the telephone, which apart from filling the rear boot, had no connections via the rear seats to the actual handset. It was all a godsend for now I could move around papers to keep in touch with the office, factory and outside contacts with no difficulty. Apart from getting tired eyes now and then, the car office worked very well with enormous time saved working and finding one's destination.

My next call was the Dorchester Hotel, Park Lane, London, without the hassle of parking. I met the trade supplier of much raw material to the abrasive trade in the USA, UK and elsewhere. At the time he was drinking jarfuls of iced water sitting in the sun of his private lounge at the telephones facing Hyde Park. I was introduced to his wife and for the first time in my life noticed someone with no eyebrows. Anyway she soon disappeared for I was enjoying very important subjects of discussion with the husband. As we neared the end of the meeting it was getting late for their dinner at 18.30 so in consequence his wife returned to chase her husband. This time as I left I noticed she had painted eyebrows on in a thin smooth black line. It was the closure of a hot wonderful sunny summer day, seeing something strange with so much ice and me late home for my dinner.

Camberley became interesting for the whole family. First of all was the vicinity of the Army staff college. A close friend from Epsom was a career soldier and today was a lieutenant colonel with two young children roughly the same age as our own. The colonel's wife was an ex Sword of Honour in her own right, and they came to Camberley to stay with their friend the Lieutenant General, now looking after a large Army training school nearby, after his appointment teaching at the staff college. The interesting thing to me was that these two gentlemen had followed each other in appointments, since leaving Sandhurst but two years apart, which they thought extraordinary too!

I joined the local golf club, took a few lessons at weekends and played with my wife's father when the family stayed. One day I played with her brother Ian who was a scratch handicap and for some reason being a 14 handicap I was playing like a professional for a few holes. Then we came to a long difficult hole; my partner fluffed his drive, while mine was beautifully straight, then he struck a beautiful second shot and I followed suit. When we approached the hole my partner took out his putter to play when I was looking for my ball, which was not on the green to see. In my mind, I thought perhaps I should look in the hole and lo and behold there was my ball, to win the hole.

At the same moment Roger appeared with my wife's father,

William MacDonald, from down below the green to proclaim, 'Well done!' yet looked so guilty for they had collected my ball and placed in the hole! On another day I had finished my round and was walking though the club house entrance to change when I noticed two men counting much money; they were the two men who were starting the great English car auction company. At the time I thought it was an odd thing to do, but I was wrong.

I now needed to prepare for a long journey to India, Malaya, Singapore, Australia, New Zealand, Fiji, Hawaii, San Francisco, New York and then home. The objective was very serious, as follows:

India was in response to a request for a mutual licence to manufacture, so to adapt our technology to their old plant and to suggest ways to improve their old machines.

Malaya was to see the country where my wife was born and to visit interesting rubber plantations developed by her father, with the family house and golf course. One addition was to find an export agent.

Singapore was to confirm an agent providing he passed the tests of solely trading on his own account with the possibility of enthusiasm for our products.

Australia was to be in the second half to meet with the largest boat builder and the largest orange juice producer, to learn about Australia and see what we could achieve for our products.

New Zealand was to meet our agent in Wellington on the North Island by the strait separating the adjacent South Island, who was extremely successful for our company with a very good monthly turnover.

Fiji was just an interesting stopover for the flight to Hawaii and possible export contact.

San Francisco was really another stopover but I did have a contact of abrasive sanders and grinders over the bridge in Hamilton.

New York was to meet my successful sole agent for Stihl, the German chainsaw and cut-off machines, raw material suppliers and other useful contacts from previous visits.

I set off for the first half with my wife, in the new Comet four-engine first jet passenger aircraft in the world. Although one had heard of a crashed aircraft or so, to me it was not unusual at the time of introduction of a new aircraft. The DH Comet was a beautiful fast aircraft almost twice the speed of conventional piston engine aircraft, and although a little tight in space it was a great experience to arrive

fresh a few hours before breakfast, arriving at Dum Dum airport near
Calcutta. The exit to the taxis was chaotic with the journey to
Calcutta so degrading, filthy and depressing with the poor people
living in such squalor. Eventually we arrived at the best hotel, old
and noisy inside and out with people milling about who seemed to
have nowhere to go. Our suite, paid for by our host, was large with
open windows to the traffic blowing hooters in opposition to the
throngs of people's voices.

I insist on visiting companies as soon as I arrive, whatever time of
day or night. I first make a visit to the office or works so that I can
orientate my information, so I have in my mind what I need to know
and think, before I take a rest. They all seem to want me to rest on
arrival, and in this case before my host arrived. I took exception to
the noisy bedroom and asked my wife to find a quieter situation but
we were in the best rooms of the hotel and the management couldn't
understand why I wanted to change. However I insisted and was
found a tiny bedroom at the back of the building next to the kitchen
and whilst not completely quiet it was far more acceptable to me.

My host was not amused when he found out my move did not fit
his reservation but all ended well. He was of the second family of
India which owned Hindustani Motors, the only Indian motor
company producing the old British Morris Oxford, with two
thousand employees. I did stay to lunch with the directors and it was
very obvious to me the company was run on the USA system of
management production and felt very efficient.

Apart from the motor company my host was in abrasives, printing,
papermaking and much more. My visits coincided with an owner of
a Swiss carbon paper maker setting up a factory in Bombay for my
host; he appeared to be paid in diamonds. I was given the same
choice but I replied, 'No,' for it was entirely wrong to my English
way of doing business.

My first task was to visit the abrasive plant which was in the middle
of Calcutta. We went with his family in my host's chauffeur driven
old Cadillac, which was bought from the American ambassador, for
imports were forbidden by law. On arrival we passed through a
guarded gate, and stopped at the office which was outside the factory.
We alighted and sat down in the waiting room.

I said, 'Please can I go into the factory to see the machines
working?' and the answer was, 'No, I will send for the chief operator

to come here.' I politely indicated that this was not my way of working, for I needed to see the workings to form an opinion before I talked over the requirements.

My situation was not unusual however. I gathered the father and his two sons did not visit the working areas whilst the operators were present. However, it was agreed to bring a person from the factory to take me down, so I went off and made my way to the major coating machine. I approached the operator who immediately disappeared and left the machine running without supervision. This was quite dangerous and in time the operator was made to return but he did not want to speak to me.

I could see, however, checking the way the machine was working and going through the raw materials and animal glue for coating, and watching the operator's method that it was excellent in view of the very primitive plant being used.

I left and found my own way to the waiting room to talk, for there was much to discuss and agree without the ladies. Much later we attended dinner with strange food with the waiter's hands in white cotton gloves and an orchestra playing. I thought it odd that the wearing of gloves did not stop the waiters cleaning the glasses and they carried fresh glasses by squeezing the glasses together on the inside. However, I had enjoyed my first day in India but it was all so strange with multitudes of people, the caste system and of course the religious cow wandering where it pleased. Obviously there was much more to come as my host was so generous towards us.

The next day was completely taken up discussion, and drawing plans to alter the plant and method in accordance with my thoughts. A small abrasive grinding wheel factory had already been modernised with equipment installed by a USA giant I knew very well, but I was disappointed to learn that a short time later the USA giant commenced to build its own large factory and plant with another family to develop the total market for itself.

My host started to show us India, the first journey by car to New Delhi, the capital, and he possessed invitations to HM The Queen's garden party which was attended by his family with ourselves. I enjoyed it very much indeed for it was my first such invitation to meet Her Majesty and be present for her last tour as Sovereign of India. Yet it was heartrending to me to see so much poverty, like some people lived on the streets of Delhi cooking from an open little

drum of fire made from cow dung, with our British vapour
perfuming anyone near. Yet New Delhi is a majestic city of great
buildings all by our dear renowned architect Edwin Lutyens who
created so much influence. After a reception in the evening on a
private floor of a hotel where it was fashionable to hold a drinks party
we rested before setting off next day to Agra, the city on the River
Jumna adjacent to the Taj Mahal.

The journey was very interesting with lots of monkeys swinging
on the branches of trees on route. We stopped to witness a village
wedding, so colourful, with the silk of bride and other ladies
unfolding and billowing away in the heat of the midday sun. Later
on we stopped on a train crossing, quite a horrendous sight and with
a shrieking noise. We were approached by a man with a very large
brown bear tethered by a rough jute heavy rope who tugged it to
perform for an entertainment fee, in the tremendous heat of the sun.
I felt so sorry for the bear but fortunately the train passed and the
long furry bear was lost to sight, for we moved on to Agra.

We settled into a modern hotel with many visitors waiting to see
the inspiring Taj Mahal in the moonlight. We of course followed the
same route some time later, because we knew the correct time for
the clear moon to provide the maximum light contrast. We stopped
near to see in the distance the awe inspiring sight of an ivory white
canopy with slender towers, and we quickened our pace to be there
to see the exquisite mausoleum in detail from the entrance. We
walked along the marble slim garden with its stream to the white
marble memorial itself, gleaming in bright moonshine.

Next day we visited the nearby massive Red Fort built in red
sandstone for the Mogul King Emperor Shah Jehan in 1648, with
military stationed there until 1857. From the Red Fort you can see
the Taj Mahal completed by 1653 on the other side of the river
Jamna, for the mortal remains of his beloved Queen Mumtaz Mahal
for ever.

From the village I purchased a small piece of white marble with
inserts of beautiful coloured stones as used to build the magnificent
memorial shrine. I still treasure this piece of marble today. We did
not have time to see the Taj Mahal early as the red sunrise behind
the mausoleum provided a spectacular vista.

Next day we set off for Delhi and then to Calcutta to fly to Malaya
to return after our long weekend to settle the final details of licence

improvements and to place orders. One order was for an electrostatic process for the orientation of abrasive grain particles, a new process that I intended for my own company's future use, but which the giants in the USA had already started using.

Malaya was a dream for my wife. Much of the food was sort of ordinary vegetables mixed with curry flavours, some weak, some very hot, some with cold sour milk to drink; being a plain roast beef man I could not find it in India or now in Malaya. Hotels were few and far between and mostly old for there was little long distance tourist travel yet to prompt the need.

We flew and touched down in Kuala Lumpur, then joined a small aircraft, a British high wing monoplane 'Islander', manufactured on the Isle of Wight, to go to a town in mid country Ipoh where we stayed the night. I did have a business contact to see and called at his premises and enjoyed a lively chat whilst he was making ironwork structures, some decorative, with a lovely charcoal fire burning. I felt a little hot in the warm humid atmosphere of the day, but I thanked him for the meeting, and confirmed that because he was a very small operator, it was better to continue to buy from his local merchant. The merchant did not stock our products, but I was hopeful he would sooner or later.

After my call we continued our progress to Sitiawan to see Lilian's birthplace at Batu Gajah's Hospital in 1922, her erstwhile family rubber plantation and home, and on to Lumut, approximately 85 kms away from Ipoh, then by ferry boat to Pankor Island.

The road was very interesting, with much vegetation, including small banana trees with small sweet green bananas, which we sampled on the way, together with flowers such as the wild red poinsettias, blue iris, then palm trees in lush green grass and more banana trees interspersed.

We arrived in Sitiawan with its multitude of shops lining the high street of our main road, and stopped to ask the way to the hospital on the nearby hills. We found the hospital easily in open grassland grounds with directions for patients. We found the maternity building marked first class which confirmed my wife's birthplace 'first class' to my smiling enjoyment.

Now we doubled back to find the family rubber plantation estate. It was large and very heavily planted with rubber trees, each holding a thin bowl on its trunk to collect the white gum juice. Leaving the

estate we looked for the family house and entered the grounds by
walking up a long curved drive after starting underneath the very
large bright red flowers and leaves of the Flame of the Forest tree.

The house was a large square building with extensions from each
corner to accommodate bedroom quarters on the first floor, with an
open veranda all around the house. My wife located her private
quarters and insisted on calling the housekeeper present to explain the
present situation of ownership, She was told the rubber plantation
was merged with another large rubber estate with the two rubber
planters in charge staying in the house.

Curiosity settled, we continued on to Lumut, and visited the golf
course her father designed, built and financed on his own, being a
Scotsman, to keep his golf to a low handicap.

Afterwards we found our way to the quayside to board the ferry
boat to Pankor Island and made arrangements to leave our car and
trusted the driver to meet us on our return. A very small bright little
boy approached to take our suitcases to the boat and decided he was
able to carry them. After a short distance the small boy was obviously
carrying too big a load so we stopped, and I took my wife's suitcase
which was the smaller, for the boy insisted on continuing with my
heavier case. He did a very good job with my suitcase lifted to his
shoulder, so you could not see the boy. We boarded the boat and I
paid with a handsome note to the little boy who I gathered was the
only official porter to the boat.

The ferryboat was quite small with ten seats under cover and about
twenty-five overall. We set course through a narrow channel with
timber houses on each side. Most were drying fish in the sun. We
continued to the open sea and after a short distance moored in a small
open cove with our small white hotel nearby. There were only a few
timber buildings mainly involved in fishing.

The small hotel was my wife's family holiday home at the time
which they used for their family holidays when away from Sitiawan.

After checking our room was safe for the night, we changed to
walk down to the beach, for the sun's heat was welcoming us to the
shade of an old banyan tree, which I thought my wife remembered
from her peaceful family holidays of long ago.

We sat down on the cool roots underneath the dense drooping
branches which seemed to be reaching for the cool sand; it was a very
hot afternoon with the sound of the limp sea waves breaking on the

sand, just a faint sparkling ripple. I was expecting an army of turtles to come ashore to lay eggs at the fringe of loose sand, for there were many turtles in this area of seascape and all was so quiet except for the almost silent ripple of the sea now and then.

Suddenly we were startled by the noise of a few shrieks, with high pitched piercing pistol shots; we had in our tranquil solitude forgotten the current terrorist attacks operating in Malaya. We felt very alone in our bathing costumes with no shoes on our feet so felt very vulnerable with almost immediately two men quickly appearing in our vicinity, walking towards us. I thought of two terrorists, being a little scared, however as they approached my wife recognised the men as two plain clothed government armed police, I was not quite as sure; they quickly approached, came very near through our shade and passed on with only a nod of acknowledgement.

Being so scared for a moment or two, we decided to dress and depart to do something else. A little later we walked down to the nearby village harbour and hired a small boat with a local fisherman in charge to visit the nearby islands. Our trip was made interesting, for we listened to grizzly tales of the past when nearing the old leper colony island, in complete contrast to its beautiful appearance, with lush green small trees dispersed between the rocks down to the clear blue sea.

We progressed to see other nearby lush green islands, and on passage between passed a swimming turtle which took no notice of our presence. When we stopped to look, the turtle to me appeared quite stunning, for turtles were previously only a dream or hearsay mainly appearing in the dry atmosphere; this one was shining wet in the calm clear blue sea within an arm's reach of our little boat.

After our so-called voyage of magnificent beautiful adventure, we moored within the little harbour in time for evening dinner within our little quiet hotel, at least so we thought. We were however served a meal of boiled dry fish with a few boiled potatoes and rice, then early to bed after a local walk in the cool air.

We enjoyed a restful night in our simple hotel, or my wife's old family holiday house, and after first light plus an hour or so boarded our ferry to return to the mainland. We passed again the drying fish in the brilliant sunshine, then approached the entrance to Lumut quay where I could see our small boy walking to greet us on our arrival, with our driver waving from the same car waiting nearby. All was so friendly and serene. The boy was pleased to insist again to take my large leather case and so again it was difficult to see him whilst walking towards the car. The beam of smiles greeting my reward was felt as a reward to me for choosing such a willing helpful junior soul. I am sure will do well in the future, for himself.

We set off from a very friendly Lumut to return to Ipoh, thinking about and trying to ignore the awaking pistol shots that disturbed our previous day.

On arrival we boarded the same little 'Islander' light passenger plane to Kuala Lumpur airport to transfer to our Comet jet aircraft and so to Dum Dum airport, in Calcutta. We arrived late evening then took the taxi drive through the same culvert of misery to our hotel for a good night of rest for we had a very full day tomorrow.

First, in the morning, it was necessary to confirm our flight to UK for the next day, and afterwards I spent the entire day completing, confirming and agreeing the future details for the modernisation of the abrasive plant. After completion we enjoyed dinner again with the family in the hotel dining room, with the same white gloved waiters to serve. After the dinner we thanked the family for their very kind hospitality, also for the very kind generosity of the flight to Malaya for my wife to visit her early life.

CHAPTER 9

Around the world

THE FLIGHT TO HEATHROW, London was uneventful, but on the way, we did think of Malaya with its multi-national population, for it sounded impossible: the Chinese running most of the shops, the Indians doing general work, with the Malays running the Government posts, all with their own schools and way of life, yet all was in perfect harmony.

I had only visited one of the many temples for I did not quite understand the faith of the large Buddha images which looked so unreal to me; however my wife better understood and would go out of her way to pray. We both knew we would return to Malaya and India, yet I was again thrilled to drink from a vibration-free steady glass and discounted the thoughts of the possible disappearance of an aircraft.

On arrival home, all was well and I settled down to organise my schedule of work for the Portsmouth Plant Technical future via the chemist laboratory situation, with development for the expansion of sales.

Our excellent sales overseas were progressing well, so there was the necessity to develop an increase in our range to compete more with the USA giants so to increase the security with our progressive agents hunting for business in their own country.

Thus there was the need to consider the visit to Australia first, for the market tended to overshadow nearby New Zealand, which also was doing very well with our product, against a lot of imported competition. Our Australian agent was a small well established abrasive company selling, in the main, animal glue-bonded abrasive sheets for the sheep shearing industry, who needed our synthetic resin bonded abrasive to modernise his process to the new technical developing market the USA were getting interesting in. Hence I agreed to discuss the possibility of a manufacturing licence to produce our type of product, thought by me to try and forestall the USA company's competition. However my programme was to settle ahead the progress in Europe and our very good progress with the machine power toolmakers in the USA.

As I was about to confirm my itinerary, I was informed I had a problem at home, for three members of my works staff had strayed from my strict compliance specifications and the method of adjustment to meet the humidity readings of the day that were responsible for our quality of production.

I called to see the persons involved, and we met in my office. As we assembled, I stated in no uncertain terms, 'You cannot do this error of judgment, for you disobeyed the strict company instructions not to do any deviations without my permission in writing.' The three explained that they thought they were doing the company a good service. I replied by explaining fully the company's product of quality and rejection procedure. Whilst I realised I had no chemist in charge at the present time, in my view there should be no deviation to alter the work specifications, without my authority. 'Thus, you are in deep fault.' There came a 'sorry, sorry, sorry' from each one of them. 'Please never do such a thing again. The meeting is now finished.'

I did not admire their initiative, for by experience I knew you cannot make decisions without calculation of the result for approval.

I decided the coming visit to Australia and New Zealand would be better extended to cover progress on India and sales introduction in Thailand and Singapore, followed by Australia and New Zealand then the Islands through the Pacific Ocean to the United States, San Francisco to New York. I also invited my daughter Dianne Gayle to accompany me with my wife, for it was quite a hectic trip.

We all, with thirteen pieces of baggage, set off for Bangkok and arrived in the middle of the hot afternoon. We booked in to the famous Oriental Hotel, flying by the new Boeing jet 707 following in the wake of our De Havilland Comet. At this time jet travel was pretty uncommon, but was also good. Hotels were pretty scarce in most destinations, for the Jet Set and reasonable air travel were still to mature for recreation.

The Oriental alongside the river Chao Phrya had many private rooms called after notable visitors: Noel Coward, Somerset Maugham and more, and was very quiet and comfortable to study or write. It was all very strange, yet so welcome near a city which was all bustle and noise.

I looked through the Yellow Pages to confirm the details of my two prospective addresses to call on next day as possible sales agents.

I then called each on the telephone to discuss my quest and to fix the arrangements for the next day.

Later with my wife and daughter we set off for the Royal Temple on the other side of the river, and visited the large Golden Buddha set in state, looking so new in beautiful shining bright gold. Then we visited a large silk market, though we did not purchase anything, and soon departed for our hotel for a fine dinner adjacent to the river which was covering itself in shimmering changing coloured light, and so to early bed.

Next morning, I went off to see my contacts, who were situated quite near together. I found them both to be bright young men who seemed to stock everything in the abrasive line, but mostly sourced from the United States. Both however considered my new type abrasive resin bond and wished to stock supplies, so I was pleased to accept trial orders and I was amazed to find both very interested, keen to participate in competition.

I telephoned my company their instructions to arrange delivery; thus my business in Thailand was complete and I would depart for Singapore the next day.

Singapore was on our list to visit, for it had just become independent of Malaya, now to be known as Malaysia, which included Brunei, Sarawak, Borneo and other local islands Consequently, we felt Singapore would grow and prosper without USA influence. Hence, we had developed a very good likely contact to be included on our direct route to Australia via Darwin.

On arrival at Singapore we taxied across to our hotel, which was painted a shiny light bright green in colour to blend in with the very large harbour and was situated near to a Chinese theme park with a huge vivid bright dragon of startling yellow and scarlet red over the entrance.

After checking our night reservation, we explored the theme park, which we found stunningly attractive. It was also a great introduction for me to the strange Chinese vivid art, which Lilian seemed to understand.

I had received no notification from my business contact who I thought would have good business possibilities, hence took a taxi to his office address. On the way I removed my jacket to carry it, for it was obvious nobody wore one. On arrival, it was all active, I was expected, there was no waiting, and almost immediately we were immersed in deep business. I was impressed with his knowledge of all the major companies concerned with abrasives both English and American, and he soon said, 'I will meet your request to stock your products,' for he knew they were superior because I manufactured using phenol formaldehyde synthetic resin. He immediately provided a signed letter, as an order in all the variety of sizes needed to fulfil the likely demand over the coming months.

I accepted the position, telephoned the order to my office in the UK; arranged despatch so forecasted the actual delivery date to my agent.

We were both very pleased with each other and later left to have a light lunch at the old English Cricket Club from where I later departed, pleased to have made a very good sales agent. I considered both of us understood each other. I was a little disappointed I did not have the opportunity to watch some cricket, which is played all the year round for the tropical temperature remains roughly the same all year. The rain is the only likely cause of no play.

Later, I met my wife and we decided to go to an early show at a well advertised theatre. It was a hypnotic performance by quite a clever man, who did not noticeably hypnotise any one of the completely full audience present, he just seemed to be talking in a straightforward way to parts of the audience and the eye of a group or a particular person who acknowledged an interest. By this time the man had looked somewhere else, and after doing the same introduction cycle, he returned to the previous location where the persons or person were either asleep or muttering something whilst walking to the stage to be told, 'Please return to your seat and take no notice of me,' which of course they complied with immediately.

After a few minutes, different parts of the audience were on the move. As soon as they got back to their seat, they turned round to do the same walk again. As a part of the audience, you wondered if it was your turn next. This situation happened repeatedly, and as the fellow passed by our position, one felt it was necessary to search the man's face for a clue, and the gentleman's face became distinctly clear, without movement of any kind, thus I could feel something but not a real compulsion to do anything. He passed several times and people were following the actions of the first few to submit. Once again he came to pass my position and this time I felt, if you do that again, I could submit too, for his face was so compelling and vivid in detail.

I asked my wife what she thought. She took a little time, then replied, 'I am going to sleep, please do not wake me.' I looked, found she looked very sleepy, so I decided we should get up and leave, for this show was somehow serious and not entertainment for us.

We had been told to walk the famous Bogey Wogey Street to see the many transvestites on parade under the very bright lights of the avenue, bordered by bright odd shops. It was quite an education to see beautiful ladies dressed in expensive clothes of fashion and being inquisitive to see if they were men beautifully made up to perfection for their status as English or French expensive ladies of fashion.

Strange, to say I could see no evidence of the male sex, but a little later my wife explained to me how to tell the real gender by looking at the models' knees, ankles and the Adam's apple at the throat. I found out she was right, thus I was so disappointed to find they were all men and lost interest in the spectacle.

We departed to find a true Chinese meal. I naturally missed my roast beef. After the pure green tea, we left for turning in for the night and whilst talking to the staff of the hotel, we were informed that the new Prime Minister was vigorously cleaning up the town and that Bogey Wogey Street was to close within fourteen days.

Singapore was so different, apart from the fact I would have preferred the territory to have stayed with Malaya for reasons such as that the whole development of Malaya seemed right with its large port to provide motivation for rubber, industry and tourism. However this was not to be and the chief minister was busy cleaning up the entertainment, the streets, and the development of the port, and calling for industry to come with advantages for all.

Next morning, we were awake early and off to fly across the islands of Indonesia to the Northern Territory of Australia. We arrived in Darwin to refuel and I was surprised to see all officials wearing white shorts and white shirts, looking robust and well fed. On talking to various officials, whilst waiting within the airport, we learned Darwin was deeply flooded at this present time owing to a tremendous tropical storm; the roads were under six feet of water and properties flooded to the first floor. Thus we were kept much longer than normal as transit passengers to Sydney. I asked to do a taxi return trip to see the floods but was not allowed to see the devastation in the city. Eventually we took off for Sydney.

The flight path journey was made under a perfect blue sky. It was clear to see over the deserted brown countryside, the boundaries of properties with the occasional water hole. The inner state boundaries were particularly clear. The captain's voice commentary was interesting and confirmed what we were looking at as we passed overhead. We passed over Sydney and turned almost a complete circle for the pilot to point out various prominent features: the opera house, the harbour bridge, various parts of the harbour and more. After landing and on the way to leave the aircraft I had the opportunity to thank the captain who was wearing a very crisp white shirt and white shorts.

We immediately booked into our hotel and I left for my late business appointment arriving just before they closed for the day. I visited the factory units and departed with the discussions timed for the next day.

The meeting was general talking but when I said, 'What are your future plans?' the owner looked a little red in the face but honestly replied with difficulty that one of the US giants was talking to them and the decision was nearly sealed. I wasted no more time and departed after a few minutes with an amicable smile. I considered carefully my company's position. I expected our sales to decline, although they considered they would not and looked at the strategy of the USA giants.

In bed that night I mulled over the situation and eventually came to the conclusion that the US giants were carving up the countries of the planet in turn to suit themselves. One had already taken Poland, a second was already starting with India, a third with Brazil on the way, although in Europe before the war three were together in England, Germany and France with only distributor merchants in most other countries.

I decided our business policy for the future would be to go to the smaller countries and avoid the USA giants, or put in other words the USA companies were not interested in the smaller countries. Thus the meeting soon in New Zealand was very important to me now.

However, we were destined to meet some important people we had been introduced to before we left England, so we organised our appointments. The first was with the ex Attorney General Sir Leon Trout in his Brisbane home, one of the brothers from an industrial family, one manufacturing fibreglass boats and yachts in Sidney, the other in Melbourne manufacturing orange juice.

Owing to circumstances, we went first to Melbourne at the time of the Melbourne Cup race day. Our friends were in attendance. The day is similar to the English Ascot. We met afterwards at our hotel, but beforehand had spent a little time to see Captain Cook's house that had been transported from England. Later we visited Captain Cook's memorial plate in Sydney which commemorates his landing in Botany Bay nearby.

We had dinner at the house and next day visited his factory with thirty huge transporters more than full of beautiful ripe fresh oranges waiting for the gates to open. It was most interesting to see his plant at work in a very hygienic atmosphere to can or bottle them. His company sales were massive, sending consignments all over the world. He thought the North American market was his best outlet, and we later visited the boatyard where he kept his small inboard engine boat on a hauled platform rig for entry to the sea at any time without any fuss.

Next day we set off for Brisbane and arrived too late for dinner at Sir Leon's home; consequently he came the following day to collect us early to look over his house and collection of art before luncheon there, a large house on top of a hill in the country in the vicinity of the city. First thing on arrival Sir Leon opened another garage door to present his short boot Bentley in fine working order and polished condition but not used for he found the car hard to drive without help.

Next with his wife we looked over their art collection housed within two wings from the main house, one wing a collection of only Australian paintings and sketches from the early days of history, including paintings by the early convicts who landed from Portsmouth, England. Their embarkation wooden gate still stands through the wall of the harbour; outside the gate just away from the sea a recent memorial symbol of a large metal knot stands, built by Australia for England.

It is interesting to know why the Australians call the English 'Limeys'. It is because certain men survived the killer disease of scurvy on voyages to the southern hemisphere by eating citrus fruit. The long voyages lasting two years and often more without Vitamin C were so hazardous with nothing but rancid salty meat and caused deaths in great numbers of crew.

The other wing of the house contained a beautiful collection of other works of art, some famous. One particular picture I liked was of a small boy standing in motion on top of a little hill with his hands in the air hollering 'I am king of the castle,' with a smile to say 'I am so pleased with myself'.

The pictures in both wings were beautiful, in their lovely situation with an engaging non shining bright light making you feel you had to stay to admire all. It was interesting to note that the owner and his wife did not have children, so the whole house and collection was to be bequeathed to a museum in the state for public view and to add if possible further paintings or drawings of the same theme.

The next day we hired a motor car to see Surfers Paradise, not so far away, and arrived about 11 a.m. We booked into a local hotel, Marriot RTS, as HQ and had booked luncheon, adjacent to the long wide sandy beach. The beach and area around was quite heavily populated, with golden brown bodies lying down facing the hot bright sun against the deep azure sky and some similarly brown people walking about going to or from the ice cream wagons, little take away cafés and eating food stalls with the hotel trying to keep an order of no sand inside. Others were just walking along the very fine beach, all with very wholesome bodies, dressed in scanty bathing costumes, with the occasional beach attendant with a tank on his back full of suntan lotion, holding up a jet spray to supply and spray the bodies for a small fee.

The sea in the near distance was clear dark blue with strong white-topped waves breaking on the sandy shore and in the distance you noticed the buoys holding the shark safety net to control the bathing area under the watchful eye of the lifeguard tower in charge of beach safety. One felt the urge to join them for everyone, family or not, was so jolly, sophisticated and enjoying themselves in the wonderful weather. Later after a hectic milling lunch we departed over the sand-hiding long thin grass waving goodbye to all.

Next day we arrived in Cairns for a day on the Great Barrier Reef. This was a fantastic short journey to the low atoll islands with the very deep ocean beyond leading to a vast area of nowhere. The reef is a haven for fishes and through a glass bottomed boat you could see the wonderful bright colours of all types of tropical fish with a large hermit crab. There was one alternative way down through a submerged tower with a window port to get a passive view of all around including the old hermit crab.

15 Open speed test unit for wheels and discs

16 Mixing basic powders for disc and wheel manufacture

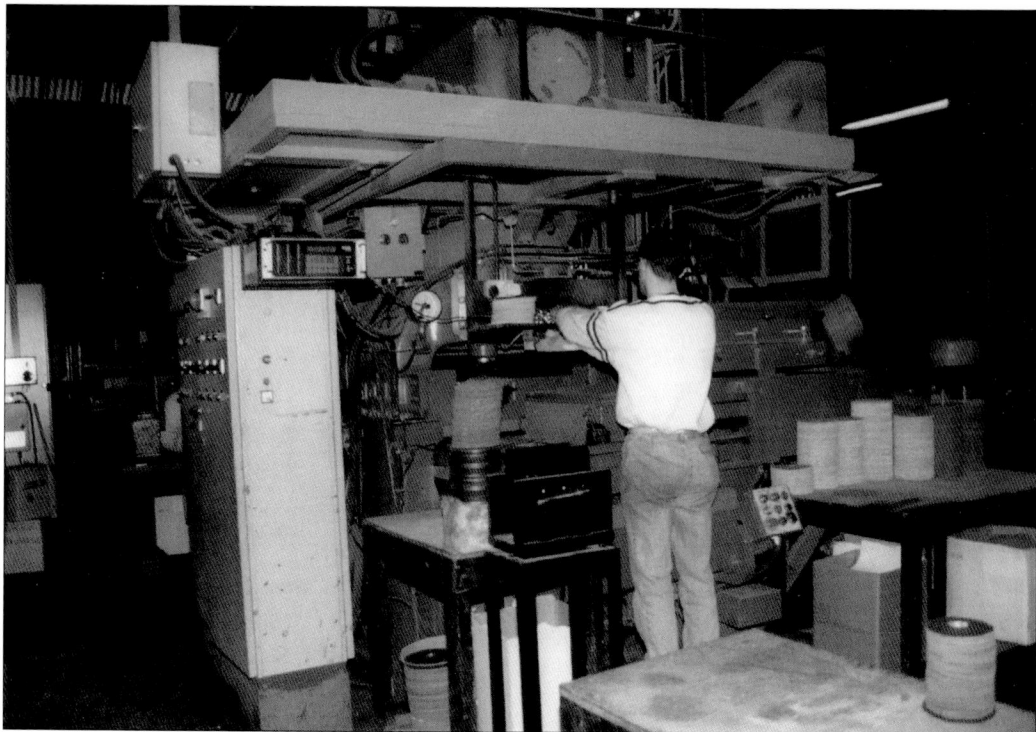

17 Hydraulic precision multi disc manufacture

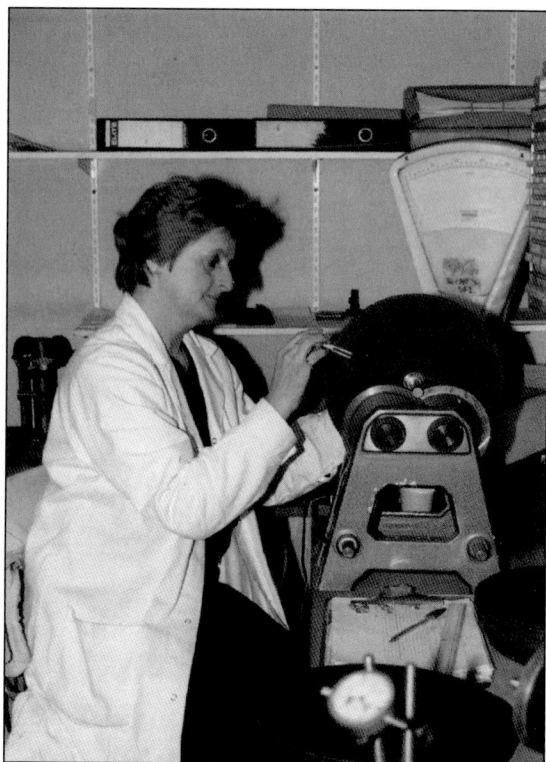

18 Accurate quality test of wheel balance

19 Presentation of British Safety Award to author's company, Arrow Abrasives Ltd

20 Arrow Abrasives – Lord Mayor's visit an open day meeting author and works director

21 The ketch launching party, despite the rain. Author in white coat, Robert on his right, then Gayle with Doodey in front followed by Lilian, Jean and Dr Bob

22 Launch of ketch – Doodey Gay

23 Ketch seasoned hull under construction, at Curtis & Pape, Looe

24 Doodey aboard the ketch

25 Setting course on the maiden voyage

26 Ketch, Doodey Gay, *on author's mooring, Hamble River*

27 Sailing through Greece

Now to Auckland, New Zealand, where we were met by my business friend Hedley Huthnance, a very good customer who wished us to take a rest before we settled down to his programme, but I said 'No!' I was anxious to start and let my wife and daughter check in at our hotel.

Hedley had made many appointments and done much work naming the possible proposed partnership of the production and engineering with my friend to do the organisation of sales and progress. I was to have the technical input with the supply of machine equipment and control. This programme was readily agreed, then I met the proposed partner, Jack Smallfield. He was an interesting fellow. While a Japanese prisoner of war he had repaired watches for the fellow prisoners and because he was so good the Japanese made him do the watches and clocks of the officers' guard and camp. When I asked about hydraulic presses and the like he replied, 'I will use old tramcar hydraulic pieces; I know they are freely available,' and I immediately knew I could readily agree work with such an exceptional engineer.

From then it was all go: the formation of the company, the agreements of all items, and my friend actually booked me to see a possible factory unit on a large piece of land in Takapuna opposite, just inland from a perfect triangular volcanic mountain. I accepted the position and height as suitable and signed up accordingly. Now I was off to an arranged appointment with the Prime Minister and other ministers in waiting.

The abrasive trade in New Zealand was through eleven distributors from eight countries that included the three giants from the USA, two from England and others from Europe; hence our local factory could supply all.

The Prime Minister knew the position of the imports and very clearly stated to us that his government could not help us in any way until our manufactured product was proved actually better quality than all sources at present imported. With our plans completed, I telephoned to my office in England details of the equipment required to be ordered for supply as soon as possible; thus the race was on. We all met for a celebration lunch with wives. My wife always practises the names of people by thinking of a similar title, for example on meeting Jack Smallfield, my new director to be works manager of New Zealand, she welcomed him as, 'Nice to meet you, Mr Freddy

Little Acre!' This caused some embarrassment until corrected, then much laughter.

Then I left to see some of the distributors and felt I should know something of these lovely two green islands of New Zealand for I was now attached to them to the delight of my wife and daughter.

First we went with Hedley to Lake Taupo where the earth is warm. Many trout streams lead into this volcanic lake. My friend possessed an outboard motor boat for fishing and I set off with him to spend the day and night fishing to return at midday the following morning, so I settled into wax jacket, trousers, and the skipper's hat found on board with provisions for the trip.

Soon we set course from shore. We eventually caught nine beautiful clean rainbow trout between six and eight pounds. Then we parked for the night against the shore, just by an old abandoned Maori smokehouse, to clean the trout, to be ready to smoke them overnight, using a nearby tea tree for smoke. The very strict rule of the lake is that you take home any part of the not eaten fish to avoid pollution to the beautiful gin-clear water.

My friend blew up his portable air tent and after a small meal on board and a smoke to keep away the mosquitoes he left for his tent for I was made comfortable to sleep on board. Next morning we enjoyed a juicy cold bacon and egg sandwich, did our ablutions then set course for more fishing after being happy to store the smoked trout on board.

We caught four more rainbow trout, stopped for early lunch and with one trout went ashore and started a fire again in a shovelled base of pumice with tea tree for the fire. My friend cleaned the fish and wrapped the entrails to take home, then enclosed the fish in wet paper with sprigs of tea tree. The fish was placed in the hollow, pumice stones on top to complete the oven. After a short period of time he moved the pumice away and unwrapped the fish, then we both ate fish from the bone; the taste was superb. We then packed up and returned to the same jetty to meet my wife who was waiting for me.

My friend set off to return home to Wellington where I was to meet him later. The pumice was interesting to me: so light and was what was left over from the ashes of the original volcano and it made a wonderful shore with masses of tea tree and bush beyond.

On the way we called in to see a fantastic glow-worm cave,

absolutely causing bright greenish light to fill the whole dark cave. Later on the road we noticed lorries pulling up in laybys to let motor cars pass, a rule of the road, and smiled at the sheep: one for every person in the United Kingdom.

We eventually arrived and stayed in a room only recently vacated by the Beatles, and went to dinner with my friend's family. The wind did blow as predicated; the city is called Windy Wellington because of the regular breeze that flows through the strait between the North and South Islands. Next day we continued across by ferry to the south, bypassing Christchurch and Dunedin, a medical university centre which takes its name from Edinburgh, Scotland, with the same facility. We crossed to get to Milford Sound, the large fiord and small town under the Mitre Peak, a mountain that mostly covers its peak with cloud.

On the way we passed through a beautiful lush green landscape, with the occasional real cowboy dressed like an American one, on a horse with an American saddle, tending to the cattle. We then reached Te Anau with the most beautiful lake I have ever seen in my life, shimmering red in the evening light with stunning swaying pink reeds on the perimeter; then to Milford Sound at just dark.

In the morning we boarded a fairly large boat which steamed to the mouth of the long fiord with high sheer black rock sides straight down from the surface depth of the clear dark blue water. Any break near the sea was full of playful seals with many large birds overhead. On return to the harbour we disembarked to walk to see the clear Mitre Peak and the Milford Mountain falls. Both displayed their best which was so unusual for this always misty raining small town which was originally reached by a Scotsman on foot. You can walk this long stiff rough trail overland should you desire.

We commenced our return journey through Arrow Town, an old gold rush town in just the condition as it was at its working height, and on to the ski mountain resort Aorak, Mount Cook Village, after passing through large areas of sheep farming. The snow was not at its best so we departed for Wellington for a last dinner with Hedley before passing Taupo to arrive in Auckland to meet the new friend Jack Smallfield I needed to work with for the future. On arrival we met like old friends and for the next day checked out his sailing yacht for a small voyage to a neighbouring island or two. We enjoyed a fine sail and afterwards ate a small meal in the Royal New Zealand Yacht

Squadron, which was often to be my port of call on later journeys to New Zealand. Each member has a locker to protect his own drinks by the bottle. The next day we were to fly to Fiji – on the way home, but not quite home yet. On the way I practised a few sextant star shots with the New Zealand aircraft pilot navigator and thought nothing had changed.

We landed at Fiji airport to be met by very tall, handsome, black haired, polite, bronzed officials in such soaring heat as to make you feel weak. The next day we boarded a motor boat for a nearby remote island to spend the day under palm trees in the shadow of the clear blue sky with sunshine pouring for all who appreciate the heat. At lunchtime we ate tropical fruit: pineapple, papaya, lychees and more, and I thought, 'How I can do something to organise to stop here forever?' We eventually took the boat to our hotel's private shore, to rest before going to the lounge bar for a drink before dinner plus a lighting entertainment of Fiji dancing ladies who seemed very cool.

As we had seen most of the island, we decided to go to the French island of Noumea, New Caledonia. On arrival there was no sign of any official so we went to our hotel with no better a welcome because there seemed some trouble with France over independence, so all seemed to be on strike, off work and waiting. Hence we took off to return to Fiji and then flew to the Hawaiian islands. Honolulu gave a great welcome with garlands of flowers thrown around our necks and dancing with music so rhythmic in the hot sunshine and all around including us.

After shedding a few clothes to conform to the Hawaiian dress of shorts and matching loose shirt of a yacht and sailing design in white and blue, we seemed happy just taking in the atmosphere in such a wonderful warm shade from hot sunshine. In the evening we enjoyed underground roasted suckling pig, sitting in a circle with other guests just taking in pineapple juice. There were merry ladies and men so courteous serving and singing. It was so unusual to us but so carefree and entreating, but one did have to remember it was all for tourism, though well done.

We spent the next day at Pearl Harbor. The devastation was immense and whilst I had seen a film or two at the time of the war and afterwards, the scene was so dramatic, it was very difficult to comprehend. We went by boat and boarded battleships and more to witness the names and memorial tributes so prominent, all destroyed in beautiful weather with the harbour at peace.

On an old Dakota or DC3 type aircraft we set off to see the active volcano island. On boarding I noticed an oil leak and oil smudges, and thought the aircraft was not as well maintained and clean as I would wish an aircraft to be, but made allowances for the situation. After about three quarters of an hour the second pilot came aft to appear at the starboard wing and engine so I looked too! Then the captain came to look; by this time there was a definite leak of oil spraying a small jet. I started to feel uncomfortable. The pilot returned to his seat and shut down the starboard engine, which was the right thing to do, no doubt due to his starboard engine's very low oil pressure.

We continue to fly on the one port engine for a moment or two, no doubt for the pilot to adjust to his new position of deciding how to respond to manoeuvre the aircraft for a safe landing. He decided to turn for home and rightly turned against the good engine. I thought, 'He seems to know what he is doing,' and waited for the next step, for instance to increase the power of the good engine to keep straight and level for the flight home and then turn to and land against it. After short time, some fifteen minutes, the aircraft was obviously unable to maintain height so the necessity was to land in the sea or find a piece of land on some island or other. Matters in the aircraft were getting a little tense; we were reducing height at an alarming rate, but to where? A few minutes later the pilot was going down to land; he turned correctly, almost in a glide to land somewhere but without any indication where.

We landed with a bump or two, ran forward between some bushes on a rough path and stopped. Passengers shouted cheers and continued with 'For he's a jolly good fellow'. We all evacuated the aircraft, and found ourselves in the middle of a pineapple plantation with pineapples as far as the eye could see.

I talked to the pilot who was very apologetic and said it was the best thing to do; I did congratulate him for his good skill in knowing what to do in such a position. After waiting until nearly dark, we were transferred to another part of the island where there was a small airstrip and boarded a light aircraft to return to Honolulu before the evening light faded. Some passengers were left behind but did not seem to mind; they were given a bottle or two to make themselves comfortable for the night and the aircraft would return in the morning for the pilot was not qualified to fly at night.

We just had time to witness the live smoking volcano before turning away for our landing emergency, but must admit I do not recall any interest or visual sighting for I believe I was otherwise engaged with the pilot.

The flight to our next call was San Francisco. We departed 25 minutes late so to make us cheerful the captain issued a bottle of champagne for a passenger draw as to the time of arrival. Much was discussed between everyone. The aircraft was full both in the normal holiday section and in the first class. We were informed about the speed we were doing, the weather report of winds, the 25 minutes late and more. My own note stated the scheduled time plus 25 minutes. The prize draw was drawn in the holiday cabin and my note was the correct answer, so I duly left my seat to receive the prize amongst cheering members of cabin crew and 150 passengers to be presented with the bottle by the captain.

Now in San Francisco, I was called by PanAm airline the next morning concerning a piece of luggage found on the aircraft which they thought was likely to be mine, so I asked my wife and daughter if they had any piece missing. My daughter replied she had thrown away a small case in the rack above her seat, so I telephoned to say so, explaining that the case was of no value so please to throw it away. The reply was they could not meet my request for the case was in the security strong room, and so it was necessary for me to identify and clear the case and contents.

So I called a taxi to go to the remote corner of the airport in accordance with the directions given, to meet the security officials. The case was brought before me, and I identified it; then I needed to check the contents. I thought the case might be locked but fortunately it was not and the little key was inside. All was agreed but I needed to cover the incident with paperwork they needed to type, for my signature; it all took a little time to complete. I apologised and left to find the taxi but had no luck for the only taxis were at the arrivals and departure buildings some long distance away, I walked and walked, spent three quarters of an hour to arrive there, and hailed a taxi to our hotel on top of the hill and told Lilian I was not really amused, more so because the thirteen pieces of luggage I had carried around on the trip had been a heavy physical responsibility.

It was possible to carry such a quantity of luggage but it was not easy for both ladies who complained of bad backs, so the system was that I put two large cases under each arm and took them to where I decided to drop them, then went for two more cases under each arm and walked to the drop with my wife and daughter carrying two light bags each, then came back for the little case now thrown away. This system was only operated when I could not find a porter. A taxi was easier for one only handled one bag at a time. I was fortunately born with arms one inch longer than most, otherwise, it would not have been possible to reach for the second handle of the second case under both arms. I considered the quantity of cases was not necessary but met with little response.

San Francisco was hilly and interesting. We tried to reach our destinations via the tramcars which went up and down at a bewildering pace; boarded a helicopter to visit Alcatraz; learned a lot about the big earthquake from documents and photographs on the wall of the hotel; visited Chinatown for a meal which although liked by my wife was familiar to me as Indian and Malayan. But fortunately very good American beef was available elsewhere, together with the fresh fish smell of Fisherman's Wharf with the lobster and fish cooked so well. I would not forget the sight of the Golden Gate suspension bridge so magnificent at near sunset.

Our route home took us through two nights in New York, including a meal at the notable 21 Club restaurant and to the new JFK airport for the overnight flight to London, Heathrow. On arrival in the early morning I completed the formalities and looked for my car, but it was nowhere to be seen and waiting produced no result. I bargained with a few London taxis until we found one willing to take us, settled the price and set off. I must say it felt unfamiliar to be trundling home to Durford Wood, Petersfield, Hampshire in a London taxi down country roads and lanes but we all arrived well to an overwhelming reception and greeting by our children who looked so well with our kind housekeeper, who was ready to prepare a meal but surprised to see the taxi. My car was apparently stationed at the wrong terminal but eventually came home to report.

Next day I reported early for work and immediately donned my factory coat for a tour of inspection to see all was well. My desk was soon glutted with mail so neatly assembled by my secretary, so I had no difficulty in sorting out what to do, although I had telephoned each day, while away, to respond to matters.

CHAPTER 10

Sailing

I HAD ALWAYS PROMISED MYSELF a sailing boat, since my conversation with Uffa Fox, the 'Flying Fifteen' sailor from Cowes, Isle of Wight in London before the 1939 war when the only experience I possessed was classical rowing on the extensive lake that fed the River Cole in my early schooldays.

During the war I went afloat on all types of craft as the potential opportunity became available no matter the type of boat, sail or power; however the opportunity to sail was rare. One unusual occasion to sail was with a Royal Air Force friend aboard his own 'Flying Fifteen' on Lake Windermere, in breezy weather, which turned too rough for us to continue. The experience however fulfilled my expectations to want more. At the time apart from the unfair weather we were filling in precious journey time between two trains, on my friend's home territory on the way to our operational posting. There were few opportunities to mature to proper learning to sail, although I was spending obviously oceans of time over the seas in my flying operations adjacent to friend or foe.

Between my wartime operations, I did break off to learn real sophisticated navigation as a Royal Air Force specialist 'N', so now could welcome the art the heavens will play with their shining bright star points to supplement the day sun noon positions and other fixes to position oneself exactly within a few hundred yards day or night whilst we are on our fast moving revolving tilted planet Earth.

Thus I was now well qualified to enjoy sailing. I had lost touch however with competitive sailing, such as local racing. I stayed moderately interested, but my dream of commanding a 'Flying Fifteen' was fading, to negotiate the planet oceans of our world. My then thoughts were just a dream, for I needed to work hard enough to find the total finance to purchase a boat, including catching trout on Lake Taupo for each one of my family to eat on the tea tree aroma of the shore, in New Zealand, enjoying the lakeside fish bream, holidays at the exciting Villa D'Est on Lake Como, only using a power boat.

Sailing the great lakes of Canada, particularly Huron, where the local weather is dominated by the effect of the water temperature and more, I can see how fickle the weather can be when dominated by lakes let alone by the sea such as the difficult oceans, like the Atlantic Ocean, I experienced in the last war.

In the meantime, through my friends of business or pleasure, I have enjoyed my personal introduction to owning a boat; for instance through my erstwhile neighbour Russel Whitely, I possessed the responsibility of looking after his Australian in-board motor boat which I moored on the River Hamble bank, with permission of course, and enjoyed entertaining my friends around the Solent area for a time.

After approximately two years I decided to purchase a proper sailing boat and considered the whole subject, then settled on a very good yacht architect, Walter F. Rayner of Poole, Dorset, whose specialty was the Atlantic Class ketch, 38 feet, built as one wished. The boatyard I chose was Curtis & Pepe, Looe, Cornwall, also the birthplace of my daughter Dianne Gayle.

I decided on a seasoned oak hull, an ocean cruising (not racing) keel, six bunks, ketch sail rig, and full navigation equipment to include a sextant and above cabin chart table, with 'Cascover' protection of the hull to prevent termite attack. So all was in hand in 1963, to await the launch date and our maiden voyage.

Naturally although I was busy with my company, Flexible Arbasives', merger with John Oakey & Sons, the oldest abrasive company in the world, I did with my family visit to keep in touch with progress and enjoyed visiting the Cornwall I had known in wartime; at the same time I promised my driver, John Pearson, he would be the first to witness the start of our maiden voyage on board, but not to sail, for the motor car needed to get home.

After the testing trials of my boat it was decided for reasons of tide or lack of water on the ebb, to move my boat from Looe to Fowey, to commence the maiden voyage with certain flexibility of time, to a buoy located outside the shore harbour of Polruan.

I wished to make my maiden voyage with just Lilian for I knew her capabilities and enthusiastic support from the report of my sailing school located at Warsash, Hamble. I did not want anyone to suggest a passage who had no serious helpful knowledge of the likely task, for on the voyage I would be testing all of our equipment and ensuring we both understood how to handle the boat in different circumstances, to arrive home to our mooring safely on the Hamble this particular occasion.

I intended to make a break in our voyage at the reserved yacht club mooring for an overnight stay in Torquay, Torbay, for we were not to take any fresh food aboard or sail in the dark.

A day or so before we were about to fix the date of departure Lilian asked if her brother Robert could come with us. I several times said no but like most men I was persuaded to agree.

All three of us boarded the yacht, *Doodey Gay*, on the appointed day. I was soon busy checking all things required to set off for a safe passage, with my driver handling most of the gear, oilskins, spare water with ice, my cut glass tumblers and wine glasses, plus the small quantity of spirit, wine, lemons, and other fruit with many other items to stow away in the appropriate places. It all took longer than I had hoped. However, eventually we were ready to sail with my wife hoisting the burgee securely to the peak of the main mast and I securing the ensign to the mizzen halyard, for our stowed dinghy, on the stern davits, was in the way of the ensign staff. I cast off my driver to go ashore and pick up the car to take home, with many messages of things to do to fill the gap caused by our departure.

I started the diesel engine and set course for the harbour entrance so to the open sea, and set course for Torbay, Devon. The passage was uneventful but a little slower than intended by our dead reckoning navigation plan so that we arrived in Torbay very near twilight with great hunger, due to the physical effort needed to carry out changes of sail rig, to testing with and without engines, and anchor checks with more safety exercises to settle our competence of sailing the ship in various circumstances on the way. Being late, I decided to moor up to a ship's barrel type buoy, in the inner entrance of Torbay. Immediately my wife's brother smoking a Havana cigar set course for the shore at Torquay aboard a launch in search of food for dinner on board.

My wife and I stayed on board with a little pink gin, to enjoy an achievement and a day well done. After forty minutes we were wondering when we might eat, when the hum of the launch was heard, and the brother came aboard with a magnificent feast: fresh cooked lobster, fresh cooked crab, with large shrimps and all the needed accessories to enhance the feast until we were all full to capacity with the pleasure of eating, so on to coffee, a cigar, then bed for an early morning start.

We cast off in good time, set full sails and seemed to make good progress in time with our DR (Direct Reckoning), yet we were drifting off our line owing to spasmodic wind change, in an atmosphere of apparent rain with definite rain on the distant horizon. We decided however not to change course until I could sight a fix, but the fix never came as the weather deteriorated. On nearing the position of Portland submarine exercise area, we were surprised and startled by a conning tower rising almost along the portside followed by the quick surface of the hull shedding volumes of sea which caused us to rock from side to side and also to slow down. We reduced sail and waited to see what was happening. At the same time we were approaching the strong Portland tide race.

With 'all's well' by Aldis signal light from the conning tower, I increased speed with the engine and eventually used the engine flat out only just to beat the race, past Portland harbour to the quiet Weymouth outer harbour to our assigned berth against the wall, reserved by the Harbour Master through my wife's very firm friends at Weymouth, members of the Royal Dorset Yacht Club.

There was much to do on our arrival, some hour and half late, for the tradespeople were about to close. We needed a long ladder to board our boat for the night to allow for the tide of some 14 feet. The head also needed adjustment and we all needed a shower or bath before a late invitation to dinner, all arranged by our dear friends Betty and Mike Whittle.

We returned to our berth well after midnight, to find our boat missing, what a fright in the dark! However, the Harbour Master had moved my boat to let a potato ship from Jersey in that needed an early unload, so my boat was safely berthed the other side of the harbour wall. It was for me a tricky move for the warps had been adjusted by me to allow for a fourteen foot tide, between high and low, and the tide was now really low. With difficulty we used the ladder at full stretch to board, to well earned sleep with a huge thank you to our friends for their hospitality and kind attention to our needs on arrival.

I awoke at daybreak to consider our position, for the previous night, I had listened to the weather report at the Royal Dorset Yacht Club; it was not favourable for a passage to the Hamble. I checked

again and decided to stay in the harbour, enjoying a further day with
our dear friends, and to divert Roger, due an exeat from his college,
from going home to meet our homecoming via the Hamble. He was
to be collected and brought down to Weymouth to meet us aboard
Doodey Gay. I also needed a technician for the head was blocked and
not working, and I needed a longer ladder of the right length to
scramble on board if need be because of the tide. Our friends, who
were man and wife, possessed a business in the town and a further
family business nearby. They met us again soon after 9 a.m. and
arranged for the head technician who owned a ships business. Such
a task of a small dry but hand pump loo can be difficult; it is not
unusual in yachts where the crew includes ladies.

All was arranged, including the Harbour Master, who also
apologised for moving my boat at 0130 hours owing to the
unexpected arrival of the potato boat from Jersey.

Our friends were magnificent and so helpful, as they had been for
many years. The two wives had been friends for a long time when I
came along at the beginning of the second world war in the Royal
Air Force and met them both. I married one, my friend the other;
he was a Royal Dorset Army Captain at the time, who had had
terrific experiences against the Germans, swimming and fighting for
the river Nijmegen and Arnhem and much more.

When my wife was taken ill with a long hospital treatment they
both looked after our children and baptised the youngest in a lovely
small village where they lived and started them off to school. You can
see the crew and *Doodey Gay* were in good hands. To this day I have
no idea where the ladder was found at 0300, but it was returned the
same day after we used it again when we came ashore next day. With
everything in some sort of order, our son on 'exeat' joined ship with
a friend before lunchtime and Dianne Gayle turned up late after
dinner and the three stayed on board to be ready to sail with us the
next day.

The weather was boisterous with light rain all day and the forecast
was little better for the morrow with much of the same. After plenty
of food and hospitality we expressed our thank yous and in the early
evening waved goodbye to our friends.

The next morning at 0645 hours we departed from the quayside,
and acknowledged the master of a sand dredger preparing to take the
berth we were just leaving. We acknowledged the Harbour Master

and passed into the bay at 0728 hours, on course for St Albans Head at 6 knots, in the misty fog with sails doing little to keep the speed intended, so helped with the engine. We passed St Albans Head then Lulworth Cove and altered course for the Needles Light Buoy, and then through the channel with the Isle of Wight to starboard until we used the Shambles Light Vessel to turn for the Hamble River and arrived at our berth at 1545 hours.

The family on board were magnificent. They all helped to crew the ship. Whilst the conditions were not very strenuous they were as one excited, like the rest of us, to complete our family maiden voyage. In fact my son hurled himself on to my jetty when the stern warp slipped the cleat to arrest the ship, with me responsible for the bow warp with my wife at the helm. Then we had to cover the sails that we lowered at the river entrance and clean ship for another day.

On 14 June, the day after we had arrived home from our maiden voyage, we left home to clear the items still outstanding on the boat, and arrived on board at 12.55 hours, I to examine my list of fifteen items and to make arrangements to put all in fine working order as soon as possible. My son released the dinghy from the davits and developed a testing routine as i/c dinghy or as officer i/c dinghy water sports carrying my two daughters (*Doodey* and *Gay*) with their friends, making six in all, continuously circling about or putting down passengers on shore to pick them up again. Anyway to them it seemed fun. My wife was having refreshments in the Royal Air Force Yacht Club, the club most local to my mooring. The Club burgee and ensign were hoisted on board *Doodey Gay* for our recent voyage, and today, after luncheon, back on board we welcomed our Hamble friends, Bill Irwin and Muriel, who had just returned from a seven-day passage on their delightful old sloop *Armada*, built and sailed by the skipper's grandfather before him.

The skipper's grandfather had commanded a public company producing tarmac coated sheet and insulation for buildings, and my friend, the son, Bill Irwin, was now in command. This friendship was the introduction of my son to assist me for the practical work of his business degree course both in England and North America, a great success.

My friend had been an Army officer in the last war, and despite desperate fighting was to be a prisoner but escaped to a lonely farm as cover from the Germans. It was a great success, living underground with the family in Belgium and spending a courageous time harassing the German communications until D-Day. In consequence, he married the daughter though he never lived with her, and amply provided for her all his life, We wished a him a 'Happy Ship' and they departed; we left at 1825 hours for home at Durford Wood.

Our next visit to the *Doodey Gay* was some five days later and we welcomed on board a Group Captain's wife of the two friends of ours we met in my Royal Air Force time in Alness, who were now Canadian, and he today was in the RCAF on a UK appointment. Although the wife lived with him on the service station, their home was on Vancouver Island where they both played golf when on leave. She was English, a WAAF officer at Alness until married, and was a very good artist. Today I have one of her water colour pictures, looking out to sky and space from a reed marsh situation. The picture is still admired for its mystery by others as well as me.

We set sail with my family, except for my son at Marlborough College and his friends. What a crew for me, being all female, because the main purpose of the sail was to test out the stern gland, the housing of the propeller bearing and my worry for the stern post heat when using the engine, plus the auto pilot which I needed for distance travel to save on heavy shift work. We were sailing well in gusty wind of force 6 or more, so I trimmed the sails to just part main and mizzen and was catching up the twelve metre American Cup *Sovereign* under reefed mainsail. We both tacked for a while, then both shortly returned to the Hamble and we moored at 1215 hours and walked over for drinks and refreshments on *Armada*. I did manage my two reports and made arrangements to fix one with the engineers at the yard; the other I had to sort out with my yacht architect.

The *Sovereign* crew was dispersed that day to meet again in London on 11 July for their flight to Boston; the boat itself was going as deck cargo to the USA and it was reported as having an exciting last fling in 40 m.p.h. gusty winds around Gosport on way to the Hamble.

It was necessary for me to pass the GPO official examination as a competent operator of the RT/DF radio equipment on board *Doodey Gay* and it was also necessary to survey the actual equipment to qualify it as an efficient piece of apparatus. The official passed the equipment, and I then passed the handling test, after which I had to send different messages to land based radio stations and afterwards to certain ships, to finally pass out using alterative frequencies to establish sea safety for all including me. I passed OK and now felt a proper 'Captain of the Ship'.

All this work made me realise what a complicated job it was to be Captain of a yacht, for you had to be efficient in all aspects of sea manoeuvres whether at sea, making harbour, or leaving harbour and in all aspects of safety, distress and navigation, whereas a naval ship's Captain had different specialist officers for all the different duties. It was fun with adventure to achieve competency as a skipper to be efficient in all aspects of the sea. My examination had made me late to meet my wife with the now Canadian lady so on being dismissed, I immediately telephoned the Yacht Club; however they had eaten lunch and gone.

Without my lunch I went on to see the yacht architect, Walter F. Roymer; he had had no lunch either, but nevertheless, we set down to business. We did a complete detailed inspection of the stern gland surrounding the propeller shaft bearings on the stern post itself. The cracks in the stern post were caused by the 'Cascover' sheeting I had suggested to prevent termite attack, for the oak had been seasoned in the Looe estuary for at least seven years and I had dried the logs out after the yacht was built. The architect was quite happy to fill in the stern post with lead where needed to ensure the same strength. When this had been done the bearing gland straightened out, and for the record it afterwards had no trouble at all.

Towards the end of July we received an old friend on board, Peter Willcox, who was our next door neighbour at Epsom for many years. Just after the war he was a Colonel in the Army, a real soldier – I am sure Army people will understand – with his friend a General who also was in command of the main recruiting centre for the British Army. We always enjoyed a sail but this time decided to go to Newtown River on the Isle of Wight. It was always an adventure to get away from the local waters and harbours we knew so well on the trials with *Doodey Gay*. Newtown is an old town adjacent to the nearby channel and was famous as a thriving town with many Members of Parliament, but only recognisable today from one building, the old beautiful town hall. The only problem with our trip was that the water at the entrance to the river is only three feet at low water, so after a lovely lunch, we arrived too late to enter. So we returned to the Hamble after a glorious sail both ways.

A few days later we decided to go to Newtown River again. This time we anchored at the entrance and waited for *Armada* to show us in. *Armada* arrived, we weighed anchor and followed them into a lovely tranquil mooring at anchor. My total crew went swimming and sunbathing, but I stayed on board, listening to the birds and the patter of the waters against the hull under a clear blue sky, until the sound of the dinghy engine disturbed my thoughts with my family returning. Both *Armada* and I sailed for the entrance of the Beaulieu river on the opposite side of the English Channel. We tied up together on *Armada*'s anchor. Here again the crew swam, very near the shore and the Captain of *Armada* and I settled down to dreaming in the strong sunlight in the lovely tranquil atmosphere. We were quite suddenly awakened by a similar yacht fidgeting about disturbing our gentle chat and pink gin refreshment. From the flag, the boisterous crew diving everywhere around us with huge splashes and noise belonged to one of the Army leisure yachts. As the yacht drifted alarmingly close, the *Armada* Captain and I went for our white topped yacht hats, put them on and turned towards the intruding yacht who then noticed an official situation developing, called everyone back on board and departed leaving our crew again in peace and tranquillity. However we shortly dispersed for the Hamble and dinner at the local inn, the Bugle.

We were so often out sailing with *Doodey Gay* on school holidays, at weekends and at other official times that we seemed glued to the ship and thereabouts. One of our sailing friends, a large farmer, set off for Spain for his holidays after the harvest was in and stored. I recall saying goodbye to him when we were just off the Needles homeward bound; such little events were always popping up. The summer was nearly finished when we decide to spend a night in Newtown River so off we went, and after a lovely sail entered and anchored mid channel. This night was the best of our local trips. Soon after arrival my daughter with my son and his friend explored the river towards its head. I was going to fish for breakfast, and my wife prepared a wonderful dinner, after which we all went to bed early. At daybreak I was awakened by the change in tide providing more smoothing ripples of water against and along the hull, dreaming in such quiet surroundings in peace and tranquility for ever. When I stirred to go to fish, I was thrilled with all things beautiful and with the birds, and caught small breakfast fish for my wife to cook.

I sat down in the saloon eating such a good fresh breakfast and thinking, 'I enjoy this life so much, I wanted to live on board to travel all year.' I had of course to return, but as I needed adventure, this yacht suited my dream.

Our next trip was to meet Captain O. M. Watts on board *South Star*, an auxiliary Buckie ketch 1947, down on the Beaulieu River near Bucklers Hard, the old town that built the fine wooden ships for Drake, Nelson and others. We were to tie up to the *South Star* and by the time we met it was dark. We expected my neighbour Russel some time later, around 2300 hours, thus it was our first experience navigating the river by night without light. It was interesting and so difficult to read the signs to manoeuvre our dinghy to the jetty to pick up the Captain's guests. Without a light was foolish and from then on we always made sure we had a good light available.

Captain O. M. Watts was a master mariner who owned a famous London yacht equipment company and was a very accomplished sailor who produced many technical pieces of equipment, such as *Reeds Nautical Almanac* and tide-tables, *The Sextant Explanation*, *Astro Navigation* and others. Our dinner together was interesting, using unbreakable glasses. To me was a little rough but a very pleasant night with us all listening to many captivating stories until we returned to our own boat to sleep. We woke up at daybreak to the lovely rippling sound along the hull and after lunch departed for a sail in freshening high winds in the Channel and so moored in my berth at 1735 hours.

Later in May it was decided to spend a few days in Deauville with my next door neighbour Russel and wife in Durford Wood, together with Doctor Bob and his wife of Marlborough, where my son was at college. The intention was to visit both old and new ports of call, and to play golf at Deauville on the new course constructed of rye grass so the grass being coarser and drier would provide teed balls all the time. We also wished to visit Honfleur, a beautiful fishing port and haven, to eat some good food and drink wine, so the date was made.

I felt obliged to ensure all was shipshape on the *Doodey Gay* with regard to the safety, accommodation and all points of equipment, with charts correct, hence the purpose of this earlier sail to call in at Cowes, for lunch at the Island Sailing Club and later anchor just off Yarmouth harbour entrance.

I completed all my checks for the auxiliary engine plus its generator and all sails, and was pleased to say that all would be well on time. We enjoyed a lovely sail in very good breezy sunny weather, my wife on the helm and my young daughter Doodey on watch. She was now approaching nine years old but was a very experienced sailor, having learnt so much from my son. We berthed at our home port at 1745 hours.

With my operations complete, I advised all to be aboard the *Doodey Gay* well before lunch so we could stow our baggage in some sort of order in view of our stay on board for some days. No suitcases were allowed except my leather attaché case of ship's papers and the three sets of golf clubs would be last aboard, with sailing gear to the fore and day shore gear, with evening wear second.

After lunch at the local RAF Yacht Club we would set sail at 1410 hours and set course for Le Havre at 1450 from the lighthouse 'Nab Tower' at 1800 hours. From 2000 hours we would take watches of two hours each. I would go to bed early for it was my intention to do my watch for the in and out shipping lanes.

My bunk was naturally in the Captain's cabin at the stern, where I had fitted a hand bearing compass so that on passage I could check the magnetic direction of the boat. There were two bunks in the fo'c's'le and two more in the saloon but I wished to stow most things not required for sailing in the stern lazaret. Russel was an experienced yachtsman and always liked to wear his old white-topped yacht club hat, which was much larger than mine, for today the hat was less wide to help it in place in strong winds.

On arrival off the Le Havre light vessel we would set course for the Trouville entrance and wait for the lock gates to open at high water. The total distance would be 105–110 miles and should take 17½ hours at 6 knots or 20 hours at say 5 knots.

The briefing was was over with all except my wife notified. We expected to meet our elder daughter Dianne Gayle coming to Trouville from Versailles, to welcome and stay aboard for our duration. The initial departure would be subject to a satisfactory weather report; however I did not expect a bad report at this time of year for June 1965.

The Deauville Yacht Club had been advised of our destination and they looked forward to welcome us all and would signal us in the inner lock. The date of departure was set and the weather was OK, so our plan was to start our trip after a good night's sleep next day, 8 June 1965, as planned.

The weather report confirmed OK, and we were all on board *Doodey Gay* on time and with all items stowed including the three sets of golf clubs. We went to lunch and afterwards we were ready to set sail so hauled in the bow and stern warps at exactly 1410 hours. We passed Hamble Point buoy at 1450, arrived at Nab Tower 1800, then set course for Le Havre light vessel and commenced our watches. I was tucked up in bed by 2115 after a nightcap and was soon sound asleep, but nervously woke up to check the compass located by the side of my head. In between I was sleeping well. However on the second watch I was suddenly awakened by Russel in his large diameter yachting hat, to tell me firmly that there was a large passenger ship about to run us down! ending, 'What shall we do?' I looked through my porthole and firmly stated, 'Immediately turn well away to starboard and be prepared to pass well astern.'

In other words I was taking the only safe decision to make in the circumstances. Any other, like across the ship's bow, is dangerous and unthinkable for normally it ends in total disaster. It's the first thing you learn when you have a busy shipping lane like the Solent. I was immediately on deck to see all was well. The ship was a cross-Channel ferry doing quite a few knots and I must say when something like this happens it all looks much larger than life, looks so difficult to control, anyway. The ship was near to my little yacht in the dark night on a vast sea and the brightness shone all around with little activity to see on board.

I felt somewhat responsible; for I had not told him what to do if one came across a ferry crossing over the shipping lanes when we were on the same route but hard to see and had to rely on our alertness. Actually, all on board quite enjoyed the exciting spectacle in the middle of the night. The trip was uneventful as far as the weather and the sea were concerned, with engine just on with all sails set trying to keep our cruising speed as planned. Later as dawn was breaking the shore lighthouse was visible flashing its coded bright beam, so comforting. We made just off the Le Havre light vessel without any alteration of heading and set off for Trouville to arrive three quarters of an hour earlier to wait outside until high water was ready for entrance to the outer harbour and so access to the inner lock yacht basin.

High water came at 1040 hours GMT and our entrance all went to plan. The real thrill was to see our daughter just waiting, waving welcome; it was wonderful, an experience of total gratification. We entered through the outer lock; then proceeded to the inner harbour through the next lock to see the harbour was full. With sails down we motored to the end of the inner harbour without seeing a suitable mooring space, so then I turned 180 degrees which is quite difficult using the torque of a single auxiliary engine with the boat virtually still, in such a small confined space with so many people watching and expecting a calamity. However, I slowly executed the manoeuvre perfectly, and some kind yachtsman let me in between a little more sparsely tied up yachts. Thus we settled in and my daughter came on board and all greetings were in abundance. Plans were made to find some French bread for breakfast whilst I reported to customs to lower my yellow customs clearance flag.

Our crew returned with large rolls of crispy fresh bread and immediately commenced eating in the saloon. I found it pitiful to watch a huge quantity of flakes of outer crust coated with French butter spilling over the deck and felt the bilge would soon get full so I withdrew down to rest in my cabin entrance, beyond the initial spillage on my very clean washed teak deck.

After the late breakfast everyone helped to clean up the situation, then we all adjourned to the Deauville Yacht Club to a great welcome reception. The Yacht Club was a great place for hospitality and the officers even held a cocktail party to introduce us all to the members.

The next day we played golf; Deauville golf club was a nice surprise, I had organised the green fees and we were received and introduced to the locker room where we received a locker each; my clubs were taken away with my shoes for cleaning and were returned in time to tee off. My neighbour plus Dr Bob thought all my preparation not necessary, particularly my caddie, but during our round the caddie was most helpful to the other two as well, for he knew the way round and the things to miss. Russel was at least eighty years old, had been playing golf since his Charterhouse School days and had been an excellent golfer, playing at one stage to an 8 handicap and today was still playing off 18.

I had married into a keen golfing family when I was at least 24 handicap. Since my retirement my neighbour co-operated to make me better through competition, to play at 14 handicap. I suddenly thought, 'Why am I taking golf so seriously?' and decided that if I wanted to become a golf professional, I should have done this in the first place! And so I declined to get any better and only to play very friendly golf at quiet times for fun and so here I was enjoying golf without all the hassle. The rye grass was very good to play on except on damp and No. 8 club possibilities.

We had a drink or two on finishing our round. I saw my gleaming clubs and shoes go into my locker then went off to meet the ladies. Over the next few days we played again and it was really a great pleasure to play on such an immaculate course.

We all did shopping, had no luck at the casino but our trip to Honfleur was most happy, with a beautiful vista and some wonderful fresh food to eat. The time went so fast, like all good things, and we prepared for the home voyage, taking on 75 gallons of water and 40 litres of oil fuel, shopping but without wine owing to the French public holiday the day before sailing. We thanked the Yacht Club for their extremely kind hospitality. I found a very nice fellow French yachtsman and arranged a lift for my daughter for her return journey to Paris.

We set course on what was a light wind, part misty, part drizzle weather report, but soon settled down to our new routine with new watches of three hours each, by mutual consent. We soon ran into fog and mist, stopping to listen in the shipping lanes for the engine noise of big ships; we also looked out for the wake movement of the ships! We made landfall at times by the code of a fog lighthouse, a light vessel or buoy to confirm our position. We eventually made Owers Light Vessel by fog horn and set course for the Nab Tower and so to Port Hamble buoy, by buoy to buoy in pouring rain with practically no visibility, and arrived at our mooring wringing wet. Almost before we could tie our warps the local customs official came on board to check our wine and spirits, and we almost had great pleasure in saying 'Nil' owing to our mistake of trying to buy some when the vintners were closed for the French public holiday. The customs official was a little persistent but in the end realised we had told the truth and smiled. It was difficult to do the same because we were so wet and cold, with wet sails to dry out! At least we made landfall the right side of St Catherine's Point, on the Isle of Wight.

Dr Bob went ashore to my local RAF Yacht Club and bought a bottle of French wine for our late meal on board. Thus we celebrated the fun we had enjoyed, then went off home.

CHAPTER 11

Roger's Year 1974

I INVESTED INTO MY SECOND venture, the manufacture of synthetic rigid resin, and glass fabric reinforced abrasive safety wheels, and had parted with my own 1963 built ketch, to have 'hands on' time, for some senior employees of my previous company did think they could do without me, so set up production at rented premises on my finance, whilst I was beginning retirement. They ran into difficulties because, in my opinion, of the lack of technical knowledge hence it was necessary to straighten out the losses by a 'quality hands-on approach'. In other words, goods sent to customers were returned because of unsatisfactory performance. Whilst it was realised quality was at fault there was very little improvement to the current in-house production, and the replacements were sent out with no better performance; that was where I came in.

I immediately stopped all production, cancelled all outstanding orders with an apology, and indicated to the staff that they could not survive doing something so silly. They should start with me at the beginning, only follow my way of in-house quality progress checks, to measure quality and feel my firm formulations only without question. Any divergence should not be allowed or you disappear from sight.

I checked all formulations plus a no wastage allowance and set the path for the only way ahead to my budget, within my official known agreed company plan.

All went well so we increased production by buying new premises nearby, to increase capacity to a possible one million pounds sales yearly turnover via a true performance budget for all operations. This initial sales figure is the hardest to get in any new business; it needs hard devotion to achieve, but once achieved you have earned yourself a niche in the market place for all time!

Business is in fact simple: all you have to do is to think of an idea that you are confident will find a place in its market, believe in it, measure performance in the market place, work hard and your reward will automatically mature. Of course you need accountancy, but you do not need professional help to start; you have to simply go by domestic rules, i.e. ask your wife to buy a petty cash book to enter cash in and out and keep to it, as well as your production and market place penetration.

It is thrilling to get started, to marvel at each stage of your progress; you quickly formulate your own budget programme of improvement for all needs. Before you start a new business, just work out what you want to do. Many afraid people will say, 'I want to borrow cash to get started,' – no sir, you just need to be tidy with whatever cash you have now. A simple, business formula is as follows:

You need to make a profit or margin to survive so to expand, so make this your first figure at the 'bottom line' and never lose it.

Raw materials	45%	
Wages	10%	
Administration	25%	= 100% total
Finance	10%	
Profit margin	10%	

You can now work out your variations to the above individual figures but you cannot extend them to a different total for the total is your only workable budget, as any housewife knows! You can work out more or less all percentages except the bottom $10 + \%$ providing the total always equals 100%. It does not matter how big or small you are.

The company was now turning over £750,000 sterling in sales, running well to budget.

My son Roger who in 1971 passed out BA with honours in business studies had always physically supported my efforts during his holidays, ever since a junior school boy; now he took charge of budget and sales performance to the benefit of the Company progress. He was a popular leader; my business staff with friends appreciated his enthusiasm for successful results, and of course envisaged him taking over from me.

At this time, 1974, Roger was working full time. Apart from the work budget and sales he helped to solve the problems of any person in difficulty and was much appreciated for working all hours to achieve a successful outcome. There was no attempt to consider my no-waste formulations for he understood my superior knowledge about the industry and also realised my own father's inventiveness, with my personal insight into the reaction of synthetic resins during their changing life, and my life with many Bakelite tutors before World War II and during my Royal Air Force service.

I cannot exist in a situation which I think is just stable or going down, for one has to expand, to know one's competitors to improve one's sales and performance, hence technical research and plant development is a common need for competitive reasons and for knowing your future. Hard work is also a necessity but that goes without saying for any direction.

At this time we were struggling to top a million sterling sales. Everything we could think of was in place but our delivery to customer was slow. My son went down to the stores to help dispatch for the day, with the agreement of the largely manual store-keeper, and worked until about 10 p.m. on Saturday night to clear the outstanding items, without a proper lunch. At home, my son collected a quick bite, then went off to meet his current girlfriend and a young gentleman just in from Canada.

The next thing I knew, I had gone to bed after a brief evening doing little and was in a deep sleep when I was suddenly awoken in the early morning by a police officer accompanied by a friend of my son, saying my son had been killed from being hit by a car going in the opposite direction without lights.

Naturally I could not believe it, but when awake I realised the dreadful news and from then on did not take interest in anything for many months except that I was pleased the two friends in the car were not injured at all.

Being on the point of retiring again, I now found the new responsibility of taking his place difficult, but I persevered and packed up everything except my new 1972 twin screw day yacht, and battled away, in the heart of my son, to create a multi million sterling business of our creation.

Never have I retired since, for I still try to live my son's life. However, I did retire from the above company, Arrow Abrasives, in 1993 and later from my work with the European Normalisation Technical Committee on Power Tools when it was completed.

I started a new business in 1995: a unique static fail-safe power tool position to activate, eliminating fire smoke, which kills people in both congested and not so congested places, using my early knowledge on the insulation of portable power tools whilst with Bakelite resins.

I must relate the many difficulties and pleasures in due course but I did think at the above precise time I would never recover from such a deathly blow. Unfortunately, later in 2004, I came up against a total unforeseen situation, recorded in a later chapter.

CHAPTER 12

Fleet Reviews

1975 – Cumberland Fleet Review

MY CREW OF FIVE INCLUDED Dr Bob and his wife. He had been a London Hospital surgeon but was now a GP and had just taken over his father's town practice as senior doctor but he still welcomed a call from the senior adjacent city hospital at Swindon to carry out minor surgery should someone be away. His wife Jean, an ex nursing sister, now looked after the practice reception. They enjoyed a busy life with two daughters at a West Country boarding school. Naturally one expected the elder to join the medical profession following in her father's footsteps, but instead she was taught biology for she was under the tutor's spell and eventually married a biology professor at Oxford University. She now helps her husband to write biology books. His first was a large volume, *The Life of a Frog*, autographed for my library.

Naturally I was the owner and Captain wearing the Royal Thames Yacht Club uniform: a six button reefer with white topped formal yachting cap to doff aloft during our salute to the club Admiral on our way past his saluting base aboard the TS *Royalist*, to be dressed overall by cadets manning the yard–arm. My wife was dressed formally in navy blue and white as were all the ladies for this 1775–1975 bicentenary occasion of the oldest Yacht Club in England, headed by HRH The Prince Philip, Duke of Edinburgh, Patron; The Earl Mountbatten of Burma, Admiral of the Cumberland Fleet; with HRH The Prince of Wales, Commodore. Later we were all to attend the Cumberland dinner and ball with our other guest, Peter Twiss, who was the first person in the world to fly well over 1,000 miles per hour as test pilot for a famous aircraft manufacturer. He was now a retired Royal Navy Fleet Air Arm Lieutenant Commander, but in charge of a yacht marina belonging to Fairey, marine manufacturers of exceptional power craft. I possessed the 'Spearfish' model, berthed in the marina.

Also on board was Dianne Gayle who was now in charge of VIPs visiting the beautiful large Château de Saran in the village near the

140

famous Champagne company in Epernay; she was in charge of our wines for luncheon to supplement the lovely picnic cooked by my wife for a full day of formal and informal celebration. My station for the Review was division 3, column B. The whole event was expertly planned with strict discipline to acknowledge within the vicinity of the Solent, Southampton Water and Isle of Wight.

We set off from our Hamble river mooring to join the fleet muster near Mother Bank thirty minutes early for the start time of 1005 hours, and joined our station to set course at 1020 hours BST towards Cowes in single file, exactly on our position astern of the column leader. Our Admiral salute time was 1133 hours after which we should double back on a reciprocal still in position and return to Mother Bank via the *Royalist* salute base at Peel Bank to disperse later.

On course for the saluting base the fleet was led by the Prince of Wales aboard a motor yacht, and following were nearly 200 yachts of which we were one, enjoying the excitement of the occasion with preparation for our official dress, for all to stand steady apart from me to doff my cap in high salute and Lilian at the stern to lower and hoist the Blue Ensign at the right moment. We arrived at the TS *Royalist* and threw our salute to the club Admiral; it was perfect, so memorable. The TS *Royalist* was dressed with young cadets manning the yard-arm but also enjoying the situation below. Many official photographs were taken by the press and others, during and afterwards. On our course home for Mother Bank for fleet dispersal, we were in the same position as going out, but we were much more relaxed, at least my crew were, for I still felt my responsibility for safety and the right judgement, so did not take a drink as they did on return to Mother Bank. On arrival we dispersed from the fleet and set course towards our fleet formal luncheon at Osborne Bay, Isle of Wight. We enjoyed a little cruise diversion on the way, with me feeling quite hungry and mildly thirsty.

It was all very impressive with all the yachts flying the Ensign and Burgee. Our Blue Ensign was the yacht's Admiralty warrant, issued only to me, the owner, and was issued to the club by the Admiralty in near ancient times. All yachts were also dressed overall at Osborne Bay, a cove just below Osborne House, Queen Victoria's house now a rest home for recuperating officers of the services.

We often anchored in Osborne Bay, such a peaceful location for a picnic on board before the younger members set out to the Solent to swim from the boat, water ski or visit local yacht clubs in Cowes. Further away are also perhaps other things for we often stayed ashore for there are many lovely small ports, rivers and pleasant anchorages in the vicinity. However the beach at Osborne with Queen Victoria's bathing station was private, so out of bounds to all.

On sitting at anchor we dressed the yacht overall; this gave us all quite a lift for a taste of my daughter's wine. More yachts were settling, large and small, many if not most joining up to commence their own idea of bicentenary celebration and fun by rafting together, a pretty and beautiful sight with such an array of flags fluttering in the breeze with the fleet dressed over all.

After some minutes the Royal barge joined the larger yachts with greetings aboard for the Admiral and flag officers and no doubt this rafting was like our top table with the start for grace then luncheon. We on board *Kinswift* exposed our picnic to the bright heavens with our midship engine locker as the table and started to enjoy our pre luncheon drinks whilst admiring our wonderful display of food and all about. Much later, after we had enjoyed our fleet menu and a cigar or two, we sang 'For he's a jolly good fellow' as though dear Robbie Burns was with us as we struck anchor in a few feet of water with the shore below so clearly visible. In fact the water was gin-clear but during lunch we needed to watch the depth as the tide receded to low water, so our departure had to be safely on time.

We returned to our Hamble mooring jetty and felt pleased that there is always at least nine feet (1½ fathoms) of water near the entrance. After mooring we proceeded to the Southern Yacht Club of which my wife and I were members to stay the night, to enjoy a rest followed by a bath before dressing for the evening celebrations of the Cumberland Fleet Dinner Ball.

The dinner and ball was at the School of Navigation, Warsash, a large building with a long jetty to the river and launches provided from 1900 to 0300 to and from the School of Navigation for members' yacht moorings. It was gentlemen's dress, club mess uniform or black tie, with dinner at 2000 hours and dancing until 0300 to music by the Royal Marines' Band or the Hurricane Force Steel Band.

Thus we boarded the club launch and arrived in a few minutes at the Navigation School jetty and after a cocktail or two sat down for dinner which was interrupted by a speech or two from our own flag officers with similar presentations by our friends of the New York Yacht Club's Cumberland cup to the winner of the Bicentenary Transatlantic race and our Emmett Cup to the line honours yacht.

Afterwards we danced all night, with champagne very plentiful. We decided to look for the launch home at about 0230 hours which quickly came and deposited our party at our own jetty. I found the club front door key of our club and so to bed in good spirits for such a wonderful day.

1977 – Silver Jubilee Fleet Review

I accepted the invitation of the Royal Thames Yacht Club to join their special anchorage within the Silver Jubilee Naval Review at Spithead off the historic Royal Naval port of Portsmouth and so made preparations to ensure my boat was in good shape for the period and my guests were informed of the special arrangements necessary.

As my company, Arrow Abrasives Ltd., was attached to HMS *Arrow*, a new frigate, and the Red Arrows, the Royal Air Force display team, I felt the need to inform the Commanding Officer of *Arrow* of my presence as a part of the Review. In return came an invitation to visit the ship on the day of the Review after the main formalities were over. I had been on board a little while earlier to present a silver salver for the best sportsman or event of the year. The captain was very pleased for the ship was entirely new so did not inherit any silver for the wardroom concerning the past.

Incidentally, the Captain, Nicholas Barker, was in command of HMS *Endurance* down near the Falklands prior to the war with Argentina, and you recall his daring mission that was not quite approved of by the Royal Navy or Mrs Thatcher at the time. To me he was an extremely efficient seaman, a delightful character who was entirely respected by all his crew, and so my guests were firmly informed.

The Commander in Chief, flag hoisted on the aircraft carrier *Ark Royal*, was host for the formalities of meeting Commanders of all ships in line, Home, Commonwealth and Foreign, in all preparations concerning the Review on Tuesday 28 June.

The ships' assembly commenced from Friday of the week before. I carried out my preparations to *Kinswift* to be ready for my station assembly located just off Gosport, in the vicinity of the Review area, dressed over all, wearing my Blue Ensign at the main masthead flying alongside the Burgee, all crew dressed as before for our own Bicentenary Review, two years earlier. Naturally all things were shipshape with the area and charts clean and all parts 100 per cent for our arrival scheduled for 0800 hours BST.

Although I witnessed the Review ships briefly arriving we waited for the Review day and assembled on time exactly and waited. Her Majesty the Queen with members of the royal family embarked on HMY *Britannia* which proceeded properly escorted to its station, Spithead, for 1230 at the head of the Review ships for their reception followed by luncheon for flag officers and distinguished guests.

Away from the general fleet activity we halted our drinks and sat down for lunch aboard *Kinswift* exactly at the same time, 1230 hours. The menu produced by my daughter and picnic cooked by my wife were efficiently presented and looked superb. At this time my crew of Dr Bob with his wife and daughter, and I the Captain with my wife and daughter indicated three hearty cheers, then we tucked into our simple feast so well presented.

At 14.25 HMY *Britannia* weighed anchor for the Queen to review the fleet until 1630 whereby she returned to the head of Review lines for the flypast at 1645 of the Aircraft of the Fleet Air Arm, followed at 1700 by Royal Navy Ships' gunfire to indicate the Review Area was now freely open to traffic apart from the other duties at sea or on the shore. The Queen was free until 2015 to dine on board HMS *Ark Royal*.

Shortly after the flypast I packed up and set course for HMS *Arrow*. After dodging a few ships I arrived beside HMS *Arrow* near the starboard gangway, and signalled my intention to board with a gift case of champagne for their wardroom. By this time I was almost alongside and could talk to the officer on deck to explain I had guests aboard, so I would be happy just to hand over my gift alongside in the bouncing sea, but my guests and I were invited aboard, so I slipped away slightly to prepare my fend offs to warp alongside which I successfully completed with assistance in the bouncing sea. We climbed aboard with me and Dr Bob carrying the wine for the wardroom.

On board we were introduced to the officers present, and enjoyed conversation over a cup of tea. After about ten minutes the Officer of the Watch called the Senior Officer and the Captain to report quietly that my boat had bounced the Captain's pinnace on station astern. Whilst I could not hear anything of the conversation I was quickly informed that the Captain's pinnace had sunk or collapsed flying the Royal Navy White Ensign and I sensed a crisis happening.

Off I proceed aft to have a look with the Officer of the Watch after the Captain had viewed the scene. Naturally I offered my assistance. Apparently the pinnace was old and needed replacement but the boat was not a priority of naval expenditure; I did however feel in a way responsible for my boat was strong fibreglass built weighing 9 tons: a very well equipped day boat, in fact there was no better. The old clinker built pinnace just collapsed as they bounced together although I had out quite large white fend offs. Anyway, at least the naval White Ensign floating with its staff was rescued and taken aboard HMS *Arrow*.

I was let into a secret appointment, whereby the Captain was to be on HMS *Ark Royal* at 1900 in time for dinner at 2015 with other captains of the Royal Navy to dine with the Queen and the Royal Family. I immediately told the Captain he could borrow my boat with no problem. Eventually my offer was declined for he had arranged for a Captain of a nearby ship to lift him to and fro so all would be well. I was pleased, relieved and quite quickly I wished to leave, so was handed my boat which was now alongside the gangway and on inspection there was no mark of the collision at all. We all made goodbyes, boarded and cast off, and departed for the Hamble to be in time for my mooring and our own dinner ashore.

I did belong to other yacht clubs near on the Solent, so was never very far from sleeping quarters or a good meal. My home afterwards could be just a simple motor car ride away and I often preferred the pleasure of getting home, to feel the garden and read *The Times* or tell stories to my youngest, then go to bed early, being often tired from the day's events.

The Fleet Review was due to celebrate the Queen achieving 25 years on the throne. Previously there had been many Fleet Reviews, started by King George III on the faithful connection of the Royals of the emerging superiority of the Royal Navy. Ten year periods was the norm but in 1887, Queen Victoria had one for her Golden Jubilee and ten years later she was too ill to attend. In 1911 was one for King George V which was followed by a special Review for our Houses of Parliament.

The previous Spithead review was for the Queen's Coronation in 1953.

I now feel that owing to the emerging political situation whereby the Government expenditure needs to be tightly curtailed and controlled, the Reviews are not necessary; for instance the Royal Yacht, still not entirely commissioned for a part of the 1977 Review, was not considered a well built ship and not a Royal Navy requirement for the future thus the current budget was not appropriate for a modern government.

I myself felt the Reviews were a spectacular success, but whilst I would miss the benefit for my country and trade in the world of our planet, I had no intention to consider leaving my mooring on the Hamble River for we were so enjoying the dream Uffa Fox injected into me so many years ago, before the Second World War. A little later on 15 July I was invited to a reception aboard HMY *Britannia* for Sunday 31 July in the same year.

On the Sunday, which is always a busy time in Cowes, particularly in Cowes week, I was dropped off on a jetty in west Cowes by my own boat *Kinswift* in time to board the Royal barge waiting at the Royal Yacht Squadron's steps, and whisked off to embark for the reception at 1830 hours until 1945 hours. I met various club members while having a drink of export strength gin and talking to our Royal Host. The time soon passed so a little later I disembarked into the same shuttle boat, and landed at the Royal Yacht Squadron steps again. My own *Kinswift* was milling about locally in the harbour under the charge of my son and his friend John Day, endeavouring to catch sight of me so as efficiently to pick me out walking to the now crowded jetty we used on arrival at the Island Sailing Club.

I had sighted my boat and it seemed my boat and I were about to coincide so I could be the first from the Royal Yacht to depart ashore. There was no real difficulty. *Kinswift* was manoeuvred for me to step aboard, but as I attempted to embark with one right foot on the jetty and one left foot on the boat, it took a sudden leap forward with me straddled across the space, and as the boat leapt forward my foot on board was dislodged. Neatly I continued to step toward the sea with my full weight to take me down below into the sea with my yachting cap floating on the surface, the water consuming my best reefer. I found myself looking through light green sea, so I surfaced without headgear. Immediately on breaking the surface I set out to swim and was fortunate the boat had not disappeared owing to adverse action. Bedraggled as I was I was helped aboard then used the ship's staff to hook up my yachting cap and departed very wet from the gaze of the amused onlookers still dressed in their best uniform.

On board *Kinswift* I had no time to discuss the whys and wherefores of the spectacular episode. Down below I discarded my heavy wet gear, wrapped myself in a towel or two, and put on my oilies without the skipper's fisherman's hat.

We returned to the Hamble where we tied up on my mooring. I immediately walked over to the Southern Yacht Club, looking like a scarecrow of oilskin that had just been retrieved from a local rubbish dump. On arrival I quickly found a bath with some good soap to wash away the green sea that tasted still of whatever.

Afterwards in borrowed clothes that fitted me not, I enjoyed a drink with our Prime Minister Ted Heath, and we all had a very good dinner. I went home to talk to Doodey who was still awake lying in her bed. My story was often a slight variation of my usual but still adored before she fell asleep. This story, repeated so often with variations always concerned with under the bridges and over the hills, was based on our journeys together perhaps on a Sunday when we would set off well before lunchtime with our large dog who was a bit slow but enjoyed walking for exercise and play

Our track was to walk through the fields from Kinley House, Durford Wood. On the way I issued commands, like: 'Quick, lie down, keep very still,' to watch the clouds flow past in the deep blue sky. My daughter and I immediately fell into the long grass in the field at the edge. We expected the dog to do the same but he was always too busy sniffing around on our way out. The command to rise, move on, was always sounded, under the bridge now. After a short distance, I would issue another command and so on until we left the hill, part of the wonderful South Downs of England, to join the stream below. On arrival we disappeared under the narrow horse bridge and looked for the small trout in the bubbling water by stepping on the water ledge just above the streaming magic of flowing stream, the small River Rother.

We spent a longer time under this old horse bridge each time we walked, until I was told off for being late for lunch, so we had a shorter time to see the trout but we never lost the magical dream of pure nature come wind or shine. Always the way home was a little more rushed but we still played 'under the bridges and over the hills' though I have to report the old dog was getting slower by this time although he did seem to try and play the same game to enjoy the quietness, the beauty of the sky and trying to be still in the long grass listening to birds, and whatever was nearby such as the odd mouse which the dog would find but never do any harm to the life that was never still.

The odd aircraft on occasion would fly above, always a romantic sight to me and I often wondered its intended destination, for I knew so many good places. However I knew I was happy with my daughter with everything so tranquil and beautiful, but now would not ever change my tranquility for anything.

CHAPTER 13

The Company

THE PORTSMOUTH NEW PLANT was well under way, the building nearly finished to provide a production unit and opposite, over the entrance road from the highway, a laboratory plus two offices, a check-in point to control entering and departing traffic, and the main telephone exchange inside to be connected to outside and inside.

The plant of roll coating machine led to covering by abrasive grain, so on to electrostatic orientation then to a hanging wallpaper type oven and movement to leave the oven at a prearranged time to be wound up and coated again with surface binding to the proper degree. It was then subjected to great heat for a number of hours to set the reaction of the synthetic resin. After hanging for the appropriate time it would be withdrawn and wound again into rolls for fabrication for whatever was wanted.

This manufacture used a similar method to the USA giants' modern fabrication to eliminate the hot spots of my single disc fabrication which was so successful and still is for special products with current production requirements. The main recipient was the large and better precision usage for the requirements of the motor industry modernisation and to supply specialties to the giant companies outlets in England.

At this time car doors were falling off at quite a rate, owing to the inadequate design of the hinges to meet the power of the new series of car. We produced a difficult double sided abrasive insert for the hinge at the request of one successful motor company to ensure the hinge holding screws did not work loose, before the general situation was eventually resolved by a new design of the door hinge to eliminate the vibration cause of the problem. Our extensive sale and precision production of hundreds of thousands of double sided hinge pads was a first and continued as unique – only possible to buy from us; it was painstaking work for the abrasive destroyed fine precision tooling at an alarming rate unless very high accuracy was obtained.

I had recently changed the second Armstrong Siddeley motor car for a Bentley which I sold for a Rolls-Royce new mass production

motor car. On a business journey to Milan both the front doors of
the Rolls-Royce became loose, and one departed, hanging on only
one hinge and in a bumpy situation so much in danger of falling off.
I stopped and tied the doors in with string, my favourite bundle
always within the spare parts carried. Eventually I found the
appropriate garage, so immaculate and clean with all the tools
showing, to leave my front doors for repair. The car was taken to the
workshop and I left to stay the night at the hotel previously booked.

In the late morning I called the garage to be told the car was ready
to take away and I was informed that Rolls-Royce had flown two
new doors overnight so the repair was easily done. I congratulated
the manager for the absolutely perfect service with nothing to pay.
Funnily I had owned the Bentley for just over eighteen months but
had not trouble with the doors and traversed rough continental roads
of cobble, ruts and ice with no problems. I just found the car of fitted
boot luggage and bulbous design too heavy to drive for long distance
travel on the continent. For many years I changed my Rolls-Royce
for a free new one each year; the waiting list was over eighteen
months or two years. The price rise was always higher, and people
were desperate to own such a car and paid over the odds to secure
such a good piece of machinery. My starting price was £6,250 but
quickly increased to eventually £120,000.

The plant in New Zealand was well on its way and my very good
chemist wanted to go and settle in New Zealand to oversee the
technical production for he suffered from chest and migraine
problems, and thought the fresh air would be the answer. I made the
necessary arrangements, and he happily departed. I was very sorry to
lose him but being a very keen trout and salmon fisherman rather
envied his opportunity with all available facilities on hand to enjoy.

A little time later the machinery was installed in New Zealand and
the initial problem runs looked extremely promising. I needed to go
to settle the quality to help my friend Hedley Huthnance with his
sales conversion possibilities, related to production standards required.

With my factory still operating profitably and with increasing
turnover I spent more time to progress the initial production at
Portsmouth and ordered increased production facilities of our single
disc production, one day soon to transfer all apart from the sales
office. At this time I was also building a second unit with a third and
fourth on the way to follow.

At home in Camberly I occasionally met for lunch at nearby large house, Pennyhill Park, now a luxury hotel, Colin Haywood, a rather wealthy gentleman, with eleven gardeners growing flowers including orchids for the house with a long holly hedge surrounding the estate, which was reputed to be the longest holly hedge in Europe. I was met at the door by a fully dressed butler who looked after my needs before entry to the drawing room with always a roaring recently laid fire, in both coldish temperatures and warm. My host would arrive to greet me exactly on the stroke of midday; the butler then brought along two flat champagne glasses, poured chilled gin with a little chilled water, added two drips of shaken angostura bitters, stirred and passed the glasses to our individual tables. My host received a tray of lemons, chose the best and sliced a good strip of rind, yellow skin only, and inserted the lemon with a squeeze longways in each glass. The drink was superb, so refreshing in front of the fire. We finished at 12.45 always, then moved to the dining room to sit at the opposite ends of a large oak table.

A second butler served and stood behind my host and the previous butler served and stood behind me, pouring the wine only for me as my host only drank weak whiskey and water. After lunch we smoked a cigar each, then I departed.

The first time I was shown through the very long heated greenhouses producing the flowers, mainly orchids, to line both sides of the long entrance corridor to the drawing room. My host always wore a rough jacket with leather arm patches, drove an old Humber motor car and was the largest investor in two English abrasive companies, one large in grinding wheels, the other an old fashioned company in the same field as mine. The reason for my visit invitations was because he was notified of my modern abrasives and found out I lived nearby; he also lived alone. Since my introduction I have always assembled my drinks exactly the same way and for some time I was nicknamed 'Pinkie' for the taste so good; however, it was expensive on the right looking lemons.

I was to meet my orchid friend Colin Haywood a little later under quite different circumstances. My programme in New Zealand was nearing completion and I thought to go in two weeks' time; however I received an interesting telephone call with an invitation to lunch to meet the directors of the oldest abrasive company in the world, John Oakey & Sons Ltd, in London. I accepted and enjoyed a fine lunch at a top restaurant. The conversation was concerning a possible mutual merger between us and I expressed my interest for this was a very old fashioned company of very good repute and financial means that saw the need to modernise into the modern world of synthetic resins and organisation to current production methods as ours.

We arrived at a decision to carry out the merger. I thought it was a very good logical step to move into direct competition and catching up on USA giants, particularly in relation to the modern progress of the technical advances caused by the introduction of Dr Baekland Resins, bought by paying a royalty to Bakelite. As in other industries today we employed plastics, otherwise various synthetic resins from the distillation of fossil fuels.

The programme was arranged for me to spend about six weeks in London to assess the future requirements necessary to make plans. I stayed in the blue suite of the Dorchester Hotel, and was collected each morning to attend board meetings and interview staff, particularly the sales manager who seemed to be running the company yet the sales turnover was no improvement over that at the turn of the century – 1900.

The company organisation was an interesting one. The son in line of the original family was managing director, but preferred playing darts at the local inn, therefore was inactive as far as the company was concerned. The directors included two Army generals, one retired with the other, the son, off on active service who knew little about the day to day running or monthly situations, and a nephew, a little active but who preferred the piano and music. The sales director I have mentioned was now there, a somewhat homosexual director inherited from a previously bought small company and seemed to be working by contacts, but staying in the factory premises overnight; by day he tried to follow various movements which I found irritating on occasions.

Consequently I quickly became the managing director without title and found it extraordinary to sort out the way forward, for we were responsible for horse grooms who were recently in charge of horse deliveries, without any firm job for them each day. We also possessed the oldest and best antique steam engine in London and the south of England, which was beautifully polished with brass gleaming for public display and had visitors who were interested in very old steam engine boilers.

The company was founded in 1623 by a piano player; the founder did travel by horse-drawn coach to Switzerland or the south of France each year. Hence, gentlemanly. I slowly introduced modern organisation and left alone those of little use, but made plans to move to a less expensive site to build a design factory to produce the same animal glue glass and natural emery products more efficiently, adding modern development production in a move forward, also considering the possibility of combining my own company on the same site.

Whilst the digestion of my proposals was taking place by the commercial bankers, who seemed to be in charge of the company accounts, I looked into estate agents for value to and realised by the sale of the current expensive value site next to the busy Waterloo railway station, got quotations for better modern equipment and looked at the best site outside London available to be suitable. With that, I set off to New Zealand.

As my new partner possessed factories in South Africa and Australia I was to include them on my way. The South African plant was adjacent to Johannesburg. I flew to Cape Town where I had a few influential friends: the Royal Air Force Group Captain now leaving the head of the Red Cross; the aunt of my wife who returned home from Kiess Castle, the neighbour to the HRH Queen Mother in Scotland. The aunt's two children, one son ex the South African Air Force and owning the agency of the US General Motors and the daughter just divorced from the son's Air Force friend, who appeared on Wick station in the extreme north of Scotland in her full length white wedding dress trailing in the pouring rain to see someone. I thought a meeting with her should be avoided.

Cape Town was glorious, with Table Mountain, the Cape of Good Hope, and the south-west tip of Africa, the meeting place of the Indian Ocean with the Atlantic Ocean. There I ate crayfish tails, so fresh and so succulent to the mouth and throat. I traversed the garden route to Knysna and Port Elizabeth to meet with my Royal Air Force friend. We then went to his home to meet his beautiful wife whom I had met before at my home in Downderry, Cornwall, just before he resigned the Royal Air Force for his beloved wife to return to South Africa. She suffered a long serious illness and now did not seem very stable but wished to see the film *The Birdman of Alcatraz* so we did, and then collected a take away of fish and chips for our supper

and departed the sad situation for both. The reason for leaving the
Red Cross was to nurse his wife full time which I admired but to me
was so different to his recognised known valuable potential in the
Royal Air Force.

In the Johannesburg hotel I had just eaten breakfast of the largest
huge avocado pear I am ever likely to see again: two halves of it. The
factory plant was simple and clean but making a loss in profit and sales
turnover mainly because local merchant competition had better
quality imported materials; with little thought I would recommend
closure and supply direct from the UK.

In Australia I found the same position and the same reason so
passed on without more todo. Arriving late in New Zealand, the
suggestion of my friendly directors was to go to sleep and do business
in the morning but I said, 'No, I wish to see the plant and machines
working now, always to orient my mind before considering my after
sleep possible working plans.'

The situation at the plant was heaven to me. It was working three
shifts a day in a clean atmosphere and tidiness, worth recording for
needing to create different grades on one simple main coating
machine is not easy, and to onlookers very confusing, so tidiness was
essential to achieve quality. I congratulated the production director,
Jack Smallfield; the reflection was on his very accurate work to get
the machines assembled to obtain such precision results on base, fibre,
cloth and paper to the technical requirements of the chemist and his
need to check samples of the material in progress to ensure
consistency quality. Incidentally I was pleased to see my chemist, who
now seemed very happy with his move to Takapuna from my factory
in England; also his health was improved.

My friend the sales director Hedley Huthnance explained he was
working many long hours to establish the customer quality with
excellent results so far, which was good news to me and I felt so far
happy concerning the future sales programme to achieve such results
to satisfy the Prime Minister of New Zealand.

I then had a very good sleep, but was awakened early by my
friends to examine the position in more detail and make further plans
and details. On entry to our factory I noticed one of the USA giants
with a very large sign outside a new factory building exactly opposite
our entrance, and was horrified within a flash thought of the possible
impact on our sales and production programme.

However I was immediately assured by my co directors that at the first sight they had urgently protested and taken the matter up with the top authorities, to find the new factory would only produce adhesive tapes from imported bulk to cut up and sell to distribution. I was not satisfied and needed proper written confirmation from the government, but I then reluctantly accepted the situation though remaining always suspicious for we were promised control of our own destiny, if quality demanded so.

I then went to Lake Taupo with my sales director to fish for trout to eat on the shore and later at evening time to fly fish the rip, the frothy boiling water leading to the lake water to the river, which I did with the help of borrowed waders and a lovely light split cane rod and enjoyed an exciting active hour with success achieved. Next day I returned to the plant and later flew out to San Francisco, New York and home, thoroughly pleased with my visit to New Zealand to see a situation so supported by two accurate enthusiastic entrepreneurs.

In New York I called in to have lunch at the '21' club with an important agent for Stihl, the large German tool company, to discuss possibilities of business. Later I arrived at JFK Airport for an overnight flight to Heathrow, London and was met by my car and so home for a good short sleep. I was tired from talking all night to an interesting passenger next to me, the president of another major USA tool company who might become a future friend.

After lunch at home I returned to work and felt busy again until quite late. The progress of Portsmouth was very good and later I enjoyed time to check on the progress of my boat and to consider the London problems I had left behind. I arranged to transfer the single disc factory to Unit 2 factory premises at Portsmouth together with as many production staff as possible; unfortunately many did not wish to move, which I completely understood; nevertheless eleven executive staff decided to transfer. Of course they were keen key personnel to me of distinguished service.

At Portsmouth we set up to manufacture reinforced cutting wheels, similar to those made in Klingspor, Siegen, Germany, made of single stage synthetic resin abrasive paper sheet or rolls by cutting out different diameters to form laminated sheets via steam hot platens of hydraulic high pressure: two tons per square inch presses, not dissimilar to my original experience of making laminated sheets for insulation and veneers for surfacing wood with all types of grain, oak, mahogany and more at Bakelite. Before my war experience, in fact, I was responsible for making such single stage resins.

Stamping out such sheets of press cured abrasive grain to different diameters was new to me and I thought very difficult for one made very accurate precision tools that soon lost their precision owing to the abrasive; however,we were very accurate, successfully breaking into the market of imported cheaper wheels and sometimes against two of the three USA giants in the grinding wheel market as well as the coated abrasive market. Our speciality was the hand held portable electric, air or petrol tool market. My emphasis was to supply manufacturers of such tools for my products were more safe thus avoiding many accidents to such user personnel. I was encouraged by UK government departments because we saved on import, so helped the balance of payment crisis and inflation. Our progress was increasing methodically, with special emphasis on the employee tool operation, and at the time I made friends with the Chief Factory Inspector.

At this time I was still travelling throughout Europe and many countries beyond including the USA and for holidays I started skiing again with the family participating first under my instruction; however I quickly realised skiing had changed too! So it was necessary for us all to learn a new way although many basics were still within the old method. However on a recent trip to the USA I purchased some new metallic 'Head' skis for me and my wife. We were the first with metal skis in Gastad, Switzerland and caused quite a stir. On the level, they were quick and light hence one needed to be careful in walkways from the lifts and pathways to the hotel.

On one occasion in the beautiful deep new snow, slightly grooved, my wife needed to be careful crossing a highway leading to the hotel to avoid a car but she did not stop in time and the driver also could not stop in time. The wheels and chain went over my wife's skis between the front and the foot lock. Immediately we examined the situation amongst quite a throng, to find no damage at all but it was difficult to stop the skiers admiring our 'Heads' and many wanted to know where we had bought them for they were the first to see the new desire.

Our family children were all skiing on hired skis but we stowed our 'Heads' singly on a special roof rack on our Rolls-Royce motor car and seemed to be the only car carrying skis from England. The admiration was quite fantastic along the whole route. In England and on the Channel ferries I am sure people thought we were quite mad with no snow to be seen anywhere around. And the little one, now three years old, was learning to ski too! And enjoyed the experience with a close friend from Durford Wood so we could traverse the slopes and country but always with a guide for safety.

On one occasion we motored to near Switzerland with our equipment and caught the small ski train to Wengen where no cars were allowed. On arrival at our hotel I received a message to say that Russel, now eighty years old, was coming to join us for Christmas and New Year for he missed us, and was so familiar with skiing at Wengen and Grindelwald on the opposite side of the valley. This friend was a very lively character, staying up late having fun which suited my wife and son much more than me. His practical worldly knowledge was of great interest to me, however, in sailing many types of boat and as the owner of a meat and food distribution company he had many connections in business around the world.

Before we would meet Russel we took a ski lift to Davos for luncheon with my family, except for Doodey, afterwards to have the famous ski run down to Wengen in the beautiful bright warm sunshine above the glittering white snow. The luncheon was superb but towards the end the sky changed to a dull atmosphere so we thought the sooner we got moving the better. On joining other people outside there was talk of staying the night which to me did not exist as an idea. After waiting and due consideration of the conditions I decided to go as soon as possible for the trail run was long; if we waited we would end up in the dark.

The family assembled behind me, plus another twenty-five people behind them, and we set off. I was not sure whether the real lack of visibility was due to cloud that would clear en route or fog that would not. It was difficult skiing for you could not see beyond your own skis, hence you needed to be guided by your feet, to feel and stare for confirmation just beyond your ski. I eventually made the run just as it was getting dark to cheers of my many followers. Unfortunately the episode did damage my eyes; I could now see two images instead of one and thought why? My eyes worked happily flying before my war years and after, and I now needed to adjust by wearing glasses for all time, but I was not hindered in the future.

On another occasion we caught the narrow-gauge railway to the last station just below the Eiger Mountain peak for a ski down to base, with Russel who had skied all his life in this area. I then noticed his very old wooden skis with no metal edges, his very old boots with virtually no laces, and a simple spring as a boot lock which was not safe at all. So I told him, 'There is no way I will ski with you for you are so unsafe on a modern steep piste,' to which he responded, 'Look, my friend, I know more about skiing than you, I have been perfectly happy with my equipment before and intend to go down the track without you, so off I will go now.'

Off he went rather erratically down a simple almost flat slope to the real run and then disappeared. I was concerned so set off a little distance behind so that he did not think I was watching him. On arrival at the first moderately steep slope he was nowhere to be seen in the valley so down I went and noticed a new ski track going off piste, but no one in sight. I thought, Where the hell is he? For it was all beautiful shiny snow everywhere.

I followed what I thought was the new track half way down the first slope. I went quite a long way and as the track was looking indistinct I stopped for further assessment and lo and behold thought I heard a faint cry for help. I decided to investigate so I approached the very deep snow and came across my friend in a hole he caused eight or more feet deep. I helped him to partly stand up in his stocking feet on top of his ski to prevent him from falling further down, then fitted the skis still in his boots, then helped him stand properly on his skis. I could not find his ski sticks but he used mine and so we set off with my help slowly towards the mountain railway line for I thought we should find a safe objective.

On reaching the railway I took off both pairs of skis and in our boots we started to descend the railway line, I noticed on the way up that the track through the deep snow was only just wide enough for the train, so arranged what to do should a train suddenly appear. We did practice drill on my command, every few yards: I said, 'A train is coming, jump up the bank of snow,' and I took the skis with me for there was no room each side of the track. We practised many jumps, fell down and scrambled up again for this was a very serious situation should a train appear. Worn out with our efforts we eventually arrived at the half way station looking a bit peculiar. We crossed the track and made for the waiting room and for me a glass of Campari although my friend wanted brandy and drank a few to relieve his tension. He did buy the drinks and profusely thanked me for saving his life for he thought he was finished in such a deep hole with snow piled on top of him to prevent any rescue; it was cold too!

On New Year's Eve my family except me, for to me the celebration means a mathematical nothing and I get to bed early, went off with our friend to spend the night away with the local ski instructors and others and felt a little hangover tiredness the next day. Should the New Year begin on the winter solstice day (the shortest day of our year) I might be interested but it would mean changing our calendar and that is too difficult now.

We always go to snowy mountains to ski in the Christmas holidays, but also sometimes the Easter holidays. I tried to finish my continental business just before, to make it less time and easier to ski, as I was interested now to buy Italian machines and raw material. To save on price I often ended my journeys near Milan or Turin so did skiing at Cervinia situated at the head of the Aosta Valley.

Cervinia was an excellent resort for skiing but did have variable snow. We stayed half way up the mountain but could not get out of the door if there was too much snow and sometimes the same area would be soft so one took the ski lift down to the town. At weekends, being near to the Turin car company, it was a little dangerous to do anything but sit in the sun.

On arrival at our hotel, Mount Gravena, we were shown a very nice room with a balcony but when I looked out, next door was a veranda terrace full of beautiful ladies in very small bathing costumes, bare to their tummy getting bronzed under the Easter sun. The room was only reluctantly approved by my wife, however I did occasionally see the spectacle again. I think someone may have complained, leaving the weekends free for the beautiful ladies to bronze.

At home again I needed to settle the items I left behind in London and elsewhere, as the untitled managing director insisted I organised a directors' meeting to make a decision and to complete our future programme forward, then to progress the proposed changes that needed to be made. This was difficult for the actual managing director was mostly in the local inn playing darts.

After a hectic week with little accomplished for certain, I went home for the weekend and had a little gardening to restore the lawn from the devastation caused by our wild nocturnal badgers looking for may bugs a few inches under the surface. I had changed the house name from Brockhurst so I think the badgers knew and enjoyed their excursion at different times to make me ponder. Also at this time I was thinking of moving to Portsmouth for I was heavily engaged with the progress of the new plant and the running in of production staff and I found it tiring being driven down each day, working in the car and returning late at night.

My wife was also expecting a child so I delayed Portsmouth as long as I was able but needed to rent an apartment to be on the spot. I found one behind the grassland just off the sea at Southsea for me to spend the night when I was late working.

I find it difficult to record the first night at my new local address. I went to bed about 11.30 after a hectic day manufacturing the first run of coated abrasive into my new hanging motive automatic through oven containing about £30,000 worth of material and after completion of this first stage went home to sleep so I could awaken early to see the result of the quality, before winding the contents and placing all through a second stage for coating fermentation before the second hot oven cycle. At 3.13 I was suddenly awoken by a very loud knocking on my door, so staggered to open the door to find my night watchman saying, 'What do I do?' The whole corner of the oven track hangers had fallen to the floor but the oven was too hot to enter. I did not need time to think. I put on a light dressing gown then two overcoats with a thick scarf tied round my neck and my hat over a further thin scarf around my head, thus was ready come what may!

On arrival at the oven I was greeted by my maker manager and four operatives who looked bewildered for the oven was at 160° centigrade. I said to all, 'I am going in.' All looked in amazement as I unlocked the door and entered with a torch to see what to do. After the initial look to see I came out, and said, 'OK, we have a problem. We need to get the material back up on the hangers and wait until the oven cycle has finished to start the automatic movement to withdraw the whole.' The response was again that the oven was too hot, so I asked for three volunteers to dress up and accompany me to do the job. There was now no difficulty. We proceeded to the trouble corner with ladders and heavy leather gloves, and assembled the fallen material on the track. By this time I was feeling so hot and roasted there was no way any of us could stay any longer. The accident had been rectified and all was well again until tomorrow's shift which of course was in four hours' time.

I gave all the volunteers an extra week's wages, and we enjoyed no trouble again because we handed the problem to the engineering department manager who would be responsible for the future situation of the machinery working properly, otherwise they would need to do the repair, even if the oven was too hot. Of course after this the oven always worked properly because the maintenance programme introduced made it so.

The engineer in charge became a very accurate maker of precious precision tools that would cope with the grains' abrasive action and as far as I was concerned he could feel the situation very well to the extent I was pleased to have complete faith in his ability to understand the likely problems. Later I confirmed his appointment as director of all engineering which now was to include all present and future plant and buildings. I joined my engineer, Gordon Ford, in Italy to introduce him to my new plant sources in Italy and found his knowledge and detail to work with computerised plans of my future plant splendid with respect for my outline decision for the future. I was not so happy with my administrative manager who was good to start with; although highly qualified from university and with a doctorate from a commercial business school his ego was developing in place of ambition. Despite my warning his conceit and self interest seemed not to allow him to work as efficiently as the promise expected.

My chemist for the vacant position as my previous chemist was now in New Zealand came from the largest UK abrasive company. He was a good learner and technically very good, so was making good progress of understanding our synthetic resin way of working with the quality needed. His new ideas were always discussed with me before any self action.

At this time I was having difficulty with the largest British trade union. The aggressive approach was unpleasant o me; however I gave freedom to approach my employees as long as they did not disrupt my working hours. My work force was not so interested for their wages were above the standard union rate, but this did not stop the union parking a big long union marked recruiting van with aggressive persuading staff inside to force their view at the one and only entrance road to the factory day and night. Whilst I found the attempt of recruitment distasteful and crude, after about a month or so they disappeared and worked in a different way. I have never objected to any of my staff joining a union of their choice. Should they approach me individually I always said, 'If you feel they give you something please do, I have no objection.'

A little later I did have difficulty with working out production costs, so employed a union cost specialist from a large company east of London. He was excellent, a little too painstaking for me but he made such a difference. He went on to become my works manager and later a company director.

I was often away on holiday but never failed to telephone each day to sort out whatever the business needed. The conversation was also helpful to relax myself for other work or play. At this period, I enjoyed very good business with two UK companies of the USA giants, who to me were getting smaller and friendlier and admired two who were also helpful with standard technical information without conditions. I was buying abrasive grain, silicon carbide and aluminous oxide from Norton, and supplying the other Carborundum with special depressed centre sanding discs, Also owing to their introduction I joined the AIA (Abrasive Industry Association) to discuss the merits of consolidation for particular aspects of interest. I was greeted into the AIA with open arms for no new company had entered the ranks of the industry for many ages.

I always looked forward to my short weekends at home, catching up with family events and social things I missed or had to do. My wife was so near giving birth. I ended up going early on the Monday without result, so I left behind my car and driver just in case of some urgency concerning the birth. Strange that just about one hour after I left for my factory in Portsmouth, apparently all problems broke loose, pains giving notice of childbirth, the nurse concerned with the birth now imminent to be collected in readiness now, and to contact the doctor to attend the birth. All was in place at the ready, but everything had to wait for a new awakening spasm which happened very soon. Although my driver was at the ready all the time he was in a more urgent position for he had only taken the midwife back to duty to have to go and find her again. The nurse arrived on time and told my wife she had delivered a wonderful little girl named after my driver, who she thought was the husband and father. My wife of course told the nurse the gentleman was not the father, and explained the situation which would not have happened if we could have had the doctor present. I received the garbled situation on my call as soon as I touched base in my office; I was rather amused at such a ridiculous situation but it did make me think for a moment.

Another adventure for me at home was foolishly caused by me; before the question concerning my son Roger at his prep school and the details to date, I had just driven home to be greeted by my son. Before I could open my car door properly he promptly came aboard the seat next to me and said, 'Please Papa, can you teach me to drive. I vacated my seat and said, 'Move over, I will explain,' and sat in the passenger seat, feeling very senior and pleased to know someone interested even if it was my young son. After explanation of the instruments, I finished by restarting the engine and he knew he could not reach the pedals so was not worried at all.

Next my son ducked down below the steering wheel and heavily put his foot on the accelerator. At the same moment the car leapt forward and before I realised what was happening we were shooting through our large hawthorn hedge, then grass, then a holly hedge, then a wooden boundary fence, then down a steep six yard bank where we were confronted by the neighbour's house. Without knowing what to do in the circumstances and feeling we were approaching the sound barrier I somehow wrenched control by turning the ignition key, so eventually came to rest within inches of my artist friend's studio wall, whilst he was painting a lovely model reading a book with her back directly in line with our likely entry through the wall!

We were so surprised we did not have time to be angry, and were so thankful no real damage was done. Needless to say I did arrange repair of everything and noted my son seemed to enjoy his little excursion.

We often talked over my regular absent weeks so we decided all the family would move down to my apartment in Portsmouth, if need be. I therefore took steps to market and sell the renamed Brockhurst (Kinley House), so to move and find a new home nearby my work. Almost immediately after the picture and details appeared in a country magazine we received many agents' requests to view. Before we could take action however a fellow decided he was going to buy the house without looking at the property. This caused me a little heartache for I was away thus could not oversee such an urgent request, so I refused, with the need to plan our own situation without rushing to meet someone else's proposal. The result was that the gentleman was not finished; he proceeded to offer immediate cash and would bring the cash with him if I would meet him. Well, after a little thought I stated to my agent, 'I have no intention of accepting cash so if he wants to deal with my solicitor he can, however personally, I do not wish to be present.'

The gentleman involved did eventually purchase my property with possessions we wished to sell, so I had no time to find new accommodation before the completion date. So one Saturday we all moved into my little apartment to lead an interesting life for about a year or so, but we were six in such a small place. However my resourceful wife decided as follows:

Doodey, the baby girl of one year, did not take too much space. The housekeeper, Mrs Wright, who insisted on moving with us slept in the kitchen and to fit in required to put her legs into the hot or cold oven at nights. Roger and Dianne Gayle went boarding in their respective ballet and prep schools but were happy, though with a dislike for leaving on the railway train at the end of the holiday. We lived on the edge of Southsea Common just away from the sea; the common flat grassland was where the would-be soldiers and people for the Navy were collected before putting to sea for battle, exploration or whatever, and the whole sea front of Portsmouth is now protected, What a piece of forced pressgang history.

Apart from the many historical battle memorials on the sea promenade there was much to see: HMS *Victory*, Admiral Nelson's flagship lying in the world's first dry dock; the stairs on which the Duke of Buckingham, the chief administrator for Charles I in 1623, was assassinated by an aggrieved soldier; the birth place of Charles Dickens when his father was employed at the dockyard; and King Henry VIII's view of the sinking of England's biggest new battleship, the *Mary Rose*, in the Solent.

I regularly sat in the same seat for thirty-five years at a very good small restaurant that I used for lunch and the entertainment of my business guests and sometimes met my children on arrival from overseas. Their particular delight was always cold thin slices of smoked salmon with French fried potatoes. The two owners of the restaurant were Polish with tremendous World War II records who walked through German lines to England to fight for freedom.

My factory was now composed of four production units, with one unit a modern heating system attached, plus a laboratory with executive offices and a separate wooden administrative building for sales, accounts, purchase and general office work including a private cycle rack, with an adjacent power station and a secure solvent store. I cancelled the company Klaxon hooter system from working and all clocking-in cards, except for overtime working, so the personnel was all level as far as possible. This was much appreciated with only an occasional hiccup to sort out. Many of my business friends thought I had gone quite mad to trust everyone.

I now needed to apply for more finance. The banks were not an option and in my opinion were letting the country down with monopolistic principles between themselves to cover their own mistakes of investment for the future. So I decided to increase the loan I already possessed and an expensive deal was done. With my present loan at 17½% my total combined loan was to be at 17¼% without any increase in special shares. I had accomplished something but was unhappy at the high levels of interest we were expected to work with, to develop a serious business profitable to the government's negative balance of payments. This economic problem was via a system organised by the banks of England and Scotland with no responsibility for the banks themselves.

Later owing to the business success the company was asked by the loan company for me to lecture other not so successful companies on how to work, to make a successful future for them. Certainly I did talk the suggestion over with the titled chairman of the loan company 3i and we both came to the same conclusion that it would be better to keep our own expertise and whatever we were both doing but not to play politics that would consume a lot of our valuable time which was so effective for our own responsibility but not so much for others.

It is difficult to believe that my business in Scotland was small. It seemed to me Scotland preferred its own nationals to conduct business with. My competitor, a famous English company, was busy trying to prevent my progress and employed five sales representatives in Scotland and three of the five decided to set up business on their own. The parent company was furious and refused to supply any of their wide range products to them. They asked me to supply instead and I readily agreed and said I would supply my products with deferred payment for six months to help them get started financially. As my agents for Scotland the three served me well, and quickly became some of my very best customers. I withdrew my sole salesman to divert his efforts to my new friends and so introduced our customers to the new agent.

Naturally the Scottish incident of change did not go without notice. We suffered great bouts of competition with English and American companies whether operating from Germany or elsewhere; however with our resolute ability to survive, the partnership was always paramount, the three became two but the agent bond from the beginning was so strong with many tales yet to tell.

CHAPTER 14

Medical and dental

MY WIFE, UNTIL I WAS fired, with my regret, from what I had considered a congenial marriage, with her divorce in 1983, had always looked after my medical matters in great detail, so I had no idea of who to go to and where and became really shy at my demeanor. Anyway, I had to learn how to make the required appointment. Eventually I could look after myself, with my secretary keeping a watchful eye on me.

It was absolute necessity to keep well and fit for my business schedule, for it took much of my life's time, even with staff, a secretary and managers with the need to meet important people hands on.

Suddenly, whilst flying to Los Angeles, I landed with a sharp toothache on a Sunday, hence my teeth needed urgent attention whilst in the USA. With help, I called a dentist on this Sunday afternoon and in fact he came from his home to open his premises to see me.

As soon as I opened my mouth he said, 'I am not a dentist, I am a periodontic,' and explained his position, 'nevertheless I will do what I can to help your pain.' What he did I cannot recall except he stopped my severe toothache and did say, 'Go see a periodontic when you get home, your teeth need urgent attention.' I was in Los Angeles and found only this man to offer to see me at his Hollywood premises.

At the time I did not know what a periodontic was, but he explained, to put me on track. After my return I set off to seek a periodontic in London, but it was difficult for I could find only two, the address of one St Anne's Place in London. Little Hollywood had over twenty, and everyone seemed aware of their work. Off I went to my London periodontic who proved to be a fine fellow. The periodontic looked into my mouth and said, 'You have come just in time, maybe,' and proceeded to give me a comprehensive treatment of the gums and put something in my mouth to clean my blood to help stop all current disease with hope for the future.

My periodontic, John Zamet, recommended a dentist, Harold Prieskel, another fine fellow who was writing a book of comprehensive dentistry in German. This was in 1983. I could not read German but he did a fine job on my teeth after my specialist gum surgery. The dentist also did fly aircraft, so the affinity was the most interesting part of my dentistry, surgery and replacement.

Apart from losing a few teeth and using a plate for a while, I had my plate teeth inserted into my jaw; the combination was very good. By this time my dentist was flying a Lear Jet and his son, a hospital dental surgeon, was also a capable pilot. I believed everybody should learn to fly. I obtained the latest flying school information from Colorado, as USA flying was much more productive, as the weather was so much better than UK. This was for my own friend in need of learning to fly to become a commercial pilot.

Eventually, owing to my near retirement business circumstances I decided London was too far for my teeth and found a local interesting dentist, near retirement, who was living in a property I knew well from my Durford Wood days, who did my cleansing and limited periodontic work.

This dentist, Brian Osborn, a qualified yachtsmaster and keen sailor, was interested in cruising the seas which was my own recreation, so we became good friends via teeth and yachting PC simulator of interest, but in a different way of ocean cruising. He had written a splendid book called *Scallywag*, published in 1999, concerning Turkey and the Mediterranean waters in a haphazard way; whereas I needed to be tidy, with precise planning and ship-shape conditions, Anyway, he soon retired.

I found a qualified pupil of my London dentist and am pleased with his performance which includes a visiting periodontic.

Strangely, in fact to me stranger than fiction, whilst staying with my younger daughter Doodey in Greece in 2006, I accompanied her own daughter to her very fine lady friend dentist in Athens, who used to fill in for my *Scallywag* author dentist whilst he was away on sailing breaks from his practice in Petersfield.

My heart has been a problem since the effort of my aviation doctor, and I eventually packed up private flying and now refuse to use all the bad things such as beautiful XO Brandy, lovely Pinkie lemon-sliver chilled pink gin, or a really dry Martini stirred not shaken, so now only appreciate local wines. I take no spirits ever, in fact today

I enjoy the difference in wine with its fine aroma and mellow fruity taste, so like to think I appreciate better food. In fact I do chase very good restaurants and three star Michelin chefs for the enjoyment of myself and my guests when possible.

My London doctors or consultants I will never give up but I combine them with my GP who I find a very good modern younger doctor who supports my need to have a medical knowledge of my condition so as to behave correctly and to avoid excess, except of H_2O, the marvel of life with the sun heat at source.

I called on my London Cromwell Hospital consultant, Dr Stephen Jenkins, who looked after my heart for years, to establish an operation to put my heart beat regular, for the fourth or fifth time. He looked up on high and said, 'It's not up to me now, but depends on what you think,' so I looked up on high and said, 'Yes please,' so it was done, but for the last time; for today I resolve to take the modern excellent medication available from my GP, Dr Stephen Buckley.

My left leg has always been a participant of my medical misfortune. I broke my left leg playing rugby at school; I was shot in the left foot by the Germans in World War II; it let me down when boarding my boat after a Royal Party, in the Cowes green sea though apart from getting immersed, I was safe. Recently, in 2005, I was involved in a serious accident after a tough fillet of beef lunch, when I stepped on nothing, and the fall put my left leg straight through my shattered left pelvis, so I asked my French guest please to pull my leg out straight and line it up with the side of my right leg, afterwards learning to walk again after nearly six months but my excellent surgeon Michael Moss, also a member of the Royal Yacht Squadron, said it would take twelve months. It has in fact achieved its best after two years, so I think I am right handed and left footed.

I lost the top part of my hair very soon after World War II, with Teepol, so my Leslie Howard look disappeared.

Like most people I have had skin blemishes. One was a few years back when I had a black frog grow on my forehead. My skin consultant, Ian White, who I recommend to all my friends, decided to remove it and ordered a surgeon to arrange the operation which, whilst expertly done, was not painful at all. The surgeon said to me, 'I have taken a little more to allow for your eye needing surgery later on. So instead of looking like the Russian Prime Minister, Mikhail Gorbachev, I was clean with one fewer wrinkle too! However since,

I have had my eye lenses replaced and now look like a little one eyed pheasant, but with perfect vision.

On a business visit to the USA, I met with my best salesman, David Winch, who I had just appointed my USA manager. We met at Boston Airport, to hire a sedan for our journey to Gainesville, to meet with our very important Norton contract customer. My friend said to me, 'If you will just take my two bags off the carousel I will book the sedan to save time.' I agreed and waited for his two bags that I had no thoughts about, but when I came to pull the first off the carousel it was like trying to move and lift the Tower of London. I stopped lifting to slide it off but of course the second bag was fast appearing so I frantically hauled the second bag off; both bags were absolute dead impossible weights, I had a groin shudder and immediately knew I needed a hernia operation. I eventually needed two operations, first the right, then later a left operation by the surgeon who had become President of the Royal College of Surgeons so I was in good hands.

I feel the need to explain a little more concerning the serious accident, when my left leg stepped on nothing to cause such a major hospital casualty to me and everyone else involved. I lay on the floor and could see my leg was in the wrong place; it reminded me of my rugby football fall at school when my foot was in the wrong place, looking backwards until it swung round to the front, which is why I took the action already described so to ambulance and hospital via a most painful ride of huge leg vibration movement.

The venue was a very old historic castle, situated in West Sussex in the south of England, used today as a highly rated hotel cum restaurant. Naturally it is not possible to change the structure in general to conform to modern basic standards, but it is of course necessary to ensure modern safety standards for visitors and staff within and outside.

The accident happened on 25 April 2005, best described in my letter to the solicitors who act for the proprietors of the hotel, and my 90th birthday thank you letter to a retired employee of fifty-odd years' service to my old company, below. At the moment that is where the matter rests without any real response.

My Dear Arthur

I must apologise for my delay in replying to your generous supply of good friends who sent me wonderful wishes for my birthday of ninety years in 2004.

I was away with my family in Greece, but celebrated the occasion with a fine dinner with a toast to you all and a thank you to all.

Arrow was a great experience for us and I am so sorry the Arrow Abrasives demise took place after my term; but the Chardonnay was a great help to ease my pain.

One of the reasons for my delay: I was involved in a very serious accident in a restaurant, just after lunch, when I stepped on nothing and my fall put my leg through my shattered pelvis. The result was that my leg stayed inside my pelvis and I had to get my guests to pull it out, then wait for the ambulance to take me to hospital.

The complication of a shattered pelvis and leg femur joint prevented an operation for three weeks to initiate the bone regeneration, and in fact the original hospital thought I was unlikely to walk again.

However, the second hospital consultant became a sailing friend in need. He carried out the eventual operation to repair the shattered pelvis by grafting the pieces with metal, at the same time replacing the femur leg joint with an artificial joint, so to mash up the sawn-off bone to sculpture a new pelvis joint to accept the new femur artificial joint. All was expertly carried out and I lay on my back with no respite for many weeks.

Last month I was passed fit for crutches and movement, to learn to walk again. Today I can walk slowly with sticks and I have set myself to walk with one stick by 6 December 2005, to meet my daughters in Greece. This is not easy as my legs have not been used for months, but I will make it OK and will return on 29 December, for I now have so much to do.

A Happy Christmas to you all and I wish you Good Fortune in 2006

It is a pleasure to write so sincerely.

Towards the end of September 2005 I was motoring home from Chichester, West Sussex and was just about to pass through the village of Chilgrove, driving along in perfect sunshine at peace with our lovely green countryside planet, when a pheasant decided to cross the road as I was slowing down for quite a large bend in the road. The pheasant was the leader of about fourteen others, so I slowed even more to a virtual standstill with my brakes hard on, ready for the off as the pheasants passed in single file. As I was waiting suddenly a car hit my stern without warning at 60–80 m.p.h., and came through my rear boot, into the interior of my vehicle, pushing everything forward including myself, the engine, the gear lever, locked wheels and all. I was visibly shaken, my neck, head and chest, but most of all I was trapped within my vehicle with nothing working; my car had been totally immobilised by the impact force. Eventually, extracted from my car, I came home on my local garage's breakdown truck; all liability was with the car that had caused the accident, so I eventually received full recompense for the car and my part medical needs. My leg recovery was not yet complete from the Castle luncheon fall; in fact I still needed two sticks for any movement at all, and I received the addition of whiplash with the effects of the huge forward thrust.

Immediately after the crash, various no win–no fee lawyers offered action for me and were very good, but they only work within restrictive limitations of consultative action, understandable for the method restricts the expense.

Thus my first request was to meet with an independent solicitor to check through the evidence available to suit the no win–no fee basis of operation. Next was to have an independent medical examination with a consultant physician and surgeon at a hospital in Surrey, despite the wealth of medical information available from other sources.

The medical report was most comprehensive, but during my discussion with the consultant I mentioned a report of mine sent to my own GP complaining about the action of my teeth and eyes apparent some 6 to 9 months after the second accident which roughly stated that the trouble with the eyes and teeth was considered to be due to the terrific impact thrust.

The consultant said it might be possible but indicated it would be difficult to prove, so in conclusion these implications would be left out, but such an injury as whiplash would be in for it was obviously caused by the impact. This advice or observation I found not uncommon throughout the medical field. Yet I am positive my view is true and is confirmed by my medical history, also by my need to grit teeth automatically on impact so fiercely that my teeth moved to a new position from their stable position; on the other hand the first accident could also be at fault for the same reason.

The information on my eyes is that the strong good eye had a macular hole yet the weaker other eye has taken over to give perfect vision via laser treatment; all this ophthalmic work is so delicate to provide a wonderful revival of sight throughout the planet, cure or system. I believe it will soon prevent macular degeneration taking place.

It was in August 2005 when I first visited my GP concerning likely prostrate troubles; however the problem symptoms were dealt with and the position became tolerable. In 2006, however I seriously became victim of a painful condition, and felt no relief after my visit to a local consultant for tests. The results showed an enlargement bladder situation but no sign of cancer. Somewhat relieved, that same night I took a laxative and lo and behold, my painful symptom disappeared and all came well. The previous irritation, often at night, was relieved.

So I appeared doubly grateful for all the advice I received from my many friends, who were not as fortunate as me. Some time later just after the hot weather had departed I thought perhaps I had had dehydration due to taking wine without enough water.

CHAPTER 15

1984 – my new wife

I MARRIED MY SECOND WIFE in Chelsea Register Office, Kings Road, South London, with John Day, my friend of Roger's time, who was working for me at the time, as my best man. Debby had her attractive cousin from Brussels Common Market European Office. The ceremony took little time but was long enough to make us all late for a taxi to my helicopter transport from the River Thames, Battersea Heliport then to Paris, then by limousine to my favourite Maxim's de Paris restaurant for luncheon. Then we did a little shopping to end in time for the limousine so to board the helicopter for return to the River Thames before dark.

The luncheon was late but the food delicious: fresh oysters, a little fresh Dover sole followed by tender medium rare thick Aberdeen Angus fillet steak, without potatoes but with light brown toast and fresh warm foie gras. Naturally we enjoyed throughout champagne, a ten-year-old Dom Perignon. I personally proposed the toast to Her Majesty the Queen of Angleterre, and a toast to the memory of Roger, my dear son killed near Midhurst, West Sussex, in 1974. Followed by the invention recipe of Monk Dom Perignon, the appointed cellarer of Hautvillers, situated on the Mountain of Rheims, which we all know as the real sparkling wine of today. Of course I did thank God for the occasion, via a simple grace before our meal commenced.

I was well versed in Champagne by my daughter's frequent invitations to Château de Saren, a Moet & Chandon VIP château in the valley of the River Marne, where she was in charge for a time. I learnt all about the manufacturers of Champagne and their wines in detail and thus became quite an expert on the subject in the UK. I like my Madame Bollinger story. I often eat in the Spread Eagle Hotel, Midhurst, West Sussex, which is a wonderful half-timbered building, which has been welcoming guests since its origin as a tavern in 1430. I have used it to accommodate my overseas visitors, and have birthday parties or conferences in their Jacobean Hall with field banners flying. There is a lovely bedroom with a four-poster bed, with a wig cupboard, a small study for entertaining or having breakfast, wearing your wig of course! The very large golden eagle with wings spread that adorns the hotel outside was reputedly given by the pre second world war German, Herr J. Von Ribbentrop.

On the wall just outside the dining room with Sussex puddings hung from the ceiling, is a simple framed authentic black and white photograph with the message as follows:

> 1890–1971 Madame Lily Bollinger's photograph shows herself at a halt with her bicycle in the foreground of her estate after inspecting her vineyards, and she says of her own champagne, 'I drink it when I'm happy and when I'm sad, sometimes I drink it when I am alone; when I have company I consider it obligatory. I trifle with it when I'm not hungry and drink it when I am. Otherwise I never touch it – unless I am thirsty'!

I also admire the Sèvres porcelain *coupes* which were moulded from the breast of Marie-Antoinette and once adorned the Queen's Dairy Temple at Château de Rambuillet. Now the sole *coupe* survivor is in New York, according to the exhaustive study of the subject by Patrick Forbes in 1957 in his wonderful book title, *Champagne*. However in the 2006 *Debrett's People of Today*, Anno MMVI, you find a different story.

> The legend has it that the open top *coupe* was modelled on one of Marie-Antoinette's breasts. There is no truth in this at all, nor was it modelled on any of the breasts of Madame de Pompadour, Madame du Barry or Empress Josephine. The *coupe* was actually created by Venetian glassmakers in England around 1663 and was designed specifically for champagne, so it pre dates all four women (and indeed all eight of their breasts) by about a century; however I believe what I will.

After such a satisfying luncheon, we set course for the fashionable street to buy something for my new wife Debby. It proved a little hilarious, to try on dresses with a little time to spare, to consider alterations and so eventually all was accomplished with the limousine waiting or following along our footsteps. Thus we were whisked back to our helicopter for the flight home which seemed to take much less time than the way out. We landed at the River Thames heliport to be met immediately by Her Majesty's Customs & Excise Officer, who was waiting for our touchdown. He commenced immediately to examine our wares and parcels before we could recover our UK sanity, and he was very difficult despite our explanation to him, which he seemed to consider all was a frivolous nature, that we had no alcohol or perfume which seemed to disappoint him. I paid VAT and duty on my purchase of my wife's wedding present of a dress and some simple no value items. I thought I must not let the incident spoil my intentions for the day, so home we went to change and refresh, then went to the famous Annabel's nightclub, of which I was a member, for an early meal. Anyway, we changed our mood and forgot the unhappy-happy man at our river heliport drop.

Next day we all returned happily to work, except the cousin who travelled to see her family in the Quorn hunting countryside. I recommenced my hectic appointment schedule, held by my Portsmouth secretary, together with much technical work to do in the factory. However, I returned to my wife in London at the weekend and later on Sunday we settled into my very pleasant temporary rented home, just outside Odiham, Surrey. where we enjoyed a great welcome from my lady help and the weekend students of my new wife's London Business School programme.

Before marriage, I had requested my future wife should have to learn business, for I needed a replacement to fill the unfortunate position left by my son and considered I was fortunate, for my future new wife agreed to do so. My only suggestion was the London Business School, with the famous high international standard; in fact I thought the only competitors were the Manchester Business School and Harvard in the USA.

Thus she set off to compete for the Sloane 12-month course entry, and was accepted, to my surprise, for at the time there were very few ladies in the business world. It all was very interesting. I discussed the work expected to be done, partly to confirm my own standing, and we looked up details of my major customers' progress of development. the future market dimensions of my industry plus other adjacent interests. It was so absorbing to me, I did wish I had more time to study the work of the London Business School and hoped my future wife would take the Doctorate of Business after the Sloane, but it was a little distant at this moment.

My wife had possessed two black Pekinese dogs. They had been in the care of a nice dog-loving lady's family home, from early puppies, and now was time to collect them and bring them home to Odiham. In the process we passed two Shetland ponies for sale adjacent to the dog lady and Debby wanted to put them for recreation in the unused large water meadow, a piece of farmland that belonged to my rented property. Now at Odiham I possessed two dogs and two ponies, and this episode seemed to set off an invasion of all types of dogs, ponies, donkeys, thoroughbreds and Arab horses throughout my new marriage. Little did I realise at the outset that I needed to become so involved with them over the next fourteen years in England, France, South Africa and the United States of America.

I experienced a strange thing on getting to know Debby; I discovered she was driving a Mini Moke, an open top car like a small Land Rover or old Jeep, without a licence to drive. I was horrified and found it difficult to believe, but I had to for she had just received a police reprimand for going the wrong way along a one-way street; of course she needed to provide an answer to the South London Magistrates Court. I was further horrified that she had used someone else's name without the permission of the person involved, but it did not seem important to her or the lady involved. The case to answer fizzled out but not before I found that the Moke was not insured or taxed as required by law!

Naturally I held a very serious talk with Debby and insisted on no more driving of the Mini Moke at present. It was also in need of repair, it was so old. I took along to the person who sold it to her and found out she was behind with payments on the instalment price, yet the seller was not the slightest worried and carried out the repair free of charge and indicated he had a better Mini Moke coming in and would she like to change.

Debby only used the Mini Moke, really, to store her very many paintings, but now she could not drive until she had passed a proper driving test. This she was determined to conquer but stated she was nervous passing an English driving test; it was impossible, she had tried but the examiner walked away for her driving was so bad! Within a short time she found someone who would help and he lived in the Bahamas. At this time I was about to go on business in Tokyo, followed by Lisbon through Moscow and Paris, and these two appointments in Japan and Portugal were very serious for my business development and were fairly urgent. In Lisbon I had to meet a good prospective supply agent for coated abrasives and we were to exchange products of our manufacture, also I had stationed my PR salesman in charge and I was to meet him on time with the company owner. Hence I said to Debby, 'OK, I will help with the driving test by meeting your friend to see with you his plan.'

Just prior to my business journey I had started flying again but naturally I had to pass a medical and flying test. The flying began with my talk to Debby, concerning the fact that I wished everybody should learn to fly for it was so rewarding to be in the third dimension. Just being a painter as an artist, you will find it difficult to achieve survival recognition, particularly from your abstract way of sex and pleasure. Debby had drifted into Epsom art school from Battle Abbey School, which was the main part of her education. She spent much of her early time in Malaysia, at that time Malaya, with her family, following her father on Royal Air Force Duty as a navigator.

Today, she was still painting but in different locations and was in Spain painting when she already had an appointment for her initial flight at Goodwood airfield. I duly arrived at the airfield to find no sign of Debby at the appointed time. I was with the Chief Instructor who was a lady; she suggested I take her place. I was pleased to do so and off we went in our PA-28 Cherokee aircraft. Just after take-off at approximately 500 feet the instructor said, 'You take over,' and explained the controls to fly on. I was pleased to do so. Flying a light aircraft is fairly safe providing you follow the discipline of the aircraft and feel part of it. Hence I continued along at 500 feet following the circuit as instructed. We eventually came to part of the South Downs when the wind heavenly gusted, and made the aircraft bumpy and rough so I automatically moved the control column to compensate, so continued ready and steady to land as told, until the instructor whispered, 'I will take over to land, OK?' We duly taxied to the flight office and stopped. My instructor immediately said to me, 'You can fly, can't you?' I replied, 'Yes, I used to be a Royal Air Force pilot, but that was some long time ago.' She then stated, 'It was so good, please take up flying again if you wish.'

Thus we wrote to the Air Ministry for guidance and she gave me the address of the local doctor for aviation to arrange a medical examination for me. The Air Ministry indicated I could fly providing a cross country solo was executed and I was certified by the Chief Instructor as fit to fly solo. All went well and I started to fly again for my private licence renewal.

Time to fly was very difficult to fit in, for I had my business to

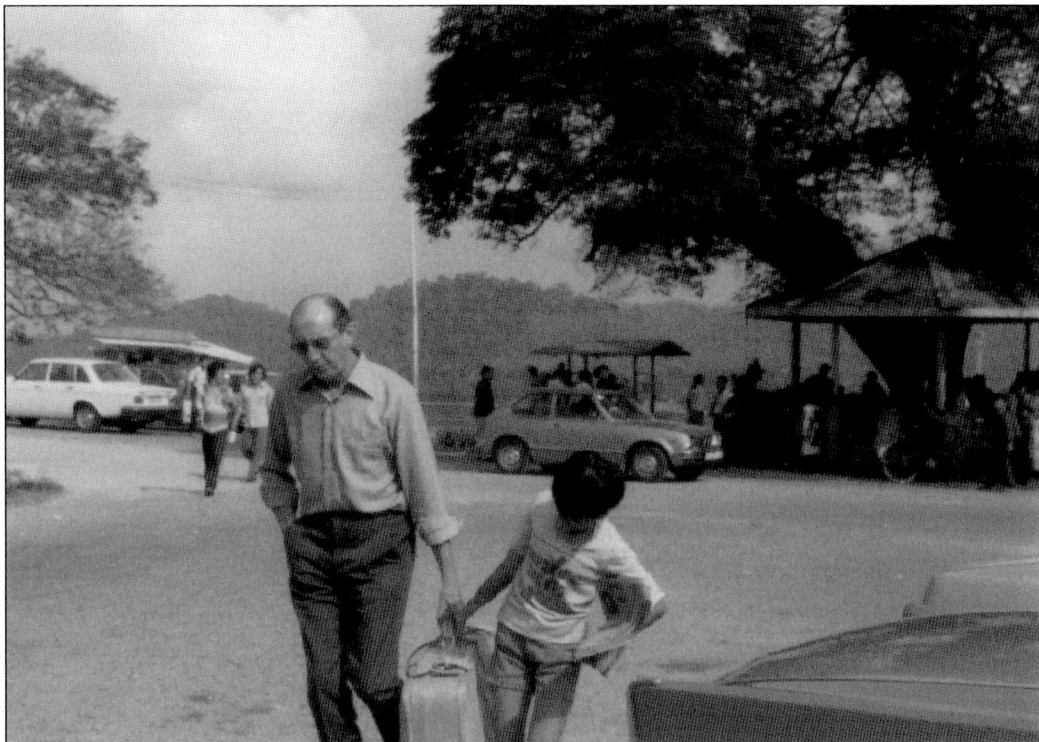

28 The small boy who insisted on carrying our cases, Malaysia

29 The author on right Marki Galiatsatos, the Deep Singer, left is Roland the Albanian artist, Kefalonia

30 Teaching family how to fish with two friends

31 Author beside the River Tay, ready to fish for a salmon for dinner with John

32 The author reeling in brown trout whilst teaching the family, Bibury

33 My various split cane rods, with green sea rod from my ketch and one carbon fibre belonging to my son

34 Second marriage to Debby Camp at Chelsea Register Office

35 The helicopter to Paris after the wedding

36 Debby with the Mini Moke

37 The 12th-century house, Little Langley Farm

38 Little Langley Farm from the air

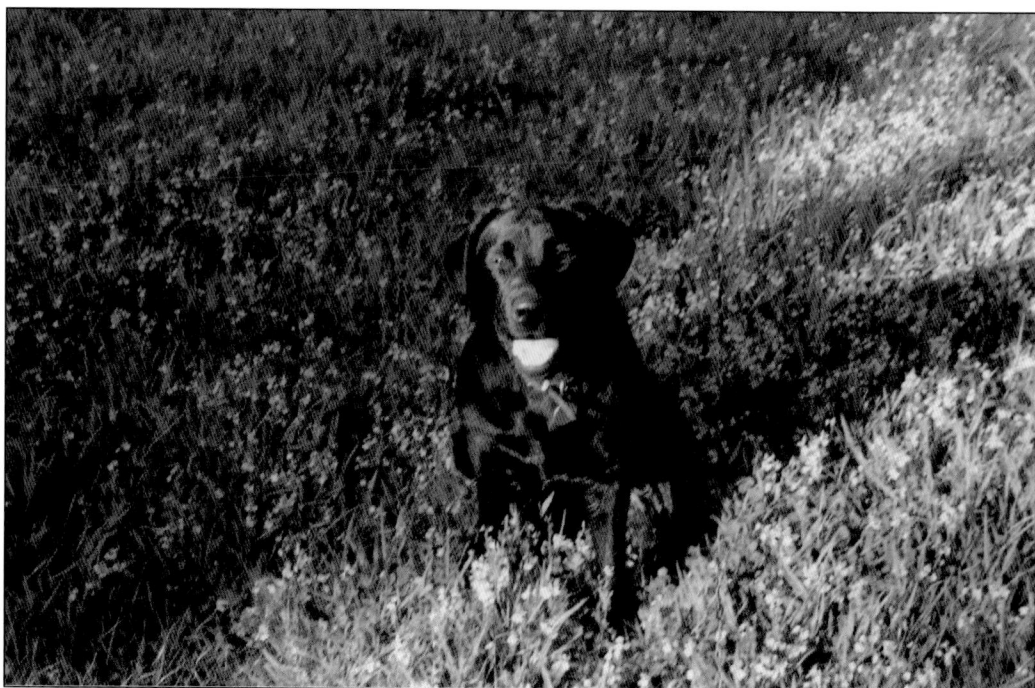

39 Prince, my wonderful dog

40 Three Shetland ponies at Little Langley Farm

41 Debby competing in jumping event near Forest Mere, Liphook

42 My portrait by Juliet Pannett

43 Iron stones, Little Langley Farm

run and at weekends worked most Saturdays, hence was only free for my boat on Sunday, but I did enjoy myself for a while, with Debby flying solo too! I encouraged Debby, who responded for only a little while; I felt she did not like the flying discipline, which really was my only reason for her to learn. I thought she was a little reckless with little discipline painting, living or driving an automobile.

Debby and I set off on our journey and arrived at the Bahamas for one night, for the next day we were due to call at the address on another island, but the telephone did not answer our call. I became suspicious and thought we might be wasting our time to call in person, so decided to drop in on the local police station by taxi. We entered the police station and sat down to wait for attention. Eventually an officer met with us and asked what we wanted. I told him the story of looking for a driving licence test. The officer departed, saying he would look into the matter in his office; after further waiting some long time, I decided we should leave and did so via our waiting taxi. I asked the driver what he thought of our situation. The reply was that we should visit the other island in question and he would arrange a taxi to meet us at the airfield.

Next day we arrived at the other island, where we were met by a very old large Cadillac limousine, full of rust and scratches. We retold our story, and set off to the address given to Debby; it was empty and closed, so went to the local police station to tell our story again. On arrival the taxi driver suggested it would be wise for him to go in first, so off he went while we waited in the car. After some time the driver returned to say the officer in charge wished to see me. So I was ushered into a semi dark office – the sun was so bright outside – and was asked to sit down before the Chief's desk. He said he was pleased to see me for he thought he could help and would accept previous test results to confirm the results after speaking to Debby, but gave me a high price to pay. We all sat in front of the Chief's desk and he thanked Debby for coming in and said that the money required would be put to good use for he was trying to wage war on the drug offences of the island, he appreciated our generosity to help. At this the Chief rose and looked through the window and said, 'I see you have been driving a very difficult large automobile and so you get my note for the licence office and Mr Simpson, please pay my fee in the outer office. Thank you once more for coming in.'

Debby thus received an International driving licence for 12 months and promised to pass a UK test very soon, as she now felt relieved and less nervous.

We continued to Japan, did some welcome business and appointed the agent but I was doubtful if the business would survive for ever, after a day looking around. The Hotel Okura was international so was OK for me, but Debby wanted to feel Japanese so we went out to sit on the floor to eat, The restaurant also enjoyed a European section but not for Debby, she just wanted to sit on the floor as she had done often in London.

Next day we joined the overnight flight to arrive in Moscow to refuel in the morning. We had to leave the aircraft for the refuel but there was nothing to see or do, everything everywhere looked so drab, people so communistic and lazy, so we were pleased to join the aircraft again for our Paris stop overnight before the flight to Lisbon. We slept in separate beds; at breakfast time I went to get out of bed and fell on the floor. I could not move anything, although I called my brain to do something, so I sweated out in an unbelievable panic about what to do. The hotel doctor got me into a wheelchair in time to arrive at the airport a short time before our flight. We switched wheelchairs, boarded the aircraft and were dumped into a front row seat just before the aircraft took off. I started to recover the use of my limbs; by the time we arrived at Lisbon I was mobile again.

We progressed to the main arrival hall and met my PR man, John Day, plus the manager of the company we had promised to meet, but to my surprise there was no owner. We got to our hotel for the night and all had a meal. I did try a little Chardonnay and felt much better and alert. I went to bed early sometime after 8 o'clock and enjoyed a very good sleep; however at the breakfast call I again could not move my limbs to get up or even move, yet my brain was clear and alert.

I struggled with the situation for a while to the desperation of all. I again and again told my brain to move my body or some part of it but there was no response at all, except I thought I might go mad with the desperation of trying. Eventually I could feel some movement. I felt horrid but at least I was moving and making progress; later I dressed, had a little to eat and drank some tea, and became well enough to board our train to near Porto. It was a long all-day journey; on arrival I felt OK so went to visit the factory premises and confirm our reciprocal agreement, but still without the owner who wished me well from the USA. To make up for my disappointment of missing the owner I was presented with a bottle of 100-year-old port, which I decided not to taste, but again at dinner I drank a glass or two of Chardonnay, and again felt much better. After a good night's sleep, again I had the same difficulty of movement but not so prolonged, and prepared quickly to fly to the UK to find out what was wrong with my health.

The next day I decided to visit the aviation doctor, and enrolled my wife to come and confirm my position at my meeting. Off we went, my wife parked the car and said to me, 'I will come with you to your interview with the doctor, but I would like to speak first.' I agreed.

We duly entered the doctor's room and sat down, and whilst I was introducing my wife she got up and said in an extremely loud voice, 'You are a quack! You make and keep my husband ill, for you want him to pay in Champagne to satisfy your demand.' Then walked out immediately.

Afterwards I was recommended to the consultant physician at St Thomas's Hospital, London (whose father was recent chief of the hospital as Florence Nightingale was). The consultant cardiologist, Stephen Jenkins, did a few tests, put me on wine only raher than spirits, and still looks after my irregular heart today with my GP in charge, as I now live in the country and go to London less often. Strangely I also still go occasionally for my hairdresser to cut my hair.

To finish this episode: I wondered what had happened to set off the train of events. I considered it was all due to the aviation doctor and the medical before my solo flight. The doctor had passed me fit for a medical flying certificate for Australia, the United States and the UK, but as I was leaving suggested I take some pills for blood pressure which was thought a little on the high side. I took the pills in accordance but, up to this date, I had never taken any pill of any kind. It created low blood pressure, below my ear balance, thus I could not use my limbs; the anxious time in trying to make my brain to work the limbs caused much stress. Hence my thyroid could not take the strain which was why my heart eventually became irregular with the story of distress. At my local hospital in Midhurst the young doctors administering the electric shock to stimulate the heart back into rhythm did not remember that you cannot put a heart back to normal with an abnormal thyroid, combined with only giving two shocks instead of a possible six attempts.

Later my wife and I gave a fancy dress party in a marquee at home in Odiham, to welcome my return from my local hospital. She dressed as Cleopatra, and I was in authentic hired full Admiral's naval uniform with all the gold braid and a cocked large hat. I was not entirely well but the young hospital doctors attended and looked after me. The party was a great success but I pushed off to bed very early, so left the revellers to stay to the early hours.

To return to my story: I did give up flying, but spent my spare time on my boat and at various parties on and off the boat at Cowes, Yarmouth and Lymington, with more across the English Channel in France. In fact I never closed any of my membership of local yacht clubs since my days of sailing the ketch-rigged yacht I had had built at Looe and sold in 1966 to sort out my new company with the time required.

It is interesting to record at least two artists, one for painting and one for drawing.

When I was a young boy of ten years, I was yet to be properly interested in art, but a new resident came to be our neighbour in Paradise Lane, rural Birmingham. After a short time a welcome introduction took place without me being present, which resulted in a reciprocal event taking place in the next property. In fact it was a jolly affair. I was requested to attend the next day to the gentleman's art studio.

I duly attended with my brother and sister to sit for a personal drawing or sketch, and after about a half hour sitting each, we were finished and returned home, with a little sweet inducement. My father explained the gentleman's name was Norman Pett, a life artist appointed in charge at the Birmingham Central School of Art. My father kept the framed drawings for very many years, for all to see, stacked on the wall one above the another. Eventually the family heirlooms including our own pencil portrait drawn in 1924 by Norman Pett passed down to each of us.

He was most famous for his cartoon of Jane. I expect most World War II veterans remember the stirring episodes of the thrilling *Daily Mirror* strip cartoon with the scantily clad Jane, a real life model chosen to be Jane, always losing some part of her apparel, with the dog Fritz watching, in some difficult hopeless predicament or other. I must say the effort during the war of the response to Jane was absolutely a phenomenon and was referred to by the government ministers, so the troops, land, sea and air, used the strip as a symbol of hope and glory.

The strip was withdrawn from the *Daily Mirror* after the war; however the image still remains for all to muse on, as one can see in *The Times* report of 1990 of Jane attending the Imperial War Museum with such stars as Dame Vera Lynn and Spike Milligan. In 1994 there was a story in the *Daily Mail* with Jane talking to Lester Middlehurst. *The Times* in 2000 reported 'Farewell to Jane' and 'Ripping yarn added vim to Allied victory'. Finally a book was published: *Jane – A Pin up at War*.

It all proves to me that my friend Norman Pett was an extremely clever artist.

My next artist, Juliet Pannett, was a gifted painter and draughtsman, very versatile whether portrait or landscape and in 1963 she executed a portrait of my whole family. Her reputation was already well known and she had been most prolific since her eighteenth birthday. She had access to a reserved seat in a House of Commons to sketch scenes for the *London Illustrated News*, and in 1964, drew Winston Churchill leaving the House for the last time.

In 1938 she married a captain of the Devonshire Regiment and was commissioned to paint their Colonel in Chief, Princess Marina, Duchess of Kent. She painted many royals in the seventies for the Queen. In 1989 she painted a portrait of the Queen herself for a hall in the city, admired by the Duke of Edinburgh.

Today she is survived by her son and daughter. I was proud to own, apart from my family portraits by such a prolific artist, a painting by her son Denis entitled 'The Green Tarpaulin', a beautiful Sussex landscape summer scene with a haystack covered by a green tarpaulin, whispering summer breezes. However in my movements this wonderful picture has disappeared without a trace and today I miss this wonderful water colour. I still have however my Sussex Downs water colour showing the temperamental skies with cumulus clouds so white supporting the switch of a perfect summer's day by Juliet Pannett, his mother.

The sketch of a jumping horse by her daughter Elizabeth, I gave to my horse loving friend and it was so much appreciated. I think what a wonderful thing to inherit the skill of Juliet Pannett, a wonderful artistic brilliance and so prolific.

I have naturally met many other very good artists. I was friendly with Ivan Hitchens for a time as he lived nearby. I admired his work and tried to hang one, but I could not quite cope with with the idea of abstract trees and landscape although expertly painted in the brightest colours.

Next I owned a series of Michael Ayrton's sculptures with working drawings partly from his African tour, which expressed some beasts not traditionally admired. His figures of man and woman were to me rather heavy. Unfortunately the profound artist died at a young fifty-four years; however his work is still in demand today.

Roland Shtembari, a brilliant Albanian artist working in Kefalonia, Greece, I have been friendly with for some years and today admire his unusual work, either sculpture or painting, both with a futuristic beautiful abstract feel, with a flair for public exhibition in the open air, similar to but not the same as Henry Moore. Roland has a flair in his painting of portraits, accurate to the smallest detail with a perfect design to be slightly futuristic and will today become famous.

My last mention is a Greek artist who lived nearby when I was in Peania. He is Costas Chitziris, and is unusual for although his paintings are in exhibitions and museums his work is simple, say head and shoulders on a dark background. The main background can be a dark blank to further your contact with the glance of the thinking eye of the painting. Again, unfortunately he is not well so I forgive his lack of artistic work available today.

Plate 29 shows Roland Shtembari on my right, while on my left is Marki Galiatsatos who is a well known tenor, but although often requested to perform in Athens and elsewhere he will not leave Kefalonia. However he is an artist too and did the drawings in my daughter's book on *The Herbs of Kefalonia*.

CHAPTER 16

Horses with Debby

AFTER I WAS MARRIED TO Pickle, her family name for Deborah (Debby) in May 1984 we lived in Williams Mews, Knightsbridge and then moved to North Warnborough, a village near Odiham, near the Royal Air Force Station, servicing in the main the battle-scarred cracked helicopters from the Falklands war.

On the way to North Warnborough we collected Debby's two Pekinese dogs which were staying with two dog devoted ladies near Slough. As I have said earlier, on the way in through the field to their house, Debby fancied two Shetland ponies munching away on grass. They were duly bought from the two ladies and named Pickle and Moppet, and this was the start of our future home for dogs, horses, ponies and donkeys. I was rather nonplussed for I never had possessed my own animal and my previous wife was allergic to fur of any kind. The Pekinese were in charge of the house, food and leisure, and the Shetlands spent their whole day just munching away in the paddocks until nightfall when they slept in a small wooden barn with a supply of hay to eat.

As you know, my wife was attending the London Business School, hence she only came home at weekends. As I was steadily working the animals were looked after by the daily help lady, except for weekends. At the weekend my wife would always invite fellow students in twos, threes and fours, and the guests were summoned each Sunday to walk with us, the dogs, and the Shetlands before and after lunch around the village for the population's appreciation and amusement. Within a short time Debby obtained two donkeys, Victoria and Albert, from the donkey sanctuary, so the donkeys were included in the weekly walkabout, and we needed all the guest help to control our two of each, Pekinese dogs, Shetland ponies and donkeys, for each section needed different requirements apart from lumps of sugar or Polo mints to keep them going.

The situation existed for twelve to fifteen months. By this time we had become friends with the RAF Odiham Station Commander and his wife at the airfield. Whilst this friendship was fascinating in connection with helicopters, I was particularly interested in the propeller blades, for I had before the war carried out research on honeycombed plastic filler for the core to create flexibility and light weight. My wife was particularly interested in the large horse of the Commander's wife and set course to find one like it. The first two we saw were ex riding school livery but eventually rejected for lack of spirit to be trained for jumps. The Commander's wife was a tall lady with a big horse that could jump; my wife was less than 5 ft 6 ins so competition was difficult.

Through some talk, Debby by chance contacted a lady breeder of pure Arab horses and fell in love with two one-year-olds, Henrim and Demon, so they joined the Shetlands in our paddock. The breeder ran a section of the main farm, purely for breeding fine pure bred Arab stock with a manège for training plus impeccably clean stables for some fourteen Arab horses; this was our introduction to the Arab horse.

It so happened that I decide to move to be nearer my company in Portsmouth and bought a small farm, Little Langley Farm, on the border of Sussex and Hampshire, of eight acres. Included was a twelfth century farmhouse and a matching stable building of four old type pens with office cum harness and saddle room, plus a very old wooden barn coach-house adjacent to the lane to hold the horse carriage. I carried out many up to date improvements to the house and stables, including replacement of the cobble stones, plus a new drive to make a less dangerous entrance, together with post and rail fencing for new paddocks. I built a 36 × 18 feet all weather swimming pool plus later a Dormit manège.

Soon we all moved in, everybody into their respective paddocks, except the Pekinese who shared the house with us. Our housekeeper from Knightsbridge moved into the cottage which was an old milking parlour, altered to suit. The Pekinese had expanded in number just before leaving and were now four from a litter of six.

We enjoyed entertaining our friends on my twin diesel engine 'Spearfish' power boat, moored on the Hamble River, and I had my new Cowes mooring in the harbour opposite the Royal Yacht Squadron steps for recreation on the Isle of Wight. Work days were for me very full, at home or away overseas.

The donkeys were no trouble; they did an occasional bray, if they required anything apart from a few carrots to say good morning or good night. The Shetlands came in at night to their stable, and by day we had arranged a different paddock next to our two main ones. My wife started to ride the Arabs over the local heath including Chapel Common. I was a legal commoner responsible for the upkeep and tidiness of access, to preserve the ancient rights and the preservation of the inhabitants and plants of scientific interest with the English Nature Society.

I enjoyed the effort to maintain Chapel Common's undulating heathland of fine grass and heather, occasionally interspersed on the periphery with birch and pine. In fact over the years I altered my own acreage into a mixture of open heathland which also included changing my terrace flower beds to various coloured heathers adjacent to the lawn and ha-ha which gave a clear view to the countryside beyond the paddock to the south.

Our land was surrounded by ancient boundary banks which provided entry for the moles for the art of increasing their population. I would not use traps or poison to control their activity so employed fractured glass buried about six inches, trenched in a single line at points of entry. This method was effective as a permanent barrier for the moles did not wish to harm the delicate skin of their forefeet; as a bonus it was a good method to rid of worn electric light bulbs.

My wife's riding became a full time daily exercise, jumping at the local riding school with covered manège and in our paddock interspersed with cross-country. She was involved with the breeding of dogs, horses and Shetlands; then one day Debby (influenced by a friend who was an expert at side saddle, and who organised horse shows in their horse farm location) decided to change her riding to dressage and side saddle, so of course we needed different horses. Dressage also needed a manège so we installed a Dormit manège area just below the swimming pool in the north paddock corner.

My wife set off to the dressage master at Goodwood House, West Sussex, a home of dressage participation and competition. She trained on a school horse, Maple Diogenese, and started to achieve British Horse Society standards. Later with the dressage master, she set off to search for her own qualified dressage horse, and one was found in Germany, so the two went over and bought a Hanoverian qualified experienced dressage horse, Wattau, so serious dressage commenced to the exclusion of all else. The Arab horse El Herim was loaned out to a friend and the stallion Demon was lent to a stud farm after spending a year or so trying to gallop from our post and rail boundary fence, for he was missing El Herim companionship and his own sport.

Debby brought back a black spotted white Dalmatian puppy. A little later I trained the dog for the gun on a course of six months. Somehow Debby decided to mate the Dalmatian who produced a litter of six; we kept one and found good homes for the rest. The new puppy was not trained and sometime later it decided to eat the Pekinese, and before he could find them all, the trained dog joined in! We intervened and that was the end of our Dalmatians who were found good single homes. We now possessed only two Pekinese, but my wife decided to obtain a Labrador from Battersea Dogs Home in London, so along came Prince, a lovely dog, so gentle and full of attention. However my wife took Prince out while she was riding, trot or gallop, rabbit search or not, and in consequence dear old Prince became lame and quiet. I then looked after him until he died and I missed a very good kind friend.

By this time my wife was living partly in France having bought two more Labrador puppies called Fortnum and Mason. Fortnum was boisterous and belonged to Debby; mine was placid and sensible, but as Debby was away so long living in France I decide to part with Fortnum and switched the dogs' names to part with the boisterous one yet retain the gentle one as Fortnum. All was well until eventually Debby came for a visit; she did not notice my switch of dog but wanted the two Labradors for some reason. Later we departed for lunch at the local inn. I introduced Debby to the lady behind the bar who really managed the inn for I had given the real Fortnum to her; it was a very good home.

As I went out to the car I heard quite a commotion with Debby's voice at high volume as usual. I quickly returned to find her shouting at the lady for control of the dog. I broke the fight, forcibly took Debby aside and in no uncertain terms told her to be sane; to please forget the dog's happy home for she was living in France anyway without dogs. I recall my own encounter and thought Debby was similar to a Chinese kick boxer for she had such power in punch and foot kick.

After three years or so of dressage training costing a fortune in imported new saddles and tackle, the manège and so on, with the neglect of ordinary duties, the issue became too much even for

Debby. I came home late one day to find her crying over selling Wattau for £200. I was staggered to find out why; she told me she needed £200 cash for something, so had sold the horse to a gypsy. She employed me to get the horse back. I tried but the gypsy knew the worth of dear Wattau and refused to sell although I had offered over £5000.

Debby and I eventually found out that the friend who had enjoyed the loan of the Arab El Herim had put the horse into Arab racing and was meaning to race him, so Debby wanted her returned to start racing instead of dressage which she had decided was too difficult to become an expert to win. I was amazed she had stuck the discipline of the mighty difficult training of classical riding, even with an expert qualified horse for so long.

Incidentally you need continuous discipline to follow the riders of Greek, French and Spanish classical traditions. High school dressage takes years for the horse and rider each to learn and Debby did not pass business school or flying technique, and now dressage. I wondered what racing held.

Debby liked the best of everything hence after commencing racing from home and taking the Arabs in a two-horse trailer I was not very happy. To get along with the new Arab Race Horse society, Debby was attacking everyone for information for her effective participation. Consequently we were soon knocking on the doors of Newmarket Race Horse Training with many stables, the natural heath licensed and maintained for training, plus the continual coming and going of anybody important in racing.

There was one particular Arab horse stables run by a very successful lady jockey racehorse trainer, so of course Debby introduced her Arab horses, and looked for one or two more to gain equal status and prominence as the magnificent lady jockey trainer operated from a very good position stables loaned by her successful father, a thoroughbred horse trainer.

Debby put in a lot of hard work getting our present young Arab horses El Herim and Demon fit and ready to win; however like all horses they had their own limitations, and needed the necessary jockey expertise to enhance their racing success, to come first in chosen races. All was well with moderate achievement. I quite enjoyed being involved as the owner to take a prize or two for my enthusiastic successful wife jockey, whilst meeting quite important business people or their wives, with a glass of bubbly. Soon we were providing the glass of bubbly for our new friends, also introducing our old friends who were new to the excitement of Arab horse racing.

Any day Debby would look for new Arab horses, so one day she decided to attend an auction of Russian Arabs, which occasionally the Russians organised with UK attendance to exchange their pedigree horses for hard currency. This was just after the revolution against communism, and capitalism was taking over. The Russian Arabs were high pedigree horses from the Toans Tersk stables in southern Russia, proven by the issue of winning race results to back up the expensive price. However pure Arab horse racing in UK was an amateur sport and only started in 1978 and gave way to thoroughbred horse racing, as we all know, thus there was reduced interest. To Debby and me the Russian Arab horses were very expensive so a little out of our range.

There was a pure Arab called Duma at the auction, sold to a lady but subject naturally to veterinary approval before acceptance of delivery. The horse was a beautiful sprint horse that had won many Russian races and possessed a terrific pedigree. The veterinary officer turned the horse down for suffering from an eye cataract, thus the Russian representative became running around desperate to sell, but the auction was closed, so he just milled around doing his best at any price, to avoid the huge expense of returning an unsold horse. He came across Debby who was looking for a possible cheap buy, so purchased Duma (name for the Russian parliament building) with her mother's loan. The only proviso her mother made was that I was to be totally responsible for all the upkeep, to ensure there was no more expense to her. Naturally I was not told for I was fed up with Debby buying good horses and virtually throwing them away for an idea starting on some other different tack or technical direction.

Thus Duma became under our ownership, received special attention and commenced to win Arab society official sprint races straight away, with Debby as the perfect trainer and jockey. Thus the Duma programme became paramount to all, and the two original Arabs took a back seat but still continued to give their best. They did win races too, but not the international races like Duma so gradually we became Arab society famous with eventually Debby becoming Queen of Arab horse racing in the UK.

However we had quite a way to go before the next intake in horses took place. We were collecting Arab horses, some good, some indifferent, with Debby racing as trainer jockey most weekends. Sometimes I could follow events, but I was very busy with my own company, hence missed many meetings; at the same time we needed to improve the stable of the home farm to accommodate equipment: new saddles; hanging wall fitments; rugs to keep clipped racing horses warm; and more, besides having two in-house grooms cluttering up the housekeeper's small cottage with extra beds, soiled washing, dirty boots and many more problems for my overworked housekeeper of retirement age.

Debby organised herself rental of a house with stables near Newmarket Heath and a private paddock for recreation with grazing for Duma. In all we enjoyed four or five Arabs in training with Duma, with the usual trappings. I would meet Debby occasionally and give her a lift to pick up Duma for the night. I was staggered to see her just vault on to Duma for a bareback ride to be stabled with legs flying and only a head collar. It seemed to like the actions.

Next we started international race meetings in France and England, which needed more time, horse boxes and equipment, horse passports and travel facilities. Nevertheless we enjoyed happy times with some wonderful international wins at Caen, Chantilly, Long-champs and other towns in parts of France with Arab sponsored home international race meetings, generally at Kempton with the tireless Duma always leading the way against the USA, French or Dutch. Then came the occasion when Debby forgot to enter Duma for the special Kempton Park International meeting. We were reminded by the Arab Horse Society for the sprint race would not be so interesting without Duma competing against the imported international Arabs from France, USA and elsewhere.

I tried hard to overcome the mistake, but it was too late. I did find a three-mile race entry that was not yet closed, so Debby for some reason entered Duma who had only evented the short sprint races of 6 to 8 furlongs thus was not trained for long distance. We attended the international meeting not knowing our fate and apologised to all for our lack of entry to the main sprint race. Eventually we came to the long distance race of 2½ miles, the last on the list. Duma won in record time to everyone's amazement; thus we received a beautiful Arab trophy.

The next race meeting of 1992 was at Goodwood, the beautiful country course in West Sussex. Debby hired a hospitality box to entertain our friends and Duma was entered for the sprint race. She seemed a little nervous at the start, and ran a very poor race to everyone's surprise but more so to Debby and me. There was no doubt that dear Duma was confused, unsure what was expected of her after winning a long distance race. As the owners and trainer it was obvious to all we were not the right experienced operators of the classic racing code.

Debby shrugged the whole episode off with a laugh and announced Duma was finished with racing and we would now breed pure Arab horses for racing sale. Debby left her Newmarket house and stables and stayed with a trainer jockey shipping by air thoroughbred horses to Hong Kong race track owners. For some reason Debby took another tack, to become interested in training thoroughbred horses only. Thus my Queen of Arab horse racing gave up her crown forever. Duma did provide some interesting foals. The first was sold for a six figure sum, then followed a too frequent succession of pregnancies that eventually caused exhausted Duma to die in a French breeding station of a hundred horses or more. I decided to visit Duma before she was pregnant for the fourth or fifth time, and complained to Debby at the uncomfortable situation, Duma looked so unhappy at being penned up always in a head collar with so many horses and although her position was improved she just faded away doing her best. Thus a wonderful pure Arab horse of such famous success passed on without notice from anyone in 1999.

Whilst Duma was never mine I missed such an exciting good friend, winner of 22 races, 3 classic and 3 championships.

Debby after a short stay in Newmarket became filled with the need to go into thoroughbred racehorses and went over and stayed in France, firstly working for about one year with a well known trainer who did some training with the Aga Khan horses in Chantilly. She lived in a lovely small apartment, worked hard for seven days a week and rarely came home. Later she worked for another trainer near Le Mans for another long period, eventually transferring to a part of a horse-orientated Château de Hurse with a large acreage near the tributaries of the Loire River with a part house for Debby, stables for four or five horses, a trainer's house and country riding facilities for riding and training. I bought a carpet, a bed and white goods for the kitchen and bathroom, and much of the equipment for the stables came from home. At the time Duma was in her new pregnancy with the only Arab, El Herim, who was retired as companion. I looked after both horses with my housekeeper and part time daily groom Vivien. Besides the horses we lived with two donkeys, three to become two Shetland ponies and four Pekinese dogs, one Dalmatian and one or two wild cats.

Debby therefore became the fledgling French owner and trainer and I visited the château on occasions driving my Bentley come rain, belching spray or shine. I recall one time driving in the rain from Rouen to Beauvous when I was in the receipt of a lorry deluge of spray and had been following behind the same lorry for over half an hour when we came into a straight valley in the road. I could see nothing coming so decided to pass the lorry and pulled out and sped by but as I attempted to return to my side I found my path was cut off by solid iron bulwarks with a small crossroads at the base of the valley so as I could not return to the proper side of the road. I breathlessly carried on hoping for the best but a little further I could just see a lorry approaching so I put my foot further down and just swung over on passing the last of the iron bulwarks in the middle of the road to collect the spray of the lorry going in the opposite direction. The narrow margin did not encourage future port journey routes so my future would be non direct if rain was about. Although I was a specialist qualified in meteorological forecasting, if I was in any doubt at all I would play safe with the knowledge of the atmospheric pressure.

Debby continued with the training establishment at Château de Hurse and was happy with the connection with the French aristocracy but eventually decided she had no nearby racing fraternity or hippodrome to indulge in racing so virtually leaving all behind set off for Chantilly near Paris, the home of the French racing world, the lovely horse Chateau-Estate used in 007 Bond films and the Hippodrome.

Before departure from the vicinity of Le Mans, Debby was involved in her own motor car accident by turning from the slip road into the autoroute for she hit a descending car coming at around 40 m.p.h. in the opposite direction. She was taken by ambulance to hospital, quite seriously ill, with due notification to me in the UK. I immediately took flight to Nantes some hundred-plus kilometres away from the action, and taxied to the hospital to take charge of the situation. Having met the doctor I decided there was little I could do there except somehow to pay the bill which they insisted on in no uncertain terms.

The car I inspected was a very complete right-off, just a heap of scrap metal. I was used to Debby's motor car damages, and those of 4 × 4 Rovers, horse boxes and later a special Honda coupé, but this occasion was a one off. The insurance company insisted for some reason for the pieces to be returned to the UK. Then the car was replaced plus a small percentage extra with a new model. The *gendarmerie* were less satisfied after a long interview in relation to the victim car claim.

When things settled down I again journeyed to the hospital for Debby's midday discharge after staying the night, where I enjoyed a beautiful dinner at the local Michelin star restaurant. Naturally I told Debby who demanded after a little shopping to have lunch at the same restaurant. We sat down to order our menu, but Debby insisted on a vegan meal. So Debby produced a tin of baked beans for the main course warmed with French fried potatoes, the staff politely failing to understand. My simple order of rare to medium fillet of beef with new potatoes was accepted. After thirty minutes or so our meal was delivered without the usual politeness, with the warm baked beans loaded with fried potatoes, My plate included dark, well done meat with a load of fried potatoes. Debby ate her meal with relish, mine I could not eat and after a short time we left after payment; fortunately this unfortunate episode was concluded before the majority of distinguished guests arrived.

Afterwards I was in difficulty with car hire for I needed an automatic medium size sedan or similar vehicle which was not available so was forced to take the only non automatic; also I was used to driving my car with the steering wheel on the right. Fortunately with our vegan meal we had consumed no wine so we set off to Chantilly learning to manually drive the French car safely. With no air conditioning on a hot day, the windows open with huge traffic noise, on the main roads and the auto route, there was only me reading the map with difficulty because of being on the wrong side, with Debby fast asleep. When we arrived we called her very happy friend Nicole who was exercise riding for a famous trainer.

Very soon I was back in UK and heavily in work for I had much to accomplish in the USA and Europe, with companies buying each other out causing different competitive circumstances. I was always of necessity monitoring our quality standards of production and the machine tool development of accuracy with a new programme of manufacture, particularly large cutting wheels for repair and construction of concrete against the diamond product.

On my next visit to Chantilly, at a weekend, I found Debby operating her newly acquired stables from a French jockey establishment where she was very happy, leading a frugal life and sharing domestic and sleeping quarters with jockeys both learning and qualified. Yet although she changed stables to some a little grotty ones without paddocks and grass she eventually enjoyed a situation of 'how many boxes do you want?' So she had taken boxes with a courtyard for exercise, an office and harness room and hay room, so felt quite important in the French racing society.

She bought horses and sold portions to her friends in the UK so if I carried invitations for lunch or dinner they were waiting for her to appear. Her friends included one who was the nomad son of a bishop, another was a very successful jockey from a neighbouring competitive stable with Debby singing his virtues; each successive virtue via a glassful of fruit juice seemed a little odd to me for I had only just arrived after quite a long absence to meet Debby. Of course local friends appeared too, probably for the free feast invitation. I was not worried except for the effect of these diversions on her judgement for future horse racing success.

However Debby rented new stables, sometimes part of a larger organisation of racing temporary accommodation for horses, without any personal pride; sometimes they were very old with boxes that appeared to be falling down with no real use or which provided no facilities for training or any paddock for a little grass exercise with grazing on hand. It seemed to me fresh grass was only for the horses to see only just before starting a race, a waft to make them ride with more speed. It took a little time to find the nearest good stables but desire prevailed. Debby settled into fine modern stables with fourteen pen horse boxes, an office, a tack room for clothes, a hay box adjacent to the harness room, and was now happy to be the first British French qualified trainer resident in France, with two grooms and whoever else. She improved the whole situation of the yard for training and enjoyed a cut grass section as a paddock so the horses could graze.

The stables soon were rendered complete with bright coloured hanging flower baskets over the individual horse box shutters that opened for the horse's head and neck to smell flower scent and watch all that went by. To me it was all so charming and much admired by all including the grooms but I expect the adjacent stable yard owners were not amused at all.

Debby was now busy inspecting and again buying suitable racehorses with good galloping strength hind legs. On purchase she would sell half, quarters, eighths to her friends in England and sometimes to local franchise residents; thus invitations flowed with much excitement for all involved.

I recall one of our friends, a 747 pilot with BA, had his wife so involved she hired a helicopter to take a visiting motor racing Formula 1 gentleman from Italy to witness the racing speculation situation for the portions of horses they desired to win for the future. I understood it was one hilarious party. Sometimes the yard was in hectic disarray to cope with Debby's demands of livery to friends' horses, the racing schedule and the tidiness of the horse boxes, the yard and flowers for herself and transportation of visitors coming racing. Chinese fisticuffs or kick boxing could interfere with the staff, but all would be resolved on hearing the final bell.

Naturally I was sometimes in the midst of the weekend frolics, but could not enjoy total freedom of the action. I preferred the more organised action of visiting say Longchamps or other hippodrome for a quiet pleasant lunch with less introduction to the excitement of following every tip, start and race result,. I was often introduced to too many people seriously connected to horse racing who had imagination or knowledge way beyond my comprehension and endurance.

It was always interesting for me to see Debby at race meetings in her Chanel yellow-lime coloured dress which she had acquired for the wedding in 1984. It was so good for her and she loved the display of the gold coloured buttons for they were easily recognised so felt proud at her display.

On one such occasion I was invited into the racing horse stables within the depths of Longchamps with a guest who was not afraid of the atmosphere, I lunged this way and that to avoid the moving horses being led by jockeys or grooms past me. The smell upset the intake to my lovely luncheon to make me feel queasy; being petrified I did a hasty retreat and so missed the waterfall of strongly perfumed horse relief that had splattered on my clean shiny shoes and socks.

I have really always avoided being friendly with a horse or horses since I was thrown the first time during my introduction to horses at Stratford upon Avon, Warwickshire in 1933 and here I was still feeling the same under the totally different circumstances of a polished owner with a racehorse stable, worked by a notable horse involved wife. Thus I again became remarkably less interested for the future of my involvement in thoroughbred horse racing or any of the exercise so far. So I cleaned my shoes and settled down in the enclosure with a glass of pink bubbly for comfort; however I was eventually disturbed by puffing racing gentlemen smoking huge cigars – where they were made I cannot say, but I can say the country was not Cuba. The stench was so bad it reminded me of cleaning my shoes so I uplifted myself and set course away, hopefully to find fresh air in delightful Paris. Soon I found my situation was among more of my wife's horse fraternity, so was once more isolated with nowhere to go until the gossip finished long after the last race.

I should tell you at this point I much admired efforts to help Debby in her French racing career by Alain le Comte de Saint Germain, whom Debby had met in Portugal at the Spanish Riding School, Lisbon, where she visiting under the advice of her dressage master, himself from the Spanish Riding School, Vienna and L'institut National d'Equitation, Cadre Noir, Saumur, when trying to learn dressage in 1987.

We met many times Arab racing in France with one occasion aboard the *bateau* for dinner underneath the bridges of the river Seine in Paris after a successful Arab race meeting at Evry Hippodrome. Later Alain came to my home in Durford Wood in England on his travels heading a sports safari to Nordic areas, Scotland, Ireland and elsewhere for salmon fishing, shooting game, horse eventing and racing. Comte Jean de la Sayette from the lovely extensive estate of the château adjacent to the tributaries of the beautiful Loire river, gave hospitality and assistance to Debby through the Jockey Club concerning her attempts to gain her licence, with the use of part of the large equestrian establishment for training supporting so many activities of the equestrian world whatever they may be, also once supported by our own Queen. Madame Jane D'ailleur of Paris offered so much advice and enthusiasm before Debby's embarking on the French part of her horse racing desire.

About this time I was heavily involved with business expansion and take-over talk to buy or sell, and felt like the little five-year-old boy

I had met outside the American University in Beirut, Lebanon. I had asked, 'What do you do?' The boy replied, 'I sell, I buy.' I asked, 'What do you sell?' And the boy replied, 'Sir, if you want me to buy I give you three dollars per pound sterling, but if you want to buy from me it will cost you five dollars; that is my $2+2$ table which is so simple.'

This argument also reminds me of the devout Christian traveller making his way through the dense jungle when he became aware a large lion was watching him. He immediately fell on his knees and prayed. After a little while the lion without a sound sat down beside him and too offered a prayer. The traveller remarked, 'I was praying so that you would not eat me.' The lion replied, 'Dear sir, do not worry; I am reciting the Lord's grace for the feast I am about to receive!'

I have told you about the people that helped Debby, but I have yet to tell of the horses that influenced her success too. The first horse was the pure Arab El Herim bought as a one year old with her brother Demon for all types of equestrian sport who was shunted out to a friend much later on, to our friend to take care of when she went to dressage training with Wattau for high stakes.

It was hearing of El Herim's success winning on the racecourse that set Debby to cancel all and to collect El Herim for new sport racing and although to start she started to race from home as a race jockey using a Sinclair two-horse trailer, she quickly graduated in the Arab horse society.

I was concerned, for one day I was called to an accident to the car with horse trailer not negotiating a local horse bridge, as reported earlier. I became more than just concerned for my wife, and related the story of one of her friends who had an accident with a horse trailer as follows. The friend's trailer was similar to ours with a wooden floor for the horse to stand on. Naturally the horse's feet with steel shoes vibrated about with the rough road jogging and keeping balance so sooner or later the wood struts wore out.

The accident occurred over a bump when the floor gave way and the horse dropped through. It is also likely the driver was not aware of the calamity hence the dear horse suffered terrible untold injuries until somehow the driver became aware. This is not an interesting tale but it is terrible warning for all amateur horse owners of which I am one.

To continue: El Herim survived, carried some splendid race wins and was a great influence on her jockey's forthcoming successful racing career. The prizes were not huge, say £100 for a win, but enough of a token for a proper regulated Amateur Arab Horse Society.

The next overwhelming influence was the purchase of the Russian pure Arab mare Duma in 1989 from the famous Tersk Stud in southern Soviet Union. At four years old Duma had already won nine races and was champion mare in the USSR. She very soon acclimatised and raced always to win. Her first UK race was in October and she won easily by ten lengths over a six furlongs course.

I never did understand how Duma learnt her English language, for Russian to me is not understandable; however she understood Debby's hand perhaps, for all her movements caused much success and pleasure over the next three years. As you know Duma won the Mares Championship of Great Britain in 1992 after winning 22 races, 3 championships and 3 international classics. She wore my own colours: black and white check jacket with light blue sleeve and light blue cap.

CHAPTER 17

Concorde

I TRAVELLED ON CONCORDE VERY many times, not to break any
records but purely for doing important business in the shortest
time, as I became a worthy negotiator for the strong objective of my
company to move fast in systematical quality abrasives, to meet
requests to supply large contracts related to electric, compressed air
or even petrol driven machine power tools, plus requests to supply
abrasive parts to my USA giant competitors as piece of their business.
I was one of the first to accept that Concorde was the way to travel
and for quite a long time easily reserved the front row seats 1a & 1b.
At the time most people thought Concorde's supersonic speed rather
dangerous so it took a while for the interest to mature. When it did
the aristocracy of the realm, politics and jazz called for the front seats,
so I migrated to row 2 and then 3, until I discovered the front seats
of the second cabin suited me fine, without the hassle.

Concorde, in feel, was similar to my previous Norton International
overhead valve motor bike: a small seat with a terrific thrust on
take-off, and a gentle cruise in flight even through the sound barrier
via the engine after burners. One would gently cruise at above 50,000
feet with our only companion the supersonic military fighter aircraft,
which could only last a minute or two at this height. Whilst we were
quietly flying past the speed of sound, we would be drinking superb
wines, vintage Dom Perignon champagne, Rothschild vintage red or
what you will, and at the same time be served with a good measure
of Beluga caviar, to be followed by an exquisite lunch or dinner with
politeness, today so difficult to forget.

On my first flight on Concorde I thought of my noble friend Peter
Twiss who in 1956 made the world absolute speed record of well
over 1,000 miles per hour, some 300 m.p.h. faster than the USA
record. Here I was enjoying this speed as normal, faster than a rifle
bullet. I might look through my port window to the very noticeable
curvature shape of our planet Earth. Whilst I know so much about
our solar system, I have yet to see the forty-eight moons of vast
Jupiter with three of the moons spinning in the opposite direction to

the other companions. Peter's record used a Fairey Delta 2 with a nose droop and delta wing design, later considered possible for Concorde's design. The record run was at 38,000 feet along the south coast as a U course and caused supersonic bangs to break all the greenhouse windows along the route.

Before you could finish the newspaper, half read in the Concorde lounge before boarding the aircraft, we would leave the tranquil dark blue sky to swoop into JFK airport, Long Island, New York, and take our waiting limousine with whoever to New York City by the driver called Cool John! Thus after clocking into the 60th floor of the Hilton Hotel with over two thousand rooms, with impeccable service, I would be ready in the hall for my appointment early at 10.15 a.m.

By the way, Concorde's first airline landing at JFK airport was on 19 October 1986, returning to London Heathrow the next day. My own first British Airways Concorde flight was 12 June 1987, returning to London four days later on 16 June, happy with business well done. All was normally accomplished within about five hours from leaving London airport, thus a whole day to work, particularly with the six hours time difference back.

On one occasion owing to time and pressure needing an important decision I departed London Heathrow on Concorde flight BA002 at 09.30 hours to JFK airport at 08.20 hours, then immediately on a reserved helicopter flight to LaGuardia city airport in New York. Within a few minutes of arrival I took off for Detroit airport, Michigan near the Canadian border where I was met by the person I was to see, his managing director son and his wife and taken to their abrasive plant at Ann Arbor for a heavy discussion. After a coffee break we then signed the minutes of the meeting, followed by a short car journey and lunch in town. After lunch I returned to Detroit airport with a car hire and landed at JFK airport in time to board Concorde BA 004 flight at 13.35 hours to London, so after a second smallish lunch or dinner I arrived in Heathrow, London at 22.25 hours and found my car waiting, so home to bed. This was all in one day, the six hours back out and the six hours forward taken into account, and in the morning I was ready for my appointment of the new day. All in all, a marvellous achievement due to modern machinery and technology, with so little effort on my part.

One of my flights on Concorde was with Air France, from Paris to Caracas, Venezuela, to meet with my Chile agent for a fast appraisal through many countries from Venezuela through Columbia, Peru, Bolivia, Ecuador to Brazil then to Trinidad, Panama, Costa Rica and through the Caribbean Islands to Dominican Republic and Puerto Rico.

Our export business was good with future good promise in Chile, Ecuador and Costa Rica. Our exclusive agent was a super trained Singer company top man, but who was finding it hard to compete with the cartel of USA companies. Although our abrasive products were considered superior for our small range, our distribution customers needed to buy a full range hence took in US supplies. I was here to permeate our relationship with our main customers and to see what I could do to help them compete, thus to see what could be done in relation to extending our phenol formaldehyde synthetic resin product range of abrasives.

It was hard work but the objective was achieved with the additional appointment of a sole agent for Trinidad, whose father was the ex Attorney General. I was made very welcome by my new friends who included a visit to the Test match cricket team. I promised to support again our next West Indies cricket encounter at the Oval cricket ground, Port of Spain.

The Hilton Hotel in Trinidad was locally called the 'upside down' hotel for it was built on a cliff face just outside Port of Spain and the entrance from Lady Young Road ended at the top floor reception with the other rooms and restaurant near the bottom. In many ways Trinidad was a country of extreme politics yet so rich in oil. On one occasion I visited the island's opposite shore, where there was a lovely long sandy beach with an overhanging coconut plantation, with visible oil rigs working at full blast and the sand covered with thick black oil spillage patches. However the neighbouring island of Tobago was like paradise: completely clean wonderful white sandy beaches, a little primitive but no industrial interference. In fact it was a perfect holiday island with very good accommodation at the Mount Irvine Hotel, with a lovely golf course and as you might guess I did try my hand with borrowed golf clubs. It was all so relaxing and beautifully quiet in all day sunshine. There was however a rumour of an extension to the little airport for the arrival of 747s.

It was good to remember the dusty roads of England being made into tarmac dustless roads with the Trinidad asphalt from the natural asphalt lake of Trinidad; many other parts of the world remember too! Such a revolution of good world road progress by my now important customer.

When in Santiago, Chile, with my agent Nigel Strange, I was invited with my wife and daughter to dinner with my agent's son, engaged to the daughter of the Admiral of the Chile Fleet, and I was presented with a historical book of the country's naval attachment to the UK Royal Navy, sent to me by her father who was sorry not to have been able to meet me. Chile was a most interesting country, so diverse with the famous copper mines. Our copper customer was based at Antofagasta in the north near Peru, with assembly plants of the motor cars nearby; Santiago is in the middle with so much isolated country in the south, all the land seawards of the long range of the Andes, from the north in Peru to Cape Horn in the south, where the Pacific Ocean joins with the Atlantic Ocean.

Once whilst in UK, I answered the telephone from my top important power tool customer in the USA to be told he had received a complaint from his office in Toronto concerning a consignment of special Arrow abrasives within the main supplier container, that they were the wrong type. I replied, 'I will look into it and let you know.' I called my works manager to agree a solution. I knew our manufacturing programme provided for no mistake on quality or type so the problem must be related to the special label to enhance the user's safety. Hence I decided the works manager, Bob Porter, would fly Concorde out with the correct labels to change, if this was the problem, or report to me the actual likely problem solution.

Within a day my works manager was in Toronto, Canada via Concorde to the USA and reported to me the labels were the key to the solution and he arranged the replacements accordingly to the make; all was well within three days with congratulations for a wonderful service. Naturally I had reported back to my contact in the USA about my well over a million pounds yearly customer and received his congratulations too! My works manager reported for work next day after taking Concorde home, with the thrill of doing a job well done and thanked me for the fantastic Concorde experience for a customer service.

On one occasion I was booked to take Concorde with my USA export manager John B. Day, and had decided to take my new wife Debby to give her business experience, so with three tickets, after

check-in at the Concorde lounge at Terminal 4 we awaited my wife.
The time came to board the aircraft at 10.30 yet no wife so I returned
her ticket to the staff in case she suddenly turned up. We taxied out,
took off without the possible inclusion of my wife whose was the
only blank seat in the full passenger cabin. After the normal smooth
journey we met our appointment in the early morning, six hours
back local time, and virtually completed business by 12.00 hours. On
sitting down to lunch, I was informed by British Airways my wife
had missed the next aircraft because it was full, but everyone was so
kind at Heathrow and found a seat for her on a morning subsonic
Boeing 747 due in eight hours later, so would be at our hotel about
17.30. We finished lunch then went out afterwards to carry on our
business at the Stihl agent office in New Jersey. We returned
approximately at 18.30 just as my wife came rushing into the
crowded foyer asking for money to pay the taxi, after payment via
the concierge. My wife asked for a Greyhound; I did not know what
kind of a drink it was so I asked, and was apparently a tumbler full
of grapefruit juice half mixed with vodka. I thought how delicate,
then listened to her story of not waking up in time, thought again
how unbusinesslike. With that I continued with my schedule. Off we
went early next morning to Norfolk, Virginia to my important
appointment, and stayed at a small hotel by the windswept surf of the
furious Eastern Atlantic Ocean.

My Concorde flights included Miami and Washington but
normally if going to the southern United States I journeyed direct by
conventional aircraft for Concorde plus connections took longer in
time.

We are now aware that an Air France Concorde recently was
involved in a fatal crash taking off at Charles de Gaulle airport and
today they fly no longer on the North Atlantic route. I am personally
shamed for the UK, for the Concorde was a very safe aircraft
(although I once experienced nose wheel trouble that delayed my
intended return from New York, but it all ended happily). Concorde
was modified after the French crash to make it safer still but the
Concorde story of supersonic flight was halted by Air France, with
the French government agreement, so to crash the British Airways
advance. We also know today after the initial investigations that it
was found and broadcast by TV and more that the crash was caused
by extremely bad maintenance of Air France. It is well known that

if four dangerous circumstances are added together a fatal outcome is inevitable for all, in any situation: automobiles or whatever that occurs in our life.

The four things were:

1. Wheels alignment spacer was missing from the left main under-carriage.
2. Fuel was added as surplus weight.
3. Additional loading weight was added beyond specifications.
4. The aircraft veered off the runway line owing to wheels going out of line and just missed the French president in his 747. They eventually picked up the piece of metal that burst the tyre and it caused the fuel tank to rupture; also the engineer in flight closed the wrong engine.

The pilot stood no chance, thus my historical supersonic flight travel was eliminated, also partly due to favouring the USA by supporting their Boeing 747 instead of going supersonic with Europe. Rockets and robots are taking over so the current future looks doubtful for passenger supersonic travel with pilot manned aircraft. Of course, each of us on Earth is doing 18,000 m.p.h. orbiting the sun at the present time with or without Concorde.

It is worth noting that the skin or outside of Concorde expands several inches in the friction temperature when flying at supersonic speeds when the 117° Centigrade (245° Fahrenheit) takes place. Naturally the aircraft contracts on deceleration to its subsonic standard length, through plentiful ozone altitudes to release oxygen to the benefit of all on board.

An article by Glen Collyns of the *New York Times* and the *International Herald Tribune* of Friday 13 April 2001 more than indicates the twelve Concordes, five from Air France and seven British Airways, are hobbled up in the hangars of Heathrow and Charles de Gaulle airports because of the Air France accident, but whilst many passengers are dedicated to supersonic trade many are not. There is no doubt supersonic speeds will continue by whatever source of motive power, regardless of cost.

CHAPTER 18

Crossing the Atlantic and my politics

I HAVE MENTIONED VARIOUS EPISODES of my life's connection with the Atlantic Ocean, particularly the hole through my flying boot via the German Heinkel aircraft. That reminds me today of my shoot-out just before the time of the *Bismarck* sinking beneath the Atlantic waves to the credit of the Royal Navy supported by the Royal Air Force Catalina aircraft spot navigation and more, I hope including myself.

I recall being drenched with sea waves off the coast of Wales as a little boy and being told to run home to change from my soggy wet clothes, and much later having to take charge of my Royal Air Force companions for the fourteen mile walk through the misty wet freezing cold wind of the Atlantic Coast of north-west Ireland, all through the night; however, we all made it, golf clubs too!

A little later I was flying into Tiree then Benbecula in the Hebrides off the west coast of north Scotland to meet my wife whilst she was painting my commission 'The Four Seasons' in North Uist, just below the estate where the friends of our Queen entertained Her Majesty on the annual visits of the Royal Yacht *Britannia* on the way to summer recess at Balmoral.

I arrived not on this day but some days earlier because I was suffering from some sort of muscular illness that my civil aviation doctor put down to jet lag and told me to rest. I called with an evening dinner picnic consisting of a beautiful tin of Beluga caviar plus Scottish wild salmon, with DP vintage pink champagne to cheer the atmosphere of Atlantic mist. I dressed as a chef serving whilst standing in the stream adjacent to the thatched cottage of my wife's bed and studio where I was to stay in the thatched roof space listening to the Atlantic slow westerly cold wind. The heating was just the log fire in the studio and my wife slept on a narrow bed situated opposite the wood fire.

Next day I spent an hour or so checking my salmon and trout rods and dressing in the gear that would beat the Scottish mist and drizzly rain. I settled into my boat with ghillie and set course. I felt the salmon but my arm would not work so I packed everything up. I set off as quickly as I could for the King Edward VII Hospital in Midhurst, West Sussex near my home to see what was wrong. By the time I registered my heart was irregular and I was just as desperate as the locum who allowed me in a bed for a prognosis.

At this time I had been heavily engaged in business round the planet but much of my time was spent in the USA, travelling through or going direct, consequently the Atlantic Ocean was often crossed in many different ways on all journeys. The Royal Air Force duty included learning to fly from a grass field at Prestwick, very near the Atlantic seaboard, and my reconnaissance flying programme was over the sea from Lytham St Anne's. The Hudson night and day conversion was from Silloth on the Solway Firth, a pure water haven, then I had all the Atlantic Ocean convoy patrol flying from Limavady near Londonderry, Ireland. I used to set course from Inistrahull, a small precious rocky island lighthouse, off the north coast against German U boats.

My first Atlantic sea crossing was on an armed merchant ship with a captain who was always prepared with only one gun fore and aft to fight the Atlantic raiding German battleships nearby, to Halifax, Newfoundland.

Later my return crossing was on a slow moving troopship, a coal burning ship just out of retirement that took three weeks to get ready to fill with black sooty coal bound for Liverpool.

We flew from Iceland in all kinds of weather but there was an impossible gap in the middle of the Atlantic Ocean for the German U boats to exploit raiding our precious supply lane.

Then was the Royal Air Force HQ on D-Day, ending up in Cornwall with my wife and new daughter alongside the beautiful bleak Atlantic Ocean where the innkeeper's daughter's name was Storm. She introduced me to a blackened steamroller driver who had just set a record of making a queue of forty-eight vehicles behind before turning in for his pint of ale.

So back to civil business in peaceful England and my life contract with Bakelite making the thermosetting products now called plastics, to include more variations like thermoplastics.

I started flying the Atlantic as a passenger very soon after setting up my business in 1946 with American raw materials; all kinds of aircraft were experimented with by the commercial airlines. The winner for me in the end was Pan American Airways, who made me a life member of their exclusive Clipper Club. British Airways (then BOAC) although often the pioneers for comfortable flight around the Empire with flying boats and Hanley Page land planes, plus later the amazing first jet engine for DH Comets, missed out providing a British passenger aircraft for the North Atlantic route, with Comet cancelled as the first world jet powered aircraft possibility. It was taken over a few years later by the larger Boeing 707 jet until Concorde came into fast supersonic passenger service.

I have so far neglected to record the heroic journeys across the Atlantic made by the likes of Lindbergh, Allcock and Brown and others before the lease-lend of armaments and food by President Roosevelt of the United States of America at a time of desperation in the British Isles with low supplies after leaving France to the Germans. The most important task at the time was to make the Atlantic safe so the President agreed to a plan put forward by our Prime Minister Winston Churchill. An international team of aviators formed a ferry service in the USA to fly the internal airline Lockheed, 14-passenger airliner with no armour plate or seats, called the Hudson over to the shores to help fill our Royal Air Force, Coastal Command defences against the German U boats, who at this time were enjoying their time easily sinking ships in our convoys of supply across the North Atlantic. This difficult ferry crossing was enthusiastically carried out by the intrepid pilots who found their way without the expert knowledge of the necessary navigation and the extremely rough and icy Atlantic weather. They kept up a traffic supply but of course they lost a number of pilots who crashed somewhere, ran out of fuel or missed the British Isles altogether.

This situation caused my HQ to ask me for a report on what was going wrong and how we could put it right. I carried out my survey of the situation whilst in Iceland using my specialist knowledge of navigation completed by the 'N' award passed near Lake Huron, for the Royal Air Force in between operational duty. The gap was finally closed by the USA 4-engine long range Liberator in 1944 on lease-lend to the RAF coastal command defences in Iceland and the RCAF from Newfoundland, which caused the Atlantic gap to close, and got rid of the German U boats.

I now continued with flying the Atlantic as a civilian passenger. After I had started my business it was not an easy journey because of the short range of flight of the aircraft; the seats were uncomfortable for this long time and it was not economical.

Travel became more feasible with the US Constellation aircraft with forty-five passenger seats followed by the Boeing Stratocruiser that to me wallowed in flight but carried in comfort sixty passengers with a cocktail bar below deck and a proper galley for serving gourmet meals, plus the turning of my seat into a proper bed with white sheets. I recall I felt strange trying to get to sleep with my trousers off but my shoes on in case of an emergency landing for the flight to the USA which went via Shannon, Ireland; Reykjavik, Iceland; Gander or Goose Bay, Labrador; Dorval, Montreal for refuelling; so to the then Idlewild Airport (now JFK), New York; then helicopter to the top of the Pan American Building, New York City. Thus it took a long time, some twenty-seven hours or more, sometimes with hostile weather also causing delays in take-off or difficulties by flying higher, needing oxygen or flying round the dangerous thunder, lightning and ice laden cumulo-nimbus clouds. It was not quite always so for on remote occasions the North Atlantic Ocean could be like a millpond with blue skies and the odd weather ship silently reporting on the North Atlantic route for the great circle air traffic.

In 1954 I was very busy, but fell ill with appendicitis and coming through the anaesthesia, saw an angel talking and taking me to heaven, all so beautiful pure white. It took a little while to think, it cannot be so, for I was scheduled to visit the USA before my operation. Anyway all was possible later in convalescence.

I decided to go across the Atlantic by the Cunard liner *Queen Mary* with my wife to look after me. My doctor thought this way was more civilised if anything went wrong. It was all so efficient, luxurious, and with no frantic boarding, meeting my steward in our cabin to stow our baggage away and to look after all my needs. I had booked the famous *Queen*'s grill restaurant for all meals except breakfast in bed. We enjoyed the spacious lounges, walkways and courteous service and curiously did not feel afloat. Though we had not yet put to sea we had the feeling the ship was too grand to be bustled about by any Atlantic waves and weather. We sailed from Southampton for Cherbourg to take more scheduled passengers, before setting course to cross the Atlantic. After a short time out at sea I put on my dinner jacket and bow tie for our first dinner, I did not drink for I felt not well enough but had made an appointment to see the ship's doctor for a shake-up next morning.

My quiet reserved table was for two. I did not wish to sit at a ship's officer's table, in my delicate state. The dinner looked out of this world, with Beluga caviar from a real size elegant swan made of clear ice, and a beautiful medium rare scotch fillet and more, but when it was put before me to eat I was not hungry and left the table before the dessert and so to bed not feeling well.

The ship's doctor next morning gave me a tonic, 'Metatone'; it was wonderful and only recently have I stopped the daily dose because of other medication. I proceeded to feel the good life again, enjoying the odd very dry Martini and superb food with vintage wine, until one day in the middle of the Atlantic. We joined our separate table for luncheon together, while the walkways were roped against the rough sea. Our table had the side hinges raised but the dining room was in the centre, the most peaceful part of the ship, although I had a strange feeling the ship's three funnels were nearly touching the huge waves. I decided it was safe; after all, the commodore was in charge as the ship's captain. We were just starting our second course when there was a huge bang on the side of the ship near our table, and immediately water poured through the starboard portholes as if from super large hosepipes slashed across the floor or deck. We had to lift our legs and feet to let the sea water through underneath our table without getting wet. After a little sloshing about the seawater was controlled, and we enjoyed the rest of our lunch. Our dining room lost three or more starboard portholes which were smashed to little pieces but soon all was safe. The ships of that time were not fitted with stabilisers but naturally were soon afterwards and today all ships have fitted them, some yachts too. I forgot to think of the earlier Atlantic sailors fighting the same conditions in small wooden sailing ships.

I continued for quite a long time to use the *Queen Mary*, *Queen Elizabeth* and *Queen Elizabeth II* and made one or two crossings in smaller Cunard ships. I met influential passengers and occasionally a top customer to help my company product sales, which were in demand for their quality, service and price in the United States. In fact one large customer asked me to manufacture in Nigeria for them to establish their presence. We did so in Lagos and I with my wife stayed over to initiate the progress, although I did not particularly like the beach holiday celebrations using petty thieves for killing amusement. I was pleased to see the country of two of my son's unusual Marlborough College Nigerian friends who eventually graduated as lawyer and doctor. To me, Nigeria so desperately needed to sort out the tribal administration problems and needed help to provide medicine, as so many people were using witch doctors for assistance.

Although the ship was a comfortable means of crossing the Atlantic for I had plenty of time for planning and working on new ways to operate the company, it was getting too slow in the modern era of ever increasing air traffic to provide less expensive first class comfortable travel in ever decreasing time. Gone were the old days of twenty-four hours or more. I switched back to Pan American Airways who operated a modern fleet of aircraft who were just talking to Boeing about the introduction of the large 747 at this time. The USA was dropping its interest in supersonic travel aircraft. Here in England we were at last talking of using our superior jet knowledge with the French to confirm our joint embarkation on the manufacture of the supersonic transport later to be called Concorde.

Hence came the joint cooperation between Aerospatiale and British Aerospace which led to British Airways and Air France's first Concorde commercial flight to the USA via the North Atlantic route in 1976 carrying a hundred passengers and competing with the Jumbo 747 first commercial flight in 1970 carrying 350–490 passengers at a much cheaper price and heralding the birth of mass passenger travel holidays for business or whatever.

Although the Trans Atlantic liner business declined later it became the birth of holiday cruising by ship. Concorde was withdrawn towards the end of 2003 through lack of French spares and the expense of operating such a small fleet of only twelve, while Aerospatiale continued with the medium sized Airbus and the development of the 380 giant two-tier Airbus, designed to carry 680 passengers in relative comfort. Perhaps this is the last of pilot operated aircraft except for a future supersonic aircraft much larger than Concorde and so we are ready for rocket propelled aircraft following the space shuttle of the United States development with Russia of today and in the future to make crossing of the Atlantic quick and easy for us all. Little navigation would be needed because of on board computers planning all aspects of the flight across the North Atlantic route above the weather at 550 m.p.h. However today it would take

me much longer to cross the North Atlantic than it did thirty years
ago.

Parts of the Atlantic do not appear to change. First is the fabulous
warm Gulf Stream; in drought it never fails, in floods it never
overflows; it is a solid warm river stream flowing through the cold
mass of the North Atlantic Drift, swinging through the lower part of
Gulf of Mexico, and continuing the swing just north of the equator
to acclimatise our shores for all time.

Second is the Aurora Borealis, influenced by our nuclear sun's solar
wind. It provides free of charge artistic natural requirements to
welcome a perpetual reminder of the magnetic gravity of planet
Earth, the Universe and the forever space of our bright sparkling
realm of stellar inheritance, the beautiful horseshoe of shimmering
silvered bright pink, blue, green of dreams.

Sometimes I am asked about matters concerning politics so today
I judge the need to pursue what has happened to democracy, which
always allows various protests and falling dimensional standards, as it
calls for more people to take advantage of the changing individual
technology as it comes available.

Let us look at some of the major governments of our planet Earth:
say the United Kingdom, France, Germany, Russia, USA and the
like; it seems our old aristocracy with the Parliament advocated by
the Knights of King John, who although reluctant to sign the Magna
Carta has produced the best results so far.

France after an awesome cruel long revolution that ended with the
human guillotine being introduced by their Parliament for cutting off
the heads of their remaining aristocracy, now seems stuck without
their kings or queens.

Russia cut off the heads of their aristocracy for Communism and
now is somewhat stuck too but today is democratic within the
confines of a type of KGB operation. It is about to emerge a great
energy producer.

The USA, only some two hundred years old, has a confused type
of aristocracy, owing to the inheritance from the Anglo Saxons and
the very hard work in development of their land and population.

China, a future power, is looking through Communism to create
a democracy to stabilise itself with more tolerance for its caged
deprived working people, who yet realise they may never have the
chance to be free.

Australia and New Zealand are working well with a white man's democracy, yet it is too early to evaluate their future.

Africa is difficult to compare because of the enormous existing poverty. South Africa is surrounded by so much corruption to add to the efforts of so many tribal chiefs and war lords.

India has the old Rajahs akin to aristocracy, but is now developing democracy for its many people through a Parliament to meet similar aims as China's. It would be a global world economy power, but it neglects the many village people who have no say.

So looking far and near England seems to survive better, yet the hereditary House of Lords might disappear with the politically democratic House of Lords to succeed. It means so little for whilst democracy works for the individual to progress himself for power and money but lacks public spirit, the hallmark of the aristocracy was that the public spirit was always there whether knights, lords, dukes, princes, queen or kings. All that happens under political democracy is caused by a political power surge via life peers, the small money makers without true public service, so become more mediocre. They move towards the increased future technology with lower standards of democracy, without true public service and yet not knowing that the House of Commons is in charge. Without any true gentlemen!

Perhaps the function of aristocracy is to erode by the introduction of or part replacement by the new super-rich multi-billionaires of the ex-communist states of Russia, China and India, who by lack of Governmental control in going politically democratic, succeed in slicing off huge portions of the emerging wealth industries for themselves by exploitation of the simple knowledge by self manipulation of the early emergence stages before the wealth is available to all.

Yet for reasons that concern stability of peace and peace of mind there is no public spirit included or likely to be included in this latest development.

Today is my birthday hence I feel the need to be realistic with all my dates and time. Being born in December 1914 I can look backwards though World War I and see the Battle of Trafalgar in 1805, when Emperor Napoleon of France, so supremely sitting beyond Cape of Trafalgar of Spain, decided to destroy the British fleet and invade England. However Admiral Nelson became the hero to save Britain on the second great battle that followed the attempted

Spanish Armada in May 1588. Both occasions are clearly a little back in time as are the battles before them but led to the road to democracy via our own King John with the Knights of Parliament to authorise his wishes. And so through Oliver Cromwell and the Union of Scotland and England.

My disjointed fraction of history is only to focus on changes on the way to democracy which commenced by aristocracy. The time is so short from the ancient Pyramids' construction to the technicalities of our pieces of democratic influence: mobile telephones, computers, fuel rockets, space walks, nuclear projects, inter planetary connections and more yet I have no idea what the forces will be in a thousand years or even twenty, fifty or one hundred years hence.

The greatest influence really was the coming of Christ, so beautifully presented by Leonardo de Vinci in his painting 'The Last Supper' as well as other religions represented throughout the planet Earth.

CHAPTER 19

1987 – problems with the Company

AN UNUSUAL YEAR IN WHICH I HAD many problems to solve which restricted my basic development of real company sales progress so to increase the budget with freedom to operate safe expansion.

I decided to dispense with one of my staff, the accountant inherited from my previous qualified senior accountant company secretary, who wanted time to sail his boat so decided to leave to join the Gas Board! The inherited fellow was not qualified and I could not find the extra time to watch over his artful ways. Unfortunately his eyes were shifty and so perhaps covered up a doubtful past. Why he was employed I do not know. However I had insisted on a junior accountant to run sales control and purchase control so as to get accurate budget figures more quickly leading to proper accurate account monthly figures and on time within five days of the month end.

The result was that the fellow, the inherited accountant, pressed his brother to become involved to secretly supply the Inland Revenue at their headquarters in Bristol with false information on my yacht as some sort of revenge on his departure.

It was a clever piece of work, concerning my yacht built in 1963 and its replacement in 1972 out of my private personal money from the sale of my company at the time of my retirement from the fiasco of my connection with the oldest abrasive company in the world, which had been born in 1623 with the brightest brass plated steam engine in England, plus abrasives with the same total turnover today as at the turn of the century. They did not need my expertise, my services or the utilisation of my synthetic resin knowledge so vital to their survival.

I always cover my work in great detail to ensure correct accuracy. The files concerning the boats were requested by the Inland Revenue and there was no problem to supply them; they included all building information at in stage costs with totals from my private bank account. The files were taken away and later returned in full with no comment or extraction as they were of no interest to the Inland Revenue.

Strange things happen; the Chief Tax Inspector had just departed the Inland Revenue to join the forerunner Coopers & Lybrand (C&L), a large firm with headquarters in Queen Victoria Street in the city of London. (Later it merged with the well known accountants Price Waterhouse.)

In my opinion a rather nasty young man of the Inland Revenue took over my case and spent lots of his time chasing me, spending a very long time singlehandedly making an audit of the company books suggesting major differences some ten years old but obtaining no proof.

The first real Inland Revenue meeting of the many that took place with the ex tax inspector was round the dining room table of my house with the principal nasty man sitting in my chair, also doing an inspection of the house looking for valuables and estimating my worth, much to the annoyance of the ex Chief Tax Inspector, now poacher turned gamekeeper accountant for Inland Revenue problems and C&L.

In 1992 I was on a visit to the USA. It was an important visit because the British exchange rate was faltering after the government had gone into the European Exchange Rate Mechanism (ERM) about two years previously at a rate of nearly 3 Deutschmarks to the pound sterling. Everyone at the time thought this a ridiculously high rate value for the pound and thought the Prime Minister, ex Chancellor of the Exchequer, knew more than we. This high rate had caused havoc in our European market, and also particularly in the USA, so I provided a company exchange rate with important customers, otherwise we would lose their essential sales now firmly in our budget and financial programme.

Our private company exchange rate was to follow fluctuations within a 10 per cent margin plus or minus our actual agreed set price. Should the fluctuations beat this range we would need to review the agreed set price and set a new one if possible. This was reason for my visit to the USA.

As I was about to leave Philadelphia for the airport to fly for about two hours to be with my best USA customer the next day, I received a call from my works director to say a Barclays Bank assistant had called on a normal yearly routine visit to check the company's hire purchase agreements with the assistant accountant and had motivated a private dispute about our overdraft level with the assistant accountant who had provided an inaccurate answer. The assistant accountant wanted to prove his worth for the senior accountant position, now recently vacant. Consequently I needed to return home to settle whatever I needed to settle but for me there was no problem at all with Barclays Bank figures, as all were within my budget and programme. Whilst away, on holiday or on business travel, I always updated my figures on daily contact with my office.

Thus I immediately taxied to the airport and flew home overnight; however I was slightly annoyed to miss out on the rest of my important USA visit and for the works' director's lack of effort to control the staff situation caused. In the morning I called the senior manager of Barclays Bank, who had recently replaced the good previous senior manager, to ask for an explanation and make a date for my intended visit. The conversation was a little tense but polite until the manager asked me to call with my personal Coopers & Lybrand audit accountant for he needed to talk over security matters.

Next day my C&L audit accountant came to see me. I told him the strange story and off we went together to Barclays Bank to be welcomed by the senior bank manager. The immediate discussion concerned the bank's directors' seats at the Portsmouth Football Club, with my audit accountant asking about the use of the seats for entertainment of his clients. Here agreement was settled quite quickly. I did think, 'How odd,' in view of my important visit to discuss financial matters reported to me for settlement. I should say here that Barclays Bank was well known by me and others for arranging a junior assistant to call on matters to cause a spiteful situation, so the senior manager could settle by being very polite and pleasant. To me this way of working was a farce, but here I was with no notice being taken yet of my problem visit.

Eventually the senior bank manager asked my audit accountant if he would kindly check the value of my premises and building, and agreement was reached to do so. However instead of using my usual prominent local valuation agent the two agreed to appoint a small agent via my company accountants. We departed and although I had disagreed with the new situation, I was told not to worry about the call of the Barclays Bank junior manager for all was OK. I did think the position was most odd.

For some days I talked to my staff concerning the bank incident and we agreed it would not happen again for there was no need, but they should be responsible for settling a problem that did not need to occur. All was peaceful despite the trouble with the Government and its ERM causing inflation plus a possible minus profit figure for me to add to the company's bottom line. After seven days the small valuation agent called on his own, went about the business of valuation and departed without a word except 'Hello' and 'Goodbye'.

Very soon afterwards Barclays Bank called for me to meet them. I did so to be told the valuation was disastrous for there was no value to sell in today's circumstances, because it was a specialist business, and an owner like me might not be found. My next meeting was with my audit accountant at the bank. The senior manager told me I did not have enough security to support the overdraft and also suggested I was getting a bit too old to be such an active Chairman and Chief Executive (CEO) and should take a more restful position as Executive Chairman of Directors. He suggested the appointment of an acting new Managing Director (MD) for a three month period, while I found a new more permanent MD. This suggestion was quite a shock to me yet my chief audit accountant agreed and said he would help recruit a temporary MD on my behalf.

The stage had been set for it seemed I was falling into a deep, well organised Barclays Bank trap with the southern chief office audit manager participating in the deceit heavily with them to achieve my downfall at any cost. Yet previously the bank had really competed for my business which was one of the best in Portsmouth and the south coast; the bank had said so in writing.

In hindsight the trap was well organised, for Barclays Bank had heavy unreliable debts in the Third World that they could not collect, together with the position of a fluctuating inflation ERM situation pushing them into a difficult UK position. They could not recover any long term debts from the very large companies because of the overdraft amounts to relieve their position, with the cunning way of devaluating security so that you either went possibly bankrupt or underwent a forced sale at a false low price, so to organise collection of our loan payment on the sale or bankruptcy.

To move on: I had to go along with the duplicity of the audit manager, a very flamboyant character. I interviewed the only two possible recommended likely applicants of my auditors. Of the two qualified accountant applicants the first seemed overworked and the second was under average height, back from a skiing holiday and unemployed. The audit manager agreed and confirmed the choice of the two.

I cleaned up my office position for the new occupant. It possessed three viewing windows to see what went on outside for I was conscious of staff walking about to talk to other staff, which I knew was often not necessary and if it was necessary then I would look into the problem, for the time spent carrying messages was unproductive. I also considered that the new temporary MD should see the deliveries of raw materials in and our product deliveries out, together with the in and out flow of works staff for I some time ago had stopped all employees' clocking in and out. I moved into my operations office next door. I also commenced my programme of MD initiation duties whilst I retained all technical budget and financial control yet the MD would need to work within my budget figures.

The day soon came with the new temporary man arriving late but on the right day. I was ready to guide him through his duties with the introduction of my staff, the new company qualified accountant secretary, whom I had put in charge of finance, eventually to become the chief accountant.

This temporary MD for three months was costing £250,000 a year although I thought the rate excessive and from day one he was nasty and aggressive to my mind, towards both staff and myself, as though he knew everything and wanted everything and that we all knew so little. Fortunately I had the consequences covered in my Directors' minutes, but that caused an attack about cheque signing and my superior Executive Chairman position. After two weeks of turmoil and deliberate lack of production to budget I consulted my company solicitor and family accountant together. I stated: 'I wish to fire this foolish temporary MD.' We waited until near the first month end when I issued a irrevocable immediate notice of termination of employment, which he received silently and off he went from the premises.

This ex temporary MD did not go home. He talked to Barclays Bank and the audit accountant and after a day or so the bank telephoned to tell me immediately to take this fellow back or they would close the business I had built up over the last twenty-five years or more.

Naturally after a consultation with my solicitor I ordered new accountants to come in and produce a new balance sheet and profit and loss account, which was done over the next long weekend for the bank to compare figures with Coopers & Lybrand. The bank was not interested and issued the re-engagement order to be possible under enhanced conditions; I felt I had no alternative but to agree. What I did not know at the time was that the new accountant partner had made a friendly relationship on deceitful conditions and matters to gain monetary gains for the future.

As I was losing control of some vital parts of my system I as controlling shareholder decided to sell the Company and therefore set in motion my decision via companies that had already enquired. I naturally did this exercise with my new partner accountant, who at the time I thought was honest; however when one of my giant USA rivals was exceptionally interested and came on a works inspection visit, the MD and the partner accountant seemed not interested. They were however interested enough overnight to gum up the efficient works with broken window glass. The strictly systemised production was a shambles with piles of rubbish, and the accountancy figures distorted to prevent the outlook favourable to my cause.

I suspected a deceitful manoeuvre to prevent a possible sale and this was confirmed by an inadequate complicated offer in writing the partner accountant put in on behalf of the temporary MD, which was the first of many. I was shocked to find this duplicity, hence from now on decided to control any future sale by myself, alone. I now discussed my sale programme away from the company plant with my solicitor to keep matters closed and only open to me.

Black Wednesday came along on 1 September 1992, the day the Prime Minister John Major with Chancellor Norman Lamont crashed out of the ERM; it was also the day that interest rates went through10%, 12% to 15% and more after spending billions of sterling in a doomed effort to keep the pound within the ERM range. Thus my company could now trade freely and expansion of export was assured until it covered 40% of my business at its eventual sale date.

In the meantime many distasteful events took place, Although Coopers & Lybrand had carried out the annual audit of company accounts for the year, the chief auditor, head of the southern office programme, had changed our agreed policy of presentation through the intervention of the new accountant, the temporary MD who organised a process of trying to make the company's figures worse than they really were, for his gain. I had to use the accounts to pass at my annual general meeting of shareholders, held at our Portsmouth factory plant. My system was to always add an inspection of the new working production equipment and after the business meeting to take the shareholders on a visit to the city to see whatever was old or new before lunch and afterwards they went off home.

At this friendly business meeting the new MD and the C&L chief auditor were in attendance for I, the Chairman, felt it was necessary. However the new MD chose to disrupt the meeting by bringing up a very old settlement of the Inland Revenue dispute about which the auditors had agreed and a previous AGM had approved. In saying it was not right, the chief auditor present decided to agree with the silly MD's protest. I had to calm things down for good.

Unfortunately my senior solicitor gave full details and broke the confidential no-speak arrangement agreed between him and me. He apologised but the damage was done. The information obtained was used by the new MD to make another offer to buy, but basically he had no money so was trying various ways of to get it. 3i, to whom I had paid back a original 17½% interest loan still had some preference shares so I notified them of my intentions. They were happy to sell with me, but the MD had been in conversation with them so they sent me a letter saying I could not have a consultancy fee, after the sale, above a small amount, for this method was being abused. However, when I received the MD offer it included a consultancy fee of £30,000 per year for up to five years. I eventually accepted this figure, the use of my services was challenged and I went to HM High Court and won my case. The successful challenge no doubt was the persuasion factor with 3i and used to obtain their permission; the contract payment had to be paid plus expenses. However that was not the end of the story as I will explain later.

I continued with my sales to the USA portable tool company, but even so they only wanted to pay asset value so I was disappointed but continued discussions with their take-over accountant. When I eventually received the MD offer it was a little above the USA stolen offer, but included the consultancy agreement.

I held a meeting to approve the sale and although the MD was there, he was partly difficult; however the shareholders approved my plan and were pleased at the price per share, but it was a disappointment to me, after leading my company, manufacturing technical high quality abrasives, with multi million pound sales, 40% export with a substantial USA market and thirty years work from scratch and losing my qualified company pioneering son on the way in 1974 which was a very great loss to me.

I called the MD a crook, working to the extremes of the legal rules, who was supported by Barclays Bank and Coopers & Lybrand, to complete the kill via the wicked trap set by the accountant partner that caused instability for the own personal greed of the MD and himself; and 3i for lack of resistance to defend the company's agreed policy.

This was not the end for I possessed a consultancy agreement and was still working as the technical expert in the committee of the Normalisation European Standard of safety for power tools and accessories, including abrasives. This necessitated travel to my committee friends in Germany for the Brussels HQ mandate, which is the technical quality standard today for all member countries of the European Union, akin to the safety standard of the USA and additional overseas countries.

I created an office near my garage at home and equipped it with the necessities of an office, including a computer for me to learn to use and also a word processor, via one-finger typing. From the start the MD, now the owner of my company, prevented me doing technical work for the British Standards Institution and tried to replace me on the European Committee but failed. The MD stated that I had to report to him monthly in writing. I was not to travel on the companiy's behalf. So I behaved like a gentleman should and got on with the job which required my desk and files from my vacated operations room at the Portsmouth plant.

The questions were difficult to report on or they were partly technical; obviously the chemist and his staff were told to do something abstract or from a technical book to fox me. I stuck to my task and provided reports but payments were delayed and I had to fight for them, later with threatening letters. I reported to my solicitor the difficulties.

Quite out of the blue I was sent comments from Portsmouth University on my reports. Whilst providing primitive knowledge of a chemistry nature, they were not practical to me, hence I put them on one side. However the MD kept asking for me to include the university reports as part of mine and I kept repeating my refusal.

Then the MD stopped payment of my fee. Although it took time via my solicitor, then the non QC barrister, then the final QC counsel up to the date of the High Court trial and later for its issued judgment, it indicated the MD had to pay me in full including my expenses. Almost immediately the MD's solicitor stated that if I issued court proceedings the MD and company would go bankrupt, hence we worked out a deal by instalments; but even these were difficult to obtain whether through the solicitor or direct.

The MD had since his purchase of the company changed the bank to TSB (later Lloyds TSB) and borrowed money, despite removing all assets from the company to his own personal account. He had taken in a month advance of debtors, and spent a huge amount of money on sponsoring Formula 3 drivers and cars motor racing, using company staff at weekends to waiter and serve his guests at meetings. He also did a ridiculously expensive take-over of a small company where I had competed with new automatic plant, high quality abrasive products taking parts of the turnover for free and purchased expensive cars for himself and some new sales manager.

I wrote, 'You will go bankrupt unless you pack up motor racing and the reckless spending of company cash,' so at a difficult meeting the MD promised to pay the first instalment of £80,000 in cash the next day. I sent down to collect but got no response, though I did extract the money within 14 days, on a fixed schedule. The next problem was the payment of my expenses of the High Court action. The MD plus his solicitor argued with my solicitors and would not pay my hotel expenses amongst many other things via taxation agents; and so, with the weakness of my own solicitors, I lost some £100,000 or more of my expenses concerning the solicitors, counsel, movements, and so on. That was the end, I hoped, of what I considered the crooks of the business game.

I was eighty years old in 1994, and having released myself from the turmoil of my expenses for HM High Court case, I looked around for a small business to buy and run. I met a qualified accountant agent in the south who seemed to have a few companies some of which were in financial difficulties. By this time I was hungry for work. After all I was sixty when my son was killed on a Saturday after late work helping the store manager to overcome his backlog of dispatch, when he came home and departed for an evening entertainment with his friends when he was about to be made Managing Director.

I had packed up thoughts of retirement and heavily involved myself in working to take my son's place for the future having departed my company in 1993 after giving up all pleasure activities to so work; I felt I must have to use my time.

I visited three or four small companies, one a medical company sterilising and packing medical instruments. I became interested and paid the small amount of wages to keep it from closing whilst I had meetings to verify my interest. Unfortunately I found this accountant agent was getting involved with the management and the chief director was operating some other personal companies so there was no expertise to sell and when I worked on the accounts I discovered that orders for most production was fictitious so I lost interest.

I was also given the introduction to a small 'safety tool clutch lock' partnership of husband and wife working from the dining room in their house. I was shown a small precision working model of a Fairey Huntsman motor yacht which kindled my strong interest in the workmanship of the likely small clutch, although I found the accounts overestimated sales which in fact were very small indeed and not profitable. In fact I found the partnership being worked to the accountant's own figures which were so inaccurate for he was using the participation of this small company to advertise his own accountant's business.

I took over the partnership and created a Limited Company with the idea of using my power tool knowledge to manufacture the small fail-safe clutch power tool, and increase its value: to be a complete system concerning the installation of extraction goods for the exit of smoke and fire on contracts concerning safety of personnel.

Unfortunately an unfortunate situation occurred after ten years' work which will follow in a final chapter.

CHAPTER 20

Motor cars and my clock

MY INTEREST IN MOTOR CARS has always been profound. In my early schooldays I remember the vivid image I experienced of my father's bullnose Morris coming home for the first time to face me kneeling down to watch the event. The car slowly coming up the gradient into the garage with the dark honeycomb radiator advancing looked so menacing. It was tall with a thermometer in a glass circle pedestal on the top: a terrific experience never forgotten throughout my life.

Shortly afterwards I was able to help clean the car for the first real pocket money and was happy with my welcome task. The façade of the car was real, the protrusions to be seen as you drive were instructive, advising the mechanical condition of the vehicle at all time. At this period in history of the motor vehicle there was no examination or driver's test to pass; you just learnt to drive the best way you could, mainly on your own but of course you must remember there were very few vehicles on the highways, primitive or good, to encounter.

To drive you just needed to apply for a licence year by year to be issued with no demands at all, most unlike today. I obtained my motor cycle licence at sixteen years old for the racing international Norton my father gave me, which had previously been owned by my sister's fiancé. It gave me such a thrill and pleasure with or without the sidecar; however I am doubtful of the benefit to my sidecar passenger who as I have previously mentioned was the local beauty queen who took exception to parting from me as we went each side of the side wall over the local river horse bridge to halt in situ.

Although I was now well obsessed with the wish to learn to fly aeroplanes, I was keen to develop my interest in motor cars at the time to achieve all weather transport to and fro whatever! Hence I bought a second hand dark blue Triumph motor car paid for by myself. This car had a chromium grid which to me looked a little flimsy, hiding the true honeycomb radiator; however the appearance of the polished motor car was that of a sophisticated motor car of today though a little prehistoric for today's designs.

I somehow changed to a little two seater Austin 'Nippy' in a beautiful scarlet red which was of course a gorgeous way to attract young people, but it was not so good to transport a family of three, four or over and thus caused a separation from my girlfriend's widowed mother and my actual relationship after I had learnt to fly with the Royal Air Force Reserve. However the 'Nippy' was excellent for rugby, to get to and from work, and social travel on Sundays.

All things have to change; I was posted to London and domiciled in a convenient hotel within walking distance of my new office with the need to study for my technical skills in the evenings, hence I was pedestrian bound until the weekend when I went off to fly at Hatfield or to go home to near Birmingham. Soon the company provided a new 100s Standard Blue motor car, so I let go of my faithful 'Nippy' and commenced serious weekend flying against the threat of war with Nazi Germany. So began a six-year break in the Royal Air Force from late 1939 to mid 1945. Through this break I drove other cars for leave and the Humber shooting brake that I modified for the technical navigation survey of Iceland. I did not own a car again until the saloon Austin Seven I bought soon after my marriage in 1943 on settling down with the Royal Air Force stations in the UK.

The Austin Seven was an absolute brick for work in the difficult petrol rationing period; I tried most things offered including high octane aircraft fuel mixed with paraffin, but the Seven's engine used all. After approximately 500–1000 miles it was necessary to dismantle the engine completely for the main bearings to be checked or rebuilt and ground down to fit the crankcase shoulders; all eight valves were removed with the springs cleaned and the valve seats to be reground in to the reground engine seats by using abrasive paste. The cylinder head was removed and ground to suit the valves and the pistons withdrawn to clean the rings of black carbon and any sticky stuff, so leaving the piston rings flexible to control the compression and oil consumption, A new joint gasket was fitted with cleaned and clearance adjusted sparking plugs on reassembly of the whole engine.

Naturally I did not carry out the work; it was necessary to persuade a local garage to carry out the engineering and reconditioning under my supervision to ensure accuracy as the workers were relatively unskilled at this hard time with no engine spares available.

Tyres were another problem; often the only ones available were inconsistently re-treated tyres, some lasting less than a thousand miles, being scarce and expensive too! All cars needed top-ups of grease to go anywhere for any serious joints such as both steering wheel channel joints used on the road, A hand high pressure pumping grease gun was used under very dirty oily conditions on the mud splattered car.

Eventually I returned to civilian life and my staff appointment in plastics, thus I was presented with a new car, a brand new Singer streamlined and of modern design, 1945/46 mark, Most of the large manufacturers at this time were still using 1939 designs, materials and shape; the only other car with a new design I knew of was the Riley. I felt proud of my new Singer but in 1946 decide to leave my lifelong Bakelite plastics appointment to develop a new type of abrasive sanding disc for the motor car industry, thus I forfeited my new car.

As I was living in a London mews and working close by I had no real urgent need for a car, but my two company partners possessed cars. One had just sold his Lanchester motor for a short boot Bentley. When I later moved house and borrowed the Bentley, it was super and so impressed me that I promised myself a Bentley one day. My wife agreed. We lived in Surrey without a motor car and I journeyed to and from London, Marylebone with the very early Green Line Express non stop bus as transport in the morning and the late night return the same day. It was enjoyable but tiring to get the business started and also to train my partners in the technical necessities of working phenol formaldehyde synthetic resin Bakelite to conform to specific daily multi hour shift times. I had to take the 'vital cure'. This is because we made our own ovens to my specification, but we could only manipulate sheet steel and angle iron for construction, hence the cure was inclined to be uneven which is fatal for accuracy and quality. Hence I devised lower temperature cure cycles for different stages of production quality, rewound to ensure accuracy of the preliminary stage at $80°$ Celsius, water stage at $100°$, first curing stage at $110°$ and after twelve hours or so the final stage at $135°$, all to produce semi flexible abrasives obtained by extracting the resin film situated on a flexible fibre backing, for the motor car industry. We supplied a better quality by far than the major USA giant suppliers who were just about to lose their superior position in the UK motor car industry. Three of us were working twenty-four hours daily at different times depending on the time taken for production and disassembly of completed products.

Owing to formidable quality success we eventually moved to larger premises in Hayes, Middlesex and after some time I bought a good second hand slightly larger Standard than the old one possessed before the outbreak of war. I kept this for a year or so before switching to a Ford 'Zephyr', six cylinders with almost completely new design and intensely reliable for urgent business in the war-devastated, laid to waste Europe. Many journeys were necessary to develop our quality abrasive high speed disc product at home so soon the 'Zephyr' had high mileage and was short of necessary internal space.

Being so busy, I asked my wife to call the local garage I had noticed on my way to meet an important business person at the Royal Automobile Club near my home. I was thinking about an Armstrong Siddeley 'Sapphire'. Within twelve hours my wife said to me, 'I have the "Sapphire" out for a demonstration tomorrow at 0830 hours.' I was impressed, so with the Zephyr in part exchange I switched to the 'Sapphire'. It was very good for business, though it had drawbacks for European travel because of the necessary complicated removal of the rear wheel spats or part covers which would not fit into the flying track of the quick airlift aircraft to cross the Channel to France for an important and often urgent visit to Germany.

The car was a very good workhorse until I fell under a short financial lapse in business causing me to sell it at the same time I was moving house to Camberley, Surrey to be on a straight road to Hayes for I was working long hours. (Incidentally the beautiful house was bought for less than £6,000 in 1959/60, just to keep you in touch with the prices at the time.)

I did acquire a very good old Lagonda for some time but when things financially straightened out with it not really suitable for business I switched back to the 'Sapphire' until 1962 when with the business going very well and with the recommendation of my wife for the immense amount of travel in Europe and overseas together with staying away from home at Portsmouth, for our new factory production running in, I switched to a Bentley 'Silver Cloud', a fantastically good car for Europe, UK and all duties; it gave me much working pleasure.

In 1962 owing to the Rolls-Royce 'Shadow' being massed produced for the first time I switched to the 'Silver Shadow' priced just about £6,000 and the Bentley exchanged for a little less. The Rolls-Royce I exchanged for many years at very little cost, for the cars were so difficult to obtain, with a year or so waiting list, so the would be customers would pay over the new price for a used car in reasonable condition; hence for a year or so I enjoyed a new no-cost Rolls-Royce although the price was always on the increase.

Next I fitted a portable telephone which nearly filled the boot with the handpiece in the arm of the rear seat; it was a great asset as I was able to work and telephone as if I was in my office with calls to Europe, USA and elsewhere at will. As I told you, after a few months I met a busy business man and he said he had switched his Rolls-Royce for a Spur model for it was six inches longer which made his car work that much easier; I did the same and got so much more work done travelling as I could spread the papers better in the extra space without my feet getting in the way.

So I went on until 1993 when I was forced to sell out at an active seventy-nine years old, when through necessity I parted with my old Rolls-Royce for a very low mileage Bentley which I kept for a year or so. I found however it was sometimes difficult to park without attracting unwelcome attention, so I switched to a five series BMW which I find suitable for my present needs at now over ninety years old.

I think of my experience with Rolls-Royce and Bentley. The first 1933/34 Bentley I ever noticed was when riding my international Norton motorcycle near Henley-in-Arden, in Shakespeare country; in my opinion the best of all with cycle mudguards with a black box type separate boot on the stern, lost for ever in later models. The 1962/63 'Silver Cloud' was a magnificent vehicle for the job in hand, recalling my friend's Bentley with the short boot. In 1948, however, Bentley joined up with Rolls-Royce and like everyone else one moved to the new RR, who were now responsible for both models, doomed to look alike and feel the same. About this time I was journeying to the works at Crewe to sort specifications for the next car, on the waiting list. Very much later on I was picked up from the station in a Ford car and asked, 'Why no Rolls-Royce?' The answer was, 'We can no longer afford to collect people from the station; you notice people not Rolls-Royce customers,' thus the tide changed and I was not to be the Rolls-Royce owner I thought I was!

Still, all went well for a time until my regular visits to Italy proved too much for the car. The heavy new front opening door hinges holding the doors started to break loose, necessitating tying the doors through the open window.

Democracy was changing the petty crime situation through the new expressed belief that all are all equal or intending to be all equal so why should I have a different car? For my office therefore only I used a 'Senator', to me a very superior Vauxhall car for so many diverse duties and ensuring the state of play was equal with no fingers crossed for all to see. Before this time the RR was the symbol of a company capable of safe financial standing and superior quality of product; now it was often thought the symbol of a fiddling pretentious chief of pretence. In my view the Rolls-Royce company never recovered from this status. Later of course the Rolls-Royce almost disappeared with the sell-out of Vickers Rolls-Royce plant to VW motors in Germany, but the rivalry forgot BMW's interest in the aero engine licence with Rolls-Royce and its registered name. After a period of years VW seem to have fought off the old fashioned Mercedes to now offer a consistent Bentley at £120,000 plus, depending on the new model, whereas BMW have built a factory in the south of England mainly to import German parts to create a Rolls-Royce for the very few UK and overseas markets. However the names of Bentley and Rolls-Royce have mostly disappeared for the time being. They did symbolise UK quality products.

It's unlike the Rolls-Royce aero engines that were going down the same way, but this was stopped by the Conservative government legislation some time ago, so unlike the Labour government with the last UK car manufacturers of Rover, Austin, Morris and others, having no direction either before European interference legislation or after.

I should explain that before the war, a three bedroom house would cost £650 and a new small car was £100. Naturally the demand was only just breaking out. The war virtually stopped everything except the spirit and the munitions, hence the blank years to 1945 created a low domestic volume, in bad economic circumstances; banks were short of money and reluctantly lending at 17–18 per cent interest at least, for some time. However the movement towards a 'superior domestic scene' continued at increased cost with little improvement in demand, until democracy of the people influenced the government programme, here, in Germany, the rest of Europe and later the United States of America, increasing the competitive demand for motor cars in the domestic market, until we have many two-car families. All is so different due to triggering of the demand, with improvement precision working, unfortunately causing massive inflation to account for the huge difference in price, a small motor car today costing £6–8,000 sterling.

Because of competition and demand, it has nearly saturated the Western world, to create a global problem: how to increase demand and accept more competition by reducing poverty of the poorer nations, except for China, where the communist Emperors need to change the mass population to democracy to achieve the same freedoms as in the West.

I have more to tell you about my family motor cars. After the last war, my wife's mobile transport started with my purchase of her first pedal bike with a push down back pedal brake, but after moving away to live outside the City of London, we replaced her transport with a Triumph TR3 and later considered a TR4 replacement. However she progressed to an 'E type' Jaguar, a very fine car, and after tremendous service, we switched to the improved 'E type V12', with a perfect engine of 12 cylinders. It did stop occasionally, when a kind of safety valve or thermostat cut in, if the engine became too hot, but apart from this malfunction for the introduction year only, it was so smooth and quiet. In fact I did write to Rolls-Royce and asked them to adopt the engine for their old-fashioned 6 ½ litre V8, instead of trying to obtain a foreign replacement.

The 'E type' was small for inside space and comfort, so Jaguar introduced the XJS, a beautiful design. On any trip to Europe, it would command a lot of attention and that was my wife's parting wish; however she soon parted with the XJS for petrol not paid by me was considered too expensive. Before this episode, I had acquired a Jenson 'Interceptor', a very fine motor car with a normal Chrysler USA engine. It was good and safe, except for one day. I left my boat, after mooring before lunch, to return home in a hurry to prepare for an urgent business appointment at 10.00 hours on Monday in the north of England. The weather was showery and whilst going a fair speed the car slipped on a wet corner. It decided to turn on application of the brakes; on release of the brakes the car continued turning, so I followed and waited for the car to be in the opposite direction, while still doing a fair speed. I looked to see there was no traffic, before applying the brakes to slow down, to find a place to turn so to resume my original compass course home, The car was perfectly stable throughout its circle.

My elder daughter Dianne Gayle, like all children of driving age, wanted a car, and it so happened our neighbour was selling an old Renault at a remarkable price, hence it became the property of my daughter. On her third or fourth time out, I received an urgent call to say she had broken down. I was busy so my garage brought her home. Apparently she was out visiting, and needed to refuel, for as usual she was inclined to run out. She went a little faster than usual and the petrol engine, in the rear, apparently ran out of water coolant. The engine atmosphere felt hot inside, but she still hurried on, as no steam had been visible. She still continued for further period and on running out of oil, the engine stopped with a small bang, for good. Now she opened the boot at the front and said to the first person to help, 'Let's open the rear boot,' and she found the spare engine, but it was hot and would not start. Thus the explanation of the car failure was put together, which resulted her call for assistance.

This odd situation was typical of my daughter at the time and for some time later; however she loved the red VW 'Beetle' replacement. During many years' service the car behaved impeccably, and on one occasion, I enjoyed an exceptional surprise lift. When I was safely belted in we set off to give me a new view of the countryside I so loved. We arrived a very short distance north of the village of Rogate nearby, and entered the woodlands, just south of the lane, on the ridge.

I was now taken for an enthusiastic ride, the driver carefully keeping to the grass fire breaks, horse tracks or footpaths, at quite a gentle speed, a little too fast for me though. However it was a thrilling ride, through bright shining pine trees and true green earthly nature, with even the odd hind to circumnavigate, in pure moist air, on a privileged vibrant excursion of ultimate pleasure. On arriving graciously home, I did congratulate the Beetle with a kind thank you, dear daughter!

My daughter's next was a VW 'Polo', to me a nondescript, but it possessed a good ex ballet dancer's driving seat, for she had a tall shoulder problem and at each change she took her old driving seat out, to have fitted within the new car, and threw away the new one, to the consternation of the garage onlookers.

I supplied her with a four seat Polo recently, to give more room, but again the seat was not possible and the current old one was also not possible, so after much hoo-ha, it was decided to sell the new car. We were fortunate to receive the only answer to our advertisement, from an Air Force pilot, so on my reputation of some sixty years back, it was handed over by my daughter. The pilot thought and bought.

Now she is very happy with a Toyota 'Yaris', difficult to believe, but all is well, the seat perfect for height and comfort, but no ABS (braking system) on the beautiful Ionian Island of Kefalonia, with fondest present memories of her herbal books so beautifully written and illustrated, for ever.

My younger daughter Doodey, who in England worked for the Foreign Office and was seconded later to HRH Princess Diana (later Princess Diana with no HRH owing to events we know), was on leave and married a Greek Professor of mathematics. They started off with a small Fiat and an old Peugeot from a lovely house over the hills of Athens. It is always a wonder to me how the motor cars survive, however, with the ultimate congestion on nearly all roads. I find I am more confused or congested now than the motor car; however Greece is lovely, warm sea all around and so peaceful away from the herd.

I have a little place for myself and acquired a left hand drive Chrysler 'Voyager' to help move the family and me, so also enjoyed many very interesting and pleasant informative journeys through Europe to the UK, some via Venice, Como, Paris, Basel, Marseilles, Bordeaux and St Malo, for the benefit of both grown ups and children. The 'Voyager' gave no trouble at all, except for registration, but the parting came and the programme continued in a Peugeot '307' with much better fuel consumption, a much lighter very roomy body, and really many ultra modern electronic sensors and fitments. It does miss, if you need it, the possibility of walking or at least moving from seat to seat, for the 'Voyager' had linked with Mercedes and copied the hand brake system to create space between the front seats for pedestrian traffic, if need be, for picnics and the like.

I have travelled much of Greece including the beautiful north, which can remind you of Scotland in the cool of a hot temperature, or in the snow and frost of winter, with a weather system striking from still further north; however, the modern cars are not afraid. There are plenty of trusting wild mountains, and other parts where the 4 × 4 is essential driving, not at all like the Range Rover 4 × 4 hiking the footpaths and kerbstones of suburban London and elsewhere, but not in the country pursuits.

Now I close by saying my son's motor car was originally a Triumph 'TR4' in which he accompanied a Morgan owned by his friend John through many European journeys before switching to a Ford 'Capri' for business from which he unfortunately departed in 1974.

Of course I have driven more motor car types from Saab, Mercedes, Aston Martin and the like, from all of Europe – many different country types: Italian – so small with high revving engines you expect the tight elastic to break or your feet to extend through the front. Overseas – many types but in India only one, the old English Morris 'Oxford' produced in my friend's manufacturing plant, where I took luncheon American style in the fifties.

On one occasion in the United States it was necessary to hire a big Oldsmobile because I was in the airport at Fort Lauderdale to fly to England, but the Continental Airline aircraft I was booked on was supposed to fly from Miami. Hence the dash to do the normally nearly an hour journey in thirty minutes with only my wife to guide me. It was impossible yet we tried and arrived at the aircraft thirty-odd minutes late to the consternation of the impatient passengers and a big thank you to the reception lady to the airline to say we were on the way. On seating in 1A & 1B we were presented each with a personal pack of playing cards, a quantity of personalised book matches and an invitation to luncheon with our personalised name on top of our seat and of course an immediate glass of wine. After an efficient flight making up time we arrived home relaxed to start another day. The major difficulty was not checking in the hire car when meeting at the airline pick-up car immediately on arrival. I trust you enjoyed the tale without perspiration breaking at our panic.

On one other time in the USA, near Christmas 1943 or thereabouts the snow started coming down fast, likely for ever. I was asked if I could drive a plastics colleague home and I agreed in the course of conversation with my busy host, for I was staying the night.

I opened the Buick car door in the drive, and down came a large bucketful of snow. I did not know the Buick equipment or route, but the friend did, so I set course on directions of which way to go and what turnings to take. The roads could hardly be seen, let alone directions in the internal car mist due to trying to put our head out though the windows. We eventually arrived at my friend's home, to discover I did not know the way to my host's house, my home for the night. I received details on an envelope with verbal instructions that seemed not to be of the slightest use in the returning blind snow conditions.

I travelled a long way, over one slippery hour, and for some magical reason did arrive at the right snow covered place, with heavy snow still falling, and fell into bed, whilst the party still had to finish. The Buick motor car had survived and all was well.

Garages for my motor cars were not so strange.

When I was sixteen years old I passed my comprehensive initiation into motor cars, through the entry of my father's bull nose Morris whilst I was kneeling to see through the large honeycomb radiator.

My first car had a mixture of garages because I could not use my father's garage except when he was away. I was anxious to be meticulous in keeping the mechanical and body work beautiful, nevertheless it was all a good introduction into the nature of my future demands as well my future necessity, to ensure I always provided good maintenance and replacement combined with good looks.

At this time we all started the engine with a good turn of the starting handle, in unison with the crank that turned the main engine crankshaft, so the pistons, the valves and the movement of the petrol through the carburettor.

More often than not this was a doubtful method of starting all cars, new or old, because the hand clearances were only within hand tolerance; whether a portable or fixed starting handle the overall physical major effort was the same.

Thus any responsible owner would centrally heat his garage with a paraffin taper light or composing rugs on top of the warm engine, to get a temperature that made the whole starting much less physical effort, for without the right temperature starting often failed from physical exhaustion after repeat after repeat.

I placed my early cars always in a garage, perhaps cold or warm. The system changed to cars that had become more reliable to start without the fixed starting handle, owing to few tolerances at the vital parts. Then we came to World War II which necessitated a change for all machines and people, exposing our combined effort in the need to hide our weakness by advanced precision engineering.

Throughout the years of exposure most of our combined effort was a hide and seek battle won and to this day the precision engineering makes us fall dependent on others.

However in 1990 I was running a Rolls-Royce Silver Spirit and on opening my garage doors for the first time I spied a large 10-inch cast iron pipe, beautifully warm, working off the house central heating. I naturally thought what a wasteful way to heat a house, even though it was built in the twelfth century, but strangely I could see no way of turning the garage radiator off and did not try until I engaged an engineer to do so.

I gave a lot of thought to the owner cranking up his motor car in such a beautiful heat in his days gone by. Incidentally the real garage was a wooden coach house alongside the country highway, adjacent to the main gates which of course had been used for the family horse carriage. This was a little slower than today but needed no cranking to start, just a carrot or two to move itself at breakfast or later.

Whilst being stationed in Limavady we went through the situation of having two aircraft each, one to fly, one in repair or in reserve and to us it was the system of the Royal Air Force tradition, you knew your own team and respected each other. Suddenly the modern Air Force changed to adapt more productive ideas and customs which frankly was hard to bear for me in 1943.

Aircraft maintenance was introduced to provide aircraft at a point when a specific requirement was ready and waiting, so the personal responsibility was lost and we had no idea who had done what, how, and why, or if the aircraft had been tested. It seemed to me at the time it was a retrograde step with no personality involved to talk the pro's and con's with. After all, I felt my safety was important to me and my team or crew.

Other changes concerned training: we were all pilots, general duties; now we were to graduate and have half wings in the form of navigators or air gunners. Most of all women were to be introduced as batmen in our sleeping quarters and to other official duties as plotters.

Each aircraft was instrumented with an eight day clock that seemed to one a personal item. Now we started to receive an operational aircraft sometimes without a clock; when we enquired why, through the maintenance officer in charge to supply the aircraft, the vague answer was that the item was in short supply.

Clocks seemed to be getting fewer and fewer, particularly the older aircraft that needed more maintenance but they were the aircraft we were used to flying. This situation was often discussed in the Officers' Mess and it appeared some few officers enjoyed an aircraft clock in their possession and seemed to know where to get one from.

I was having quite a difficulty in trying to get certain aircraft I liked to fly on operations. The day arrived when the allocated aircraft had no clock to wind up and synchronise before checking all controls; this situation was annoying from the start although eventually one got used to the missing clock but missed the opportunity to glance at the time to note events. The pilot always possessed a wrist chronometer type watch so one could always get by, and as navigators came into being they had one watch too, so all was not lost.

However soon it was found that certain officer pilots carried a screwdriver so if they force landed an aircraft they could unscrew the clock for themselves; otherwise the general maintenance staff were perhaps likely to be the recipients.

One day I received an old favourite aircraft complete with clock for me to wind. I set it as soon as I boarded and sat down in my seat. I decided to let my second pilot fly the take-off that I described on an earlier page and after our accident all jumped out except me, for I needed to make the aircraft safe and casually asked the departing second pilot if he had a screwdriver. He threw one at me that landed on the deck at my feet.

The clock was my friend 'Kolsman 8-day'. They are wonderful clocks and I have kept this clock forever. My wife used it as our only clock and when it went a little off recently, I took it along to my friendly clockmaker for repair. The clock needed no repair but just a clean on the outside and today I have it before me. I wind it up as soon as I sit down at my desk and think what a wonderful friend it is! The clock knows me well. I saved its life as the aircraft was due to be written off. We have done some remarkable things together and I will never discard it.

CHAPTER 21

Fishing

FISHING IS ONE OF MY GREAT loves, learning first the thrill of catching a minnow on my own bent pin using a jam jar for my aquarium, whilst six or seven years old at junior school. I found the stream or narrow river Cole, walking over the horse bridge on the way to school. It took a year or so to come by the bent pin and the fine thread from my mother's work basket; the largish jar was an old marmalade jar, easy to find for they were always stacked on the pantry shelf destined for small pickled onions. The idea I picked up from watching older children on the way home from school was to learn to fish.

The opportunity came on the first day of the summer holiday. I set off with my treasured equipment at about ten o'clock and settled down kneeling on the selected small pool bank. I placed beside me the jar after filling it with clear river water in anticipation of catching a fish in quick time. After about an hour, although I could see minnow flashing bright silver, they appeared reluctant to swim near my hook. I regret to say that after a further period of time I emptied my water over the grass to place the jar in the clear water pool. I moved backwards away from the bank, and waited for a fish to enter my jar. After some long time I noticed a fish swimming around inside my jar and I gently removed it, losing half the water on running home, so excited. I immediately showed my mother who was eating her lunch with my sister Nancy and brother Jim. I of course was told off for being late but I did not care for I had caught my first fish and although in wet clothes and muddy boots I was so happy. I was ordered to change and eat lunch on my own with the jar on the table, not noticed by anyone.

I spent a lot of my time on the near banks of the River Cole, sometimes to fish with more refined equipment or just to scramble on the boughs of the trees over the river as I described earlier. I was interested in the horse bridge about three miles further down the river, where the willows swaying in the air caused flashes of dark and light patches of water running over stones and small rocks to form running pools where the large fish would feed and play to enlighten the water with silver gold flashes. I did spend some time between the two bridges, doing various activities apart from fishing: tree climbing, trying to swim in the large deep cold pools, watching the colourful kingfisher fleeting by, perhaps on his way to fish too, looking at the water meadow in all different seasons, sometimes with a bright yellow carpet of buttercups and later cowslips and iris abounded. Fishing in this period was interwoven with serious study and sport so it was more to look at; however with a better bamboo cane and real line using hand squeezed moist bread in a pellet or worm I looked for large fish of 8 to 12 inches, and this was rewarding. Sometimes it was less so for learning real fishing was expensive in time and money, with so much competition with school activities. However my interest would return soon for there was so much to learn yet about fishing.

Towards the end of my school days I became interested and fixated on flying and so neglected my desire to learn to fish. I looked forward to my month or so flying tuition in Ayrshire, but there at times I relaxed looking for trout in the burn near Robert Burns' cottage with the vivid inspiring poetry of 'Auld Lang Syne' lightly singing along with the heavenly breeze, as it does every year and verse time, in most countries of our planet Earth, perhaps with our moon also shining bright.

I left Scotland after qualifying for my wings, later to return on the outbreak of war, to walk with my beautiful girlfriend along the frothy stream near Crieff, flowing bright white over the rocks and stones and running pools dividing the trout into their own territory, for their own skirmishes of fly catching. I was learning of the habitat and nature of trout that would dominate my future knowledge of wet and dry fly fishing in so many countries.

Soon I was stationed at Limavady in Northern Ireland, in the Royal Air Force searching for German U boats to protect our vital supply convoy of ships, just before my episode concerning the sinking of the *Bismarck*. I was night flying as only one or two had survived to be still qualified to take the very early morning or late evening sorties, so in the daytime apart from playing social tennis I spent much of my time learning to fish for trout on the river Towey, an excellent river for medium size brown trout. With practice I did catch two or three on wet fly but was quite unskilled with dry fly casting, partly due to the difficulty of casting in the close hedgerows alongside the river, causing me to realise I had still a terrible lot to learn to become a trout fisherman.

After a few months I was on the shores of Lake Huron located in the Canadian part of the Great Lakes. I looked for fish but they were few and far between owing to the commercial pollution, but I did observe the heavens, to recognise Pisces and the like. During my waiting time I did some skiing practice in the Laurentian Mountains and recall on the way from Montreal halting my car at a frozen lake to watch and listen to a gentleman trying to catch fish through a hole in the ice. The weather was extremely frosty cold and the fisherman whilst not successful in my presence enjoyed my good luck wishes on my frost bite departure.

Arriving in England and home I was immediately stationed in Iceland and left Liverpool by boat to arrive in lovely dry spring weather. Apart from the Atlantic convoy duties for more German U-boats and reconnaissance German aircraft it was possible to enjoy fishing for salmon. An officer had requisitioned the best Icelandic reserves near glaciers falling as rivers into the clear dark blue sea via fiords sided by deep shiny black high rock cliffs. So we enjoyed without much effort fly fishing and poaching fresh Atlantic salmon of ten pounds or more with borrowed service rods. There were many misty and snowy days but on the good occasions the sun would shine and enhance our pleasure; flying also experienced the same cruel conditions with limited visibility.

Next I was the specialist Navigation Officer who surveyed Iceland as there was a need for successful landing grounds for aircraft flying into the UK from the USA. On departure from Iceland I journeyed through the Cromarty Firth, the Solway Firth, and the Firth of Forth before reaching Plymouth Hoe on the border of Devonshire over the Saltash ferry river to Cornwall. I did no fishing because of lack of opportunity except at Looe where there was shark fishing, but really found no interest in it, hoping I could fish in the trout and salmon streams and rivers nearby. They were good and readily available, but needless to say I failed to find the time owing to my Royal Air Force commitments and new parenthood duties. With victory secured, soon I was anxious to leave the service for I was destined to return to Bakelite and my lifelong contract now in the modern plastics chemical field.

After the 1945 final departure with some immense regrets from the Royal Air Force I enjoyed a lovely leave with my wife's family, playing golf round the local links course in perfect weather and being with my new daughter Dianne Gayle. I settled down to my civilian business duties in London HQ with a refresher course at the Birmingham works, near where I learnt to fish as a boy. However I found the atmosphere and colleagues somewhat stale for they were hesitant to hold a conversation with me for I was one of only two returning after being away at the excitement of war.

So later with my two fine service friends, I commenced the personal business in 1946 so all my time was necessary there, hence fishing was limited to reading books of famous fishermen's tales and instructions, in particular Isaak Walton, Skues and Oliver Kyte, just before going fast asleep: enchanting but I woke up with little recollection.

After the birth of our son Roger in 1948 my wife suffered from hay fever and when he was very young she was diagnosed with tuberculosis; although Midhurst was a well known treatment centre it was full and with a waiting list. We therefore relied on a friend consultant in the West Country; eventually all was well and cured. The consultant was an excellent fisherman and I was pleased to help him to obtain waterproof cotton or wool gear during my visits to the USA, whilst England was still under food rationing and austere clothing so there was no real fishing gear for river sport.

In the meantime our friends also in the south-west on the coast were kind enough to take in our two young children, and baptise Roger like two of their own. I was proud to visit whenever possible and help fish the delightful gin-clear river with my friend. I caught little, however; the small brown trout appeared like large aberrations, silver gold darts in quest for the gods of creation against the clean brown rocks of time with current ripples to tease my thoughts.

Half way through the fifties with the company doing very well indeed I visited New Zealand with my wife and as you know I fished for four- to six-pound rainbow trout on Lake Taupo, Rotorua, North Island. The exciting river rips emulate from the lake overfill; the lake is a perfect large water filled deep volcanic crater with warm circulatory streams within the area of Rotorua, where they bury the dead above ground because of the heat and they exhibit growing trout in warm trout streams in large glass river cages. With the prolific warm underwater vegetation the trout grow quite large and are not afraid to look you in the eye! Why? They have no reason not to!

The rip of ultra clear cascading water is full of ripple generated oxygen, and the trout grow on the plankton. I was handed a nine and a half foot split cane rod complete with reel, line and fly, with advice on how to perform. I followed precisely the advice, and enjoyed without inner expertise the thrill of two bites but no fish. Some distance away were five white New Zealanders and one Maori who seemed to me far more successful, fishing the rip at dusk, yet I was thrilled and satisfied with my try.

On reaching the UK and home I decided to commence practising fly casting at weekends providing I was not working or required for home duties. I purchased a lovely 8 ½ foot split cane 'Hardy' rod with a light 'Perfection' reel. A landing net was included in anticipation of taking a fish home, rather like the jam jar, taken for my first day ever fishing by the river Cole.

Next I placed double page sheets of newspaper at precise pool differences on the lawn and changed into fisherman's clothes, and took in hand my new rod and tackle to practise casting the fly to arrive on its newspaper destination. Any failure to arrive and settle the fly on the appropriate site would necessitate continuous practice casting until proficient, before going to the next site. It was tough and hard work with no respite for refreshment; anyway, there was nobody bothering to watch my antics.

As I was becoming proficient, I sorted out where to fish and was able to become a member of the River Meon fly fishing club, administered by a member of the Royal Navy, Portsmouth, near the new factory I was building. The Meon was a lovely small complete river from its source of spring water, through tranquil Hampshire green countryside to the sea outlet near Titchfield. The native brown trout were territorial, naturally situated according to their size, depending on the river holding water from source to sea. The largest fish would be approximately twelve inches in mid stream. In the estuary and the adjacent sea lived pink fleshed sea trout of twelve to fourteen inches; one would fish for them in the dusk and dark evenings. Trout are very territorial and defend their own habitat hence the river is never mixed, thus the sea trout stay at the estuary to the sea and so on. To learn and enjoy the art of fishing I spent many happy hours come rain or shine; often my wife would descend

44 Duma being ridden in author's colours

45 Debby, the winner with Duma, in author's colours

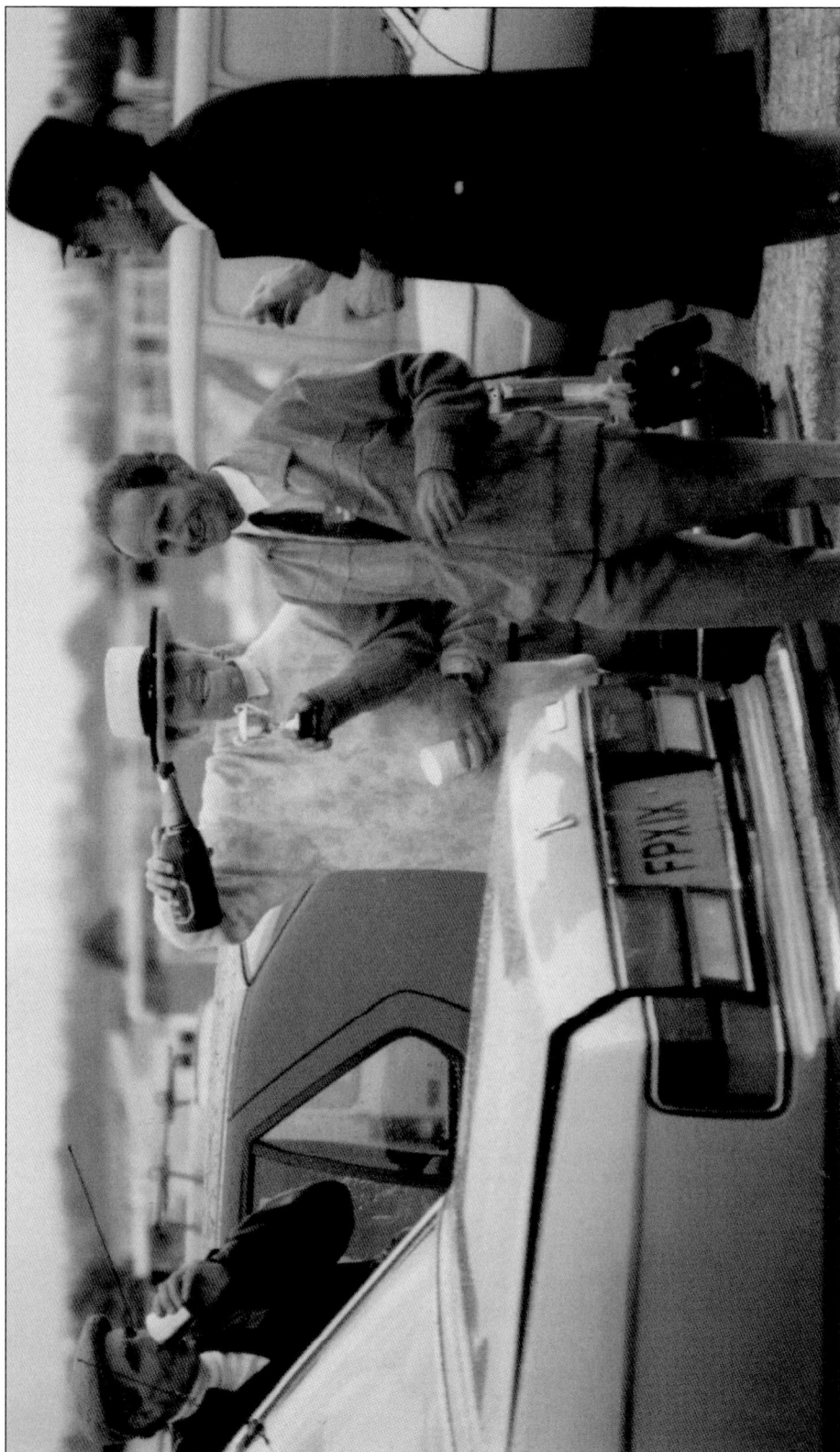

46 Fakenham 1990. Author, Debby, Clive and Cliff celebrating Duma's win. Big Bottle – Small Cup!

47 *Our stables for thoroughbred race horses at Chantilly*

48 *Our Russian Arab Duma, with foal, paddock Little Langley Farm*

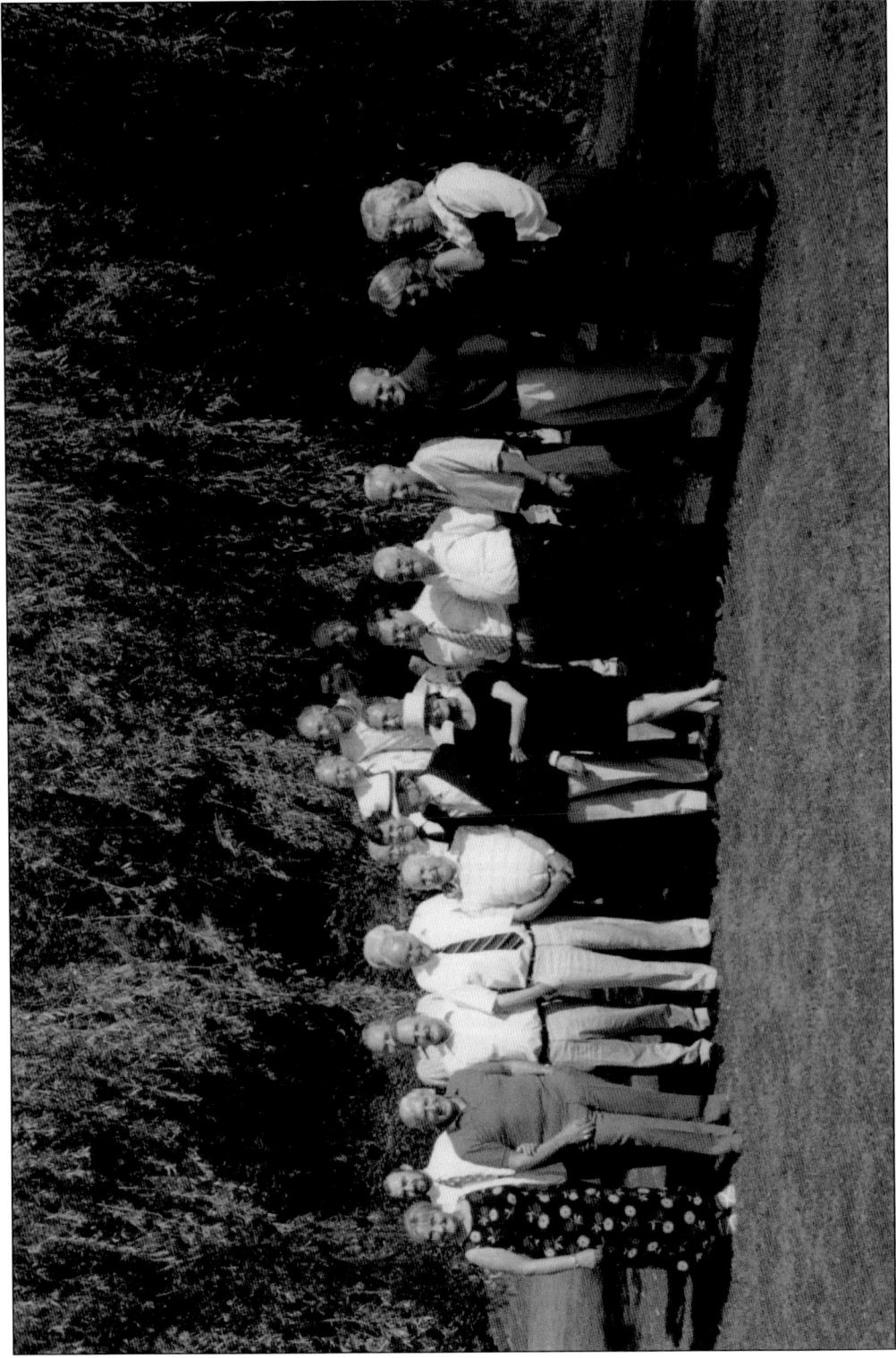

49 Employees at my open day at Little Langley Farm with me and my wife

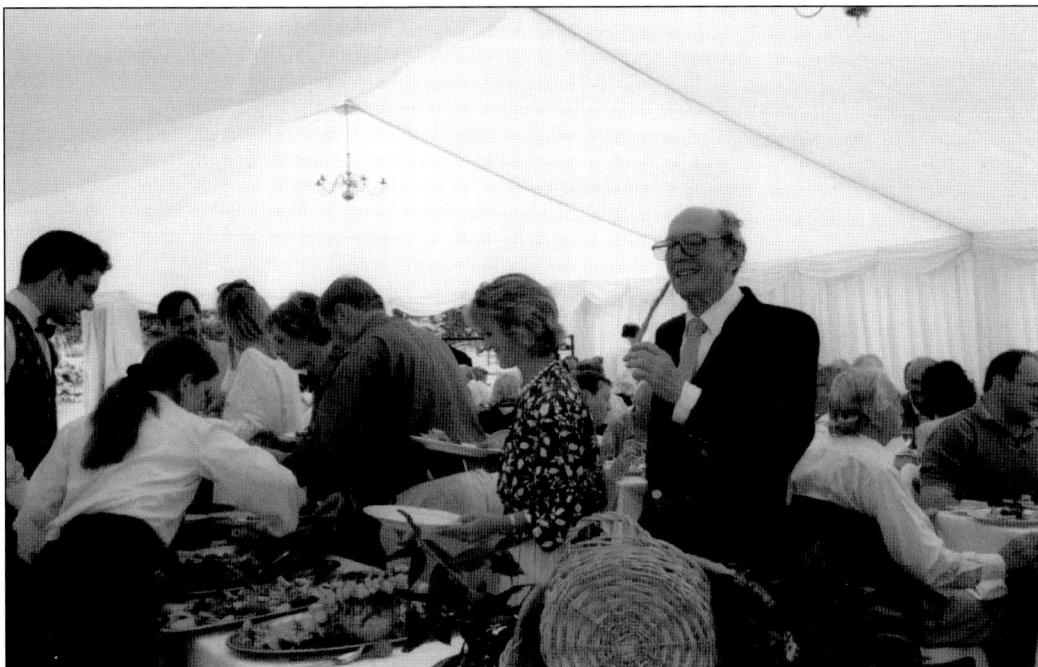

50 In the evening all were fed

51 My daughter Gayle leaving our oyster lunch on the way to Ashford Castle near my factory at Balinrobe

52 The author

53 *Walking back from the church service in celebration of the Battle of Britain. Author third from right*

54 The RAF Cranwell College Band, leading Parade of Cadets, Battle of Britain Sunday, viewed from Saluting Base

55 RAF College Cranwell, author seated second from right, next to AVM's wife. Saluting Base, Battle of Britain Parade

on my part of the bank with a lovely fresh tasty picnic hamper and we would sit down together to feast among the glorious green foliage by the water.

On the Meon, one school half term holiday I taught Roger to fish by the fast entry near the mill. He caught his first brown trout single-handed, through the air to land on the grass bank for his own dinner later the same night. The excitement was immense and so was the outcome of great fishing tales to later arrive from his rod.

Soon I was to leave the very good times on the Meon for other clear large chalk streams, by becoming a member of the oldest fly fishing club of England: the famous exclusive Piscatorial Society with fishing on the rivers Itchen, Test, Avon off Salisbury Plain with the fabulous small Wyle river of renown in the west. I also was to fish the River Kennet which runs through my son's school. All these rivers are trout fisheries but of course there is the need to cut reeds and weeds to ensure clean oxygenated pure fast running water. Out of season we fished for grayling, and of course the ferocious pike who would be pleased to eat all fish.

In 1963 I built my ketch, a 30 ft single diesel auxiliary yacht, moored on the Hamble River so sailed to the Solent and Channel harbours, and often to the Channel Islands and France. We sometimes fished for breakfast and perhaps dinner too when at sea.

On one occasion we awoke at anchor in the estuary of the river, seaward of the French town Treguier in Brittany, and my very young daughter Doodey and son Roger took me in the dinghy to fish with our fibre glass sea rod for mackerel, and very soon we caught a cluster of fish. On landing the fish into the dinghy we also hooked our young daughter's woollen jersey which caused a pandemonium of events: whether to unhook jersey or fish first! After nearly capsizing all was well for a super fresh-cooked breakfast on board.

When in the UK, I felt I should know the rudiments of fly tying and arranging the barbed hook to meet the requirements of all seasons: for example to make sure the Mayfly looked the right attractive food or enticement for the month with no noticeable alterations for the state of the weather, particularity at dawn and dusk, when the trout rise and break the surface for all to see. The Mayfly lives for one day, or less if it meets the lonely trout seeking light, breaking the surface. I was not successful as I did not have the patience or time to learn from the purchase of more professional imitations of trout fly deception, hence I packed up trying. However for the rest of my life I find it necessary to sense the trout's desire in whatever the weather, to choose an appropriate fly.

I recall the tranquil soft languid night aboard my yacht in Newtown River, such an exquisite situation alone on the Solent side of the Isle of Wight. One went to sleep listening to the ripples of water making a relaxing angel rhythm alongside the wooden hull. In this so peaceful slumber there was absolutely nothing to hold you back from beyond.

Nevertheless in the early dawn chorus I was awakened by a crunching sound of surprise, to find a yachtsman scraping alongside to an abrupt halt, to ask if he might leave his ship for a few minutes to fish for his breakfast. In my early dream mind I tied his warps fast and off he went, procured his fish, ate breakfast and set course on his voyage to the blue ocean deep. He was a lone sailor who happened to find the tide right for entry to our river, then he departed before becoming helpless without sufficient tidewater to avoid running aground on the sand base of the river.

Needless to say I went without my expected breakfast gift fish for his time to fish was very limited, but the family were now all awake. I thought of fishing for breakfast but no: we were hungry for my wife's special cooked kippers from Scotland.

I was thinking differently, of fresh oysters of Morans of the Weir, near Galway, so fresh, above the cream succulent taste of the sea. I was lost for words after my friend's departure without any fish for me after holding his ship.

I have explained before that Newtown in the ripe old days sent members to our Parliament and was a busy influential base but today it is a perfect haven of outstanding natural beauty. Today, the harvested shellfish are all exclusively exported to France for the top premier tables.

I often think of the Great Fraser River, the part in Kamloops, Western Canada, and browse over the wild salmon retuning from the northern seas, where they migrated from their first taste of the sea from downriver north of Canada where they were born, reared to a smolt, then went down river as yearlings yearning to taste the shrimp and plankton. They migrated to the rich cold water streams of the northern seas. The Atlantic salmon back for its sojourn in the northern seas adjacent to Greenland and Iceland without waiting proceeds up river, hungry to its birth place to spawn anew.

On this great Fraser River, the largest salmon river of North America, the salmon, a dark reddish colour, were gambolling and turning the river into large frothy pools, impatiently waiting for the rains to come and allow them to swim upstream to their birthplace so to renew the life cycle.

I fished many times Loch Corrib from Ashford Castle near Cong, Southern Ireland, sometimes with my family or friends in a boat with my ghillie friend in charge of the expedition. We tried to catch brown trout, or salmon returning fresh from the sea; salmon we did not catch but trout of different sizes we nearly always caught whether rain or shine. Sometimes, depending on the season, we would use a daddy-long-legs as bait, other times a wet fly.

Always wind, rain or shine we would moor up to an island with Celtic burial grounds of which there were many, for luncheon, to step ashore, light a fire and cook our trout in leaves or herbs to eat with the picnic hamper brought along with us. The meal, sometimes large but most of the time small, was always so good and welcome with a full glass of Guinness or Gorrib Loch diluted Bush Mills whiskey. Fishing in the afternoon was normally a confirmed no-catch with home early for tea, easily in time for our candlelight dinner in the evening.

Near the castle was the end of the watershed Loch Cong, where the salmon life was seriously protected until the yearling set off for the sea through the sixty miles of the loch, normally in one day. I had a close fisherman friend in Durford Wood whose father owned the sea entrance fishing rights of Loch Gorrib, but kindly allowed all fish to return to spawn.

The same cycle of birth affects all species, but the salmon are most prolific in their demand and growth. I need to say that human greed or commercial quest for easy profit concerns the south coast of Ireland near the lovely green country of Kilarney, where the commercial nets are spread across the sea bay to trap the acres of salmon returning from the rich northern seas, to collect lorryloads of fresh salmon to sell to France and elsewhere. Yes I know! For I have witnessed the dying beautiful courageous salmon being loaded from the cruel trap nets set without a thought for the future natural inheritance of the wild.

May I again repeat this part of my story by telling you how I introduced my very young daughter to the small English River Rother flowing near my house in Durford Wood, West Sussex.

The normal Sunday's weather permitting, my daughter would collect my neighbour's dog Peter. The dog was larger than she, also very much older. My daughter would meet me on the footpath leading from my house to the fields below; we would set off together through the willowy tall grass, buttercups and bluebells. I would play hide and seek, hide totally by falling down through the tall grass at the side of the path, dog as well, but sometimes my daughter found him difficult to conform. The atmosphere was electric with the silence of captivating nature.

Nevertheless we stayed perfectly quiet to listen to the birds and nature for a minute or so, then we would jump up to continue and stop again some five minutes or so further on until we arrived at the steep little horse bridge over the swift flowing clear River Rother. Underneath the arches we would look for the sign of trout, and after the fun of finding nothing we would set for home, with roughly the same procedure as on the way out, so all would arrive exhausted and ready for lunch, Peter too!

On another occasion at the Gleneagles Hotel, Auchterarder, Scotland, I was on a business trip with John, my son's best friend, still working in PR and sales for me. We stayed in the two best rooms, mine exactly above the immaculate curved garden. The hotel was not full on this quiet misty cold wintry day, with no golf. We therefore booked, through the concierge, to fly fish the river Tay the next day for salmon, with two professional anglers with hired equipment, waders, rods, nets and advice as to the best part of the river to achieve a sparkling fresh salmon to cook for our dinner later that day.

Off we went full of hope and met our anglers at their fishing lodge. We took a long time to get kitted out, owing to our fumbling through the difficult sizes of clothing, somewhat old and worn out by my standards.

However, we settled down to fish at our appointed beats and I started casting my wet fly. John was not quite so experienced and his first cast landed over the river and hooked a mature bush on the opposite bank. After a certain amount of effort and much hesitation as to what to do, it was solved by his angler's brute force and assistance breaking the line. The effort looked more as if it would break the rod and I thought of my own split cane rods which would not stand this sort of treatment.

At this time both our waders seemed to be leaking and I was feeling rather cold after my little effort to feel for a salmon. It was now nearly time for lunch, so we returned to the fishing lodge to disrobe and we all jumped into my car. Still wearing damp socks, we all migrated to the local inn to warm ourselves.

The first question I was asked was: 'Would you have Grouse?' 'Yes,' I replied. The same was asked of John who replied, 'No, I hate the stuff,' followed by, 'What else is there to eat?' Naturally the rest of us laughed! I explained, which promoted further laughs with a repeat Grouse. We all settled down to above average haggis settled with a little Drambuie. Although no fish were caught we all parted sincere friends; strangely, later the same evening we were introduced to two dinner companions to view and partake of the fresh salmon they had caught a few hours earlier.

The next family occasion was when for the first time I collected the whole family together for a fishing initiation at a fishing lodge in Bibury, Gloucestershire, where the river runs sparklingly full of large brown trout through the town for all to see. I purchased a carbon fibre rod for each member of the family, and we assembled on the river bank to receive our expert tuition; however I was the only one dressed properly to fish and the only one that seemed interested in casting and fishing. I caught a trout, but nobody else seemed interested in stopping talking to fish with the expert, who also seemed interested in talking along with my wife and all. Of course I think the situation peculiar, no one interested in learning to fish except Roger who had set off to use his new split cane 8½ foot Hardy rod away from the talkative crowd. I still have my rods to this day with all the equipment too! My twelve rods still give me extraordinary enjoyment and pleasure to see assembled, lying loose and flat ready to pack and use again.

My fishing story finishes, perhaps apart from catching lobsters in a restaurant in Aberdeen, Hong Kong, and elsewhere, finding and cooking shrimps from the sea off the beach in south England with my wonderful girlfriend just after World War II who became my wife.

Of course I have not told you about my experiences as a member of the oldest and greatest fishing society club of England. The people come from all walks of life and mostly are expert fishermen, who also try hard to help beginners to prosper on their experience for the club's waters and wherever they meet. You must always respect the advice of your elders who are profoundly interested in fishing and the fish.

Whilst my twelve rods, mostly split cane, still conjure my thoughts to breathe my past pleasure I have now given away my waterproof leather shoes with studs for the soft muddy banks with my special lightweight reel manufactured with my initials clearly etched for all time, together with my favourite flies for special occasions according to the seasons' change and feel of the running clear water, whether large swift flowing river, bubbling burn, sea outlet loch or land locked spring lake.

My personal favourite best loved venue is the River Meon where I knew intimately the whole river from the bubbling tiny chalk spring source alongside the lovely green interesting road at East Meon, and flowing forty-odd miles though the Hampshire country-side via pool and rapid, gurgling and frothing to the sea near the old village of Tichfield, to my favourite part of the English Channel where I sailed as well as fished.

My flying boots were black outside and sheepskin lined and were appropriate with or without my similarly lined one-piece suit. We had to try to stay warm for there were no heaters in the aircraft or for that matter no heaters in cars or in many houses. We took this equipment around with us, but not for my journey in the United States.

One became very involved with such good boots for they kept your feet warm and snug flying and moving about the wooden huts for meals and preparation for operations. I have already related the story about the damage to my boot during my *Bismarck* trip.

My left foot flying boot had a hole in it and although the sole of my foot was damaged it was the end of operations for my dear pair of flying boots, but I kept them in my baggage for future proof of my story about the battle.

The next problem the flying boots were faced with was when they got wet. Their normal storage was in the cupboard in my dressing room. I had moved into Little Langley farm, a twelfth century building which was much admired for its fairylike architecture, with a half oak timbered façade that was so uneven but weathered so well, giving a 'welcome home' look to all as it was approached along a drive with a twist to show one's vista.

Before settling into this beautiful building of ships' timbers possibly from Bucklers Hard shipyard (ships of the line being repaired or replaced always provided an abundance of timbers for naval officers to procure and these timbers together with some fossil oak structures formed the basic structure of the farmhouse), I needed to carry out some internal alterations. My architect who was an expert in Elizabethan and Mediaeval property created a bathroom cum dressing room adjoining my large bedroom and library. It was perfect for me. I was happy to put my preserved flying boots underneath my morning clothes that I seemed to be wearing less and less as time went on. One day I was called to my dressing room which was under water, for someone had left a tap running and it could not go to waste for this was blocked with a swallow's nest.

I quickly disposed of the water, but to my horror three or four inches of water had accumulated in my flying boots which to me looked like a disaster. I started to dry them out with a towel or two. After they were dry of the surplus water I placed them to slowly dry and after a few days I carried out an inspection. I could see some discolouration of the sole of the left boot and today it is still slightly discoloured. To me the cannon shot hole still looks the same as it was but I cannot be sure. I now preserve my flying boots where they cannot get wet, underneath my tie rack on the floor to be seen in my now new dressing room. They still are full of special newspapers to preserve the fur but I do apologise for putting my boots through the awful calamity and trust I will continue to let them slowly rest on their honour in peace.

CHAPTER 22

New life and fine dining

SHOPPING WAS ANOTHER DUTY TO mention for the way we had to tackle it. When living in London it was easy, for everything was on hand, with all the assistance we needed to cope with a young family. I personally had little to do except for business. The raw materials for the company were all subject to a government Board of Trade Licence thus needed prior approval. On the written application we needed to state the amount of the order and the cost for the licence and if necessary provide the cash with the order requirement instructions per total or programme delivery, providing our request to the foreign supplier was accepted.

The country's economy was very bad indeed. Foreign currency was quite rightly in short supply; however my company and its potential to save foreign currency, particularly US dollars, was remarkable and we were to be congratulated by the Government for our zealous response to the need to help the country free from its straitjacket of no free currency to negotiate with at all. Our potential to export for hard currency was appreciated to help fight the tight situation, so officials took time to help us through the littered bureaucracy of government who had spent all our money to fund our earlier alone World War II victory, latterly with profound thanks for American help.

I had little need for personal shopping and I don't think my wife had either for there were few new fashionable clothes and luxury to buy and time was needed to catch up on the presents I brought home during the war from North America.

We were still partly on rations: for instance two eggs a week, or an ounce or two of butter a week or month, but we did very well and had sufficient for our needs both young and adult. As trade improved we found London was a great place to shop and on moving to Surrey things rapidly got better and attractive for window shopping once more. My wife and I always thought of Knights-bridge, London, for our needs; I still do to this day for I combine the trip with doctor, hospital consultants, dentist, periodontic and the like. The necessity to stay up on business at a hotel or later in our own place in relation to business activity which was always at full stretch, was exhausting if carried on late with perhaps entertaining for foreign visitors or maybe those from Scotland or Ireland with an early morning appointment next day.

My two separated wives both thought my life business–orientated to the extreme, so in the latter years I have revisited alone and must say I sadly miss all the appointments made for me with the personal attendance of my first wife who today lives in peace on the south coast and we often meet.

My second wife did no such appointments for me at all and after a bit I had to catch up on her own appointments mainly due to horse racing which frankly I did not really appreciate at all. She now lives happily not in France but in a delightful country village nearby in Sussex but we have never met since our departure, thank goodness, for she might find it difficult to return my goods, sentimental items from my youth and my genuine property taken from a gentleman who forgives but never forgets.

Leaving the Royal Air Force in 1945 was a great decision for me for you remember I was desperate to join the service during my last year at school; however I was denied this privilege at this time. I was lucky, I suppose, to set course with an opportunity to join Bakelite without knowing the way my future was pointing. I did not know I would have the invitation of a life contract with the company. Another future was my supposed life contract with the Royal Air Force though I would have needed entry through Cranwell College for officer flight training, to progress to Air Chief Marshal of the service. Is it strange or not that neither programme was completed?

Bakelite was a destination caused by the denial of the Royal Air Force and although during the conflict of World War II I had operational flying duty and the opportunity to qualify as specialist 'N' for navigation, the requirement met for a permanent commission, it was too late to be the Marshal I had hoped for. I had missed the Royal Air Force college entry: in my opinion a specific aristocratic order of merit needed.

My progress with Bakelite was unique without a University degree; I became a considered expert on the manufacture of phenol formaldehyde synthetic resins with their new success for industry. On return from service duty I felt there was no way I could achieve my goal of a top company senior executive for I felt war service was not accepted as a natural absence of duty from a reserved occupation, so I was not happy about my future. A little later at the first opportunity I took myself to prove that I could use my skill and knowledge to work for myself.

Thus my life story continued from 1945. I married my lovely girlfriend Lilian who was a beautiful seventeen years old when we met in 1939/40 for the first time in the south of England. We were married in the Episcopal Church in Glasgow in 1943; at the time she serving in the fire service. I was the new squadron leader who used to fly from Iceland to meet her occasionally when the need for new engines and green vegetables were desired. Shortly after the wedding ceremony my chief attendant, an excellent flying officer friend, went missing without word; he is not forgotten.

My wife's family were located in Crieff, a little further north. Her father was a retired rubber planter from Malaya who had moved from the south coast because of the war civil directions. My wife was the middle daughter of three with two brothers both ex Army officers, one from the war in Italy, the other escaping from Dunkirk.

My mother and father attended the wedding from Warwickshire. My father was a retired papermaker manager. I had one elder sister, Nancy, and a younger brother, Jim, who too was an ex Army officer from anti aircraft defence. My sister was looking after her beloved husband who was in the Bakelite reserved occupation because I had introduced him to my sister prior to the war.

The wedding was a well organised by a generous aunt who seemed to have a lot of champagne with good Scottish food for the piped reception, leaving little time to catch the overnight express train to London, with a dry Icelandic bottle of Drambuie I had obtained from the Officers' Club, with us but not to drink until after arrival.

In 1946 I was living in a north London mews a little distance from Sherlock Holmes' fictional abode within a stone's throw of the lovely Regent's Park. We spent many happy hours there with our new daughter Dianne Gayle and my wife's friends. Our life was quite hectic with many visits from relatives and friends although our mews was quite small over the old stable, converted into a large garage.

The entrance ascended from the ground floor culminating in a very small gallery hall at the top of the stairs, to lead into the chintzy furnished drawing room, with fitted furniture, then through to a small fitted kitchen with the usual white goods or through to our king size bedroom. Both rooms had bay windows and were heated from below. Our daughter who was about one year old slept in a fabric covered cot, similar in shape to Admiral Nelson's cot, and a four-wheel Crown perambulator by day in Regent's Park sometimes in the kind charge of a distant relative's nurse, always in long black dress nearby, with a cheeky red-tufted green parrot saying to everybody, 'How do you do?' including my little daughter who recalls the Polly chatter to this day.

On my decision to go to work alone I was allowed certain times in the kitchen to mix chemical raw materials and cure my formula base by heated oven to prepare for my business adventure. Later I transferred my efforts to a rented railway arch premises near Marylebone railway terminal. My wife did not complain of my science endeavours, but did say on my departure that she was surprised I had not injured us with such a repugnant chemical perfume. I must agree it was a lot to ask for I felt the toxic taste of formaldehyde too, for many days after I had stopped the small experiments.

The winter arrived with quite a different scene, with snow so heavy we could not see across the cobbled mews courtyard or shop until the situation changed by snow plough or temperature. Snow and ice covered Regent's Park. Occasionally the sun appeared to make the scene of sparkling pure white trees and bushes with a spreading thick blanket over paths and grass, while a few heavily clothed people tried to break the lake edge ice to feed the many ducks who were skating about like clumsy maidens with no feet. All of us needed something hot like steaming punch at the local inn. The winter passed and I was almost blind to the change for I was out of the mews in the dark and returned in the dark, just like the old days, flying across the deep obscure cold Atlantic Ocean with no alternative but to wish for brighter times.

Spring arrived and bright colours emerged, seeming like magic: a new dawn with brighter warmer days flooding in for all to admire and feel before the April showers came to surprise us with some dull interludes to make sure we did not take the good times for granted.

I continued to be pleased with my work and with my two assistants, old service friends in need for themselves, so essential to a good quality start, with my first petty cash book taking all the items of expenditure on one side adjacent to all the incoming items of credit the other side. Only a little work was needed for accountancy so to give me full time manufacturing marketing progress.

My wife was busy too! Our little daughter was speaking some words I did not understand; however she smiled profusely, to prove she was very happy with her creative environment, with such devoted personal attention. It reminds me of when she was born in 1945 at Looe, Cornwall and arrived home on the cliff leading to the beach and sea in the arms of my dear wife to our country seaside house, full of oceans of bright yellow daffodils in the entrance, garden, nursery, entrance hall and drawing room. It was a fantastically beautiful regal display never forgotten by my daughter to this day. Her March birthday always has a display of many daffodils; of course it is the spring season yellow extravaganza of early daffodils.

It seemed out of the blue to me. Suddenly my wife said, 'I am ready for my new baby,' and everything went into panic stations. We got the doctor to take her to hospital and nothing happened for an hour or two; she then came home with a little boy, our son Roger, on 13 February 1948. They both settled quickly into a nice slumber with me in sole charge of the family of four.

The time passed quickly if a little hectic but soon we were pleased to leave our little darling mews to arrive in a beautiful terrace property in magnificent gardens of rural Epsom, and settled in to a room each.

We collected various odd pieces of furniture and kitchen equipment from different relatives to get started so we could obtain our own over the time of settling in. My wife was very busy with two children and me off to London each day in the early morning and arriving home well after dark.

We were so pleased with our move for things were going well. The business was booming with our product, so advanced as to be nine times as good as the best USA competitor, and I now looked for much larger premises. The family was not growing up entirely without me, for I made a point of taking time off to add up to a weekend of a day or two, so we enjoyed a wonderful course of family life, pointing to the stars. Soon we had a car to move around in and enjoy nature's seasons away from home.

Through the courtesy of some members, I joined the impressive Automobile Club on the Epsom Downs, where Nancy with her two boys had decided to live. The Derby comes each year to draw massive numbers of revellers each time, making the Downs almost inconspicuous under the fun time. Mind you I have also enjoyed the privilege of a race box, with all in good black morning dress and hard hat with a flower rosette.

The years living near Epsom were always exciting. You could play golf on the little downs course; I can only say it was very good for practice. My sister would say, 'I find the course challenging to test your ability to play.' I replied, 'And what is your handicap?' She said, 'Thirty-six, what is yours?' to which I replied, 'Twenty-four.' Nevertheless it is a beautiful course, a mixture of heather and chalk subsoil and a piece of historic England.

I did play a lovely course near Leatherhead with my solicitor who was prepared to fire away with no practice and see the ball a few yards away for his second shot. I did spend a little time with the club professional and I could hit a beauty over the hill. It did not impress my solicitor who was now looking for his ball only a few feet away.

My wife and I were fast moving into Europe and the USA for it was my intention to follow up my lone visit with my partner to Belgium, France and Germany where we established the initial stages of raw material purchase, competitive production and possible sales to key portable tool operators or very worth while companies willing to drop their so called clever tactics, to try and achieve elimination of a company in superior development progress, some in Germany and Italy but mainly in the USA.

Europe was in a rubble-like state and had yet to recover from World War II devastation; the roads were difficult to negotiate for distance yet once a year we would prepare a major journey to include Christmas, starting from Hoek van Holland, and through Holland and Belgium to arrive at Cologne for a meeting before making Siegen, a very important licence with prospective new technical quality.

The second visit included Dianne Gayle and Roger and on stopping near our destination they spied a frozen pond on top of the low mountain overlooking the valley. While we stopped for a breather they were so excited, trying to beat each other by not falling down, while slipping everywhere on the ice in leather shoes. After Germany with the fellow who would not talk to me, for he had been wounded by the British, yet who was vital to the visit success, we continued to Austria and skied at Obergurgl for Christmas in glorious deep crisp snow. Then we departed to Ferrara, Italy, and on to Milan, Paris then the ferry home. It was a good journey but a little tedious with only a few motorways to break the slow traffic lines.

The journeys to the United States commenced with my Bakelite friend helping, for money was difficult. I paid it back later and with her Oldsmobile it was pretty plain sailing for New York City then Toronto, flying by Stratocruiser or Constellation via Shannon. The business done was well worth the effort but I would have to wait a while for the De Havilland Comet to appear to tame the Atlantic pond.

The housekeeper, Mrs Wright, who looked after us while my wife was ill proved a welcome additional loving member of the family and lived with us some thirty-odd years, until well past retirement age, before retiring to her loving daughter whose husband had recently joined the permanent sick list of the Royal Air Force, now living permanently in his nightmare of releasing his wounded crew from the flames of his burning aircraft during a bomber raid over Germany in World War II when hit and damaged by enemy fire.

Soon we were on the move again, Roger determined to provide his packed lunch each day to eat with the old fellow tending the large surrounding gardens. Sometimes he dressed in my uniform, just the jacket, for it was nearly larger than himself and this ritual carried on until he went to his first school. Dianne Gayle was well into her junior school and was doing splendidly both academically and with her dancing. Later my wife and I started travelling again, and the children would always meet us for lunch on our return.

Visits to the USA were made by Cunard liners to ease the time, but the transatlantic aircraft, particularly Pan American Airways, despite the flavour of the dynamic Mr Howard Hughes, were now not so primitive, somewhat more comfortable and took a shorter time without so many fuelling points.

Europe was easier now we were skiing at Gstaad, Wengen and Davos, by driving though Germany via Liechtenstein; or in San Moritz with Breuil-Cervinia a favourite in Italy, mostly driving from Milan or Turin then climbing through the Valle d'Aosta. We went mostly at Christmas time when the new colder weather provided a special flavour of pure white snow and jingle bells. The car, with no chains possible, always behaved well, negotiating the roadside grit and pebbles before sea salt was used, now often the better alternative. The skis were safe above our heads lending a romantic accessory for us all, even when our new very young second daughter Doodey decided to join the jolly family throng.

The summer holidays were influenced by our friends, with my wife taking the choice; twice we had a holiday with our doctor and his wife who were friends. We played golf every day with our trailing children who helped to find or lose the balls, whilst we serious parents manoeuvered the sun-scorched fairways of a beautiful seascape golf links very near St David's Head, for two fantastically full swinging shining hot sun summers for some long weeks in both years.

We embarked with my wife's brother Robert's family, the fellow who had resigned from my original partnership to join his wife's father's estate to shoot, fish and hunt and become a full time country gentleman, for a wonderful holiday at Formentora, Spain, for two years in succession complete with a boat, car and of course the fabulous weather, beach and sea food as only the Spanish provide, to grace their beautiful summer skies.

Sometimes we stayed at home and invited family friends – in fact Roger's friend John stayed for two years – come rain and shine but mostly they frolicked without help and programme fixtures. Later the swimming pool was a great help to us all and satisfied our instincts for the sea. After our two boats disappeared all were growing up to be independent. Later tennis came into being and we programmed all family tournaments, but we were not the best or even near so tennis floundered. I was pleased for I only needed to repair the surrounding netting and eventually cultivated heather on the banks around.

I was still in communication daily with business, wherever I was located. It was also an eventful way of life to me. There was no way anybody, however important, could influence my necessary com-munications; it was vital to my clear thinking of the future. Why, you may ask? I part lived my life, as a live cell of the chemical reaction of my synthetic resin formulation; it tilted my mind and it was natural to want to understand the life and intensity of the chemical reaction progress of my future components before they ended their life plus all the reactions necessary for the comfortable final thermosetting feature.

Time moved on and we changed houses from London to Surrey to Middlesex to Portsmouth and then near Petersfield in Hampshire.

Life was never dull for a split second. We somehow included occasional nights out in London at Annabel's, the famous exclusive members' London night rendezvous, and other meeting points: Harrods, Simpson's, and Fortnum & Mason, always for Christmas puddings.

We visited first class good restaurants such as the Rib Room for Aberdeen Angus beef, the Carlton Tower Hotel, Knightsbridge, my firemen's station for business and meetings; Le Coc D'or in Stratton Street that changed its name to the notable Langhams Bistro with Mr Langham in supreme and total vintner atmospheric command. Until he gave up the chase, you could sit at Michael Caine's head of table seat, if he was absent, if you thought it a desirable feature for your bistro style meal. The fame of chief chef and owner Mr Dick Shepherd, a friend of my friend and my elder daughter, has now spread far and wide, including on the English Channel ferries.

Le Cavroche was used for my more very formal appointments for lunch. It was initially in Sloane Street, but now in Park Street off Park Lane or Grosvenor Square, for a dry martini stirred but not shaken before a serious game or venison main course if in season; there are many more.

In the countryside I think of the old partner and brother of Mr Roux's of Le Cavroche, Mr Michael Roux's Waterside Inn on the Thames at Bray, for superlative French food whilst seeing the water eddies, perhaps froth sparkling white now and then.

I would go to Cliveden Court, famed for Miss W's some time ago lurid sex history involving our Government's war minister with a Russian General spy, for a stunning dinner, politely served with seasonal game, after an aperitif of a real cold drink, not iced: pink gin with a bent sliver of outer bright lemon peel.

Stoke Poges' Country Club had a wonderfully creative golf course plus generous facilities for great feasting and wine. This was where my wife's elder brother Ian played golf with his very low handicap sons, so entertained us often with great care.

Further afield are many more interesting places to visit and eat a wholesome meal or, with a Michelin star, a delicate superb French–English repast of quality, similar to my local JSW where Jake serves my usual first course of warm fresh fois gras, an onion belini or perhaps black pudding with a suitable friendly taste, but not haggis of course.

I must not forget the stunning, sometimes most superb, small cosy inns, such as The Links, just off the tenth green on the heather blessed local course in Hampshire for country fare with beer by the pint or perhaps, say, French or New World wine by the glass or decanter. The inn landlord, Richard, used to call at my home in time for lunch on Sundays when my son was around, for my wife's great weekly meal of tender roast sirloin of beef with me often cooking the miraculous fruit dessert at the table for all the guests that day.

Overseas food is interesting and here are a few places I always enjoy to stay and eat, though the best of all is Les Prés d'Eugénie, at Eugénie Les Bains in south-west France where Michel Guerard's restaurant last served me out of this world delicate lobster of exquisite taste. The whole menu is not massive and always simple with really delicate aromas tempting you to taste.

There are plenty more such as the Petit Nice off the JFK auto route out of Marseille. It is a superb fresh seafood restaurant. I last had the best lamb I have ever tasted, sitting at my table in the best ever sea view restaurant room of the south coast, under my sleeping room, with stunning views from three sides and if you wish the subtle music of the waves will stray you to dreamland. I have already recommended it for Michelin 3 stars and it possesses three stars today.

My second honeymoon to Paris was by helicopter to Maxim's as I always made my first meal stop there to eat their finest tender rare to medium Scottish beef fillet. The restaurant still uses the metro whisperings to stir for favourite table aperitifs.

Similarly my invariable first stop in New York City was at the 21 Club for English roast beef maybe not with Yorkshire pudding but perhaps a baked jacket potato and perhaps horseradish sauce but certainly with French red wine.

I cannot finish – I love good food but I must – without mentioning Doyles of Sidney Harbour for the best fish and chips ever. It is world famous in Australia too! It is just out from the clear blue sea just below your feet with a dark blue sky and shining warm sun overhead.

My wife shopped almost entirely in London, including a little theatre or show when my business necessitated a London address; we eventually rented a house in Huntsworth Mews and later bought an apartment in the Boltons. I was also a member of three Clubs – the Royal Thames Yacht Club, the Royal Air Force Club and the Royal

Automobile Club — to rest, eat and enjoy fellow members' recreation conversation away from all time consuming business.

In 1963 came my merger with the oldest abrasive company, John Oakey & Sons Ltd, on the site of its famous old steam engine, adjacent to Waterloo railway station, that now attracted visitors from all around the world to witness the steam of the early industrial revolution gleaming gold in action.

My wife and I enjoyed our stay in the Blue Suite of the Dorchester Hotel, Park Lane, whilst I worked on the weak staff merger and considered the present sales record equal to that at the turn of the century, leading to my retirement in 1965.

Looking back, our main great joy was in our lovely Camberley home with my wife having our new beautiful daughter Julie Jackson, nicknamed Doodey, born 11 December 1956 at the busy time when I was involved with my company in Portsmouth.

Apart from home at Durford Wood, the education of our family, their great times at the various schools and colleges, their activities took first place but did involve meeting interesting friends and tutors who became famous. We steamed through different family cars of all kinds, each person looking for the best one for their own activity; I welcomed every member of the family to an interest in the sea, via my ketch *Doodey Gay* and powerboat *Kinswift*.

Out of the blue we were hit by the death of our only son, Roger, in 1974. To this day none of us can forget this. The changing world since has not diminished our sorrow at all; in fact one can say it makes it all so difficult to understand.

The family, I am pleased to say, today are deeply in touch with each other, although somewhat scattered in Europe. They will help each other in difficulty and offer the entire help needed.

CHAPTER 23

Princess Diana concert

O N I JULY 2007 I spent most of the showery afternoon into the
evening and night watching the TV concert in memory of the
princes' dear mother, who on this day would have been forty-six
years old but who unfortunately died ten years ago.

I was in Buckingham Palace on the day of her wedding,
Wednesday 29 July 1981, and witnessed Prince Charles leaving for
St Paul's Cathedral and later the dream return of the bride and
bridegroom as the Prince and Princess of Wales. I later observed the
huge crowd of delighted wellwishers waiting to welcome the happy
pair on the Palace balcony as well as cheering myself. It was for me
a momentous occasion of pure delightful happiness.

The rift of the marriage vows upset so many, including myself. My
younger daughter was on the staff at Buckingham Palace and travelled
with the Prince and Princess to many places, including Australia and
Canada. After the break, my daughter departed the Palace staff, to be
later recalled to similar duties before and after the marriage of Prince
Andrew with Sarah as the Duke and Duchess of York. Her job did
not last long for on leave for a holiday in Greece, my daughter
became in love with and married a fine and noble Greek mathema-
tician; his domain is Pythagoras.

Princess Diana, as we all know, did many good deeds, for any poor
soul or child, and died to the profound disappointment of the nation
and world. My sorrow was great and I flew the Blue Ensign from my
sailing yacht at half mast at my home for the period of mourning. I
should also mention my two young oak trees, I believe grown by the
Duke of Edinburgh from acorns of Windsor Great Park's old
magnificent oaks, which are very visible as you drive through on the
Parkway to or from Windsor.

The two young oaks were delicately conveyed to me by a dear
friend direct from the nursery at Windsor and presented to me for
my planting, to help replace the oak trees lost in the hurricane of 16
October 1987.

The trees then uprooted included oak trees which were planted too close to other trees so could not spread their branches to develop into their beautiful spreading shape.

I decided therefore to place these two very young Windsor oaks in the middle of my beautiful spacious south paddock between the haha after the lawn near the house and the southern boundary of my land.

I made a special visit to the ancient Alice Holt forest nearby to discuss my project, for they were responsible for many oaks which were planted to build our ships of the fleet long ago for King and country and the defence of England. I wanted to be sure of matching the compost of the Windsor young oaks which were still very delicately attached to their individual acorn.

Having completed my homework, I prepared the two sites for planting, and inserted my plants with a small stick to prevent the wind interfering with their infant growth. I was determined to prevent the horses eating the very few shoots, the dogs playing hide and seek on something new or the squirrels acquiring the acorns. The moles I diverted with granulated waste electric light bulbs. First I secured a small hole wire protection net around the stick then a five bar timber boundary square five feet in width and five feet in height, followed by two layers of medium hole wire netting to stop any intruders whether humans or animals.

My two Windsor oaks survived exceptionally well; they were entitled William and Harry, to always remember Princess Diana producing a wonderful gift of life to this planet, Maybe one day someone of the Royal family will visit my two lovely Windsor oak trees which I trust will grow for hundreds of years or more, as will also their little acorns for the future of the planet Earth.

The Princess Diana Celebration Concert was presented well as a wonderful memory, especially of music and dance in the great atmosphere of the new Wembley stadium, giving, I understand, enjoyment to 63,000 attending people and relayed to 140 countries and 500 million homes.

CHAPTER 24

Problems with the new Company

L LOYDS TSB BANK: Black Horse Southern Block 31 March 2004 substantiated by a letter of 14 April 2004.

Just before my second marriage in 1984 I felt uneasy, for my lady friend, Deborah Camp, promised business reasons for our marriage, an event that I consider really should be a family affair for life with a life partner. I was however feeling a little lost without my family and thought, if I marry for the second time at the age of seventy it would be important for me to feel heartfelt for the welfare of my new wife. For health reasons we would most likely be without children and she should have London Business School education for business matters.

I asked my new wife if she wished to keep her own surname, and readily she replied, 'I would wish to be known as Camp Simpson, a combination of both family names.' It was agreed and we both changed by deed poll. My passport changed to 'H.A. Camp Simpson', with a page to say, 'also known as H.A. Simpson.'

I mention this new name as it is important to remember the effect on all matters. As far as my Clubs were concerned, I sometimes lost seniority because of some staff failure to comprehend.

With my Lloyds TSB bank account I naturally changed my private account to be Camp Simpson. My Barclays commercial account, Arrow Abrasives Ltd., stayed with Simpson. This kept the two sets of information entirely separate for legal matters, accountancy, Inland Revenue for tax, and the like.

The story commences with my quest for a manufacturing unit, producing something really worth while to occupy my mind and physical need after the death of my son in 1974; plus the partly forced sale by Barclays Bank of my wonderful twenty-eight year-old company Arrow Abrasives Ltd. in 1993 with multi-million pound sales including 40 per cent to the USA giants. This had taken place when I was seventy-nine; yet I was still full of activity to continue some hands-on work. I also needed to provide my pension requirements, as my son would have done for me.

In 1994, after an examination of a number of available small companies, I came across a small husband and wife partnership which

was in extreme financial difficulties, operating from the dining room
of their house. The excellent Polish wife was under all kinds of
pressures because of her husband's lack of business acumen. They had
private education for their two daughters and an expensive old BMW
car to run without a care in the world, working only as an assembly
hand, putting together pieces of a small component, all the time
incurring a huge daily loss, despite the professional assistance of
accountants and a Lloyds Bank account.

I was interested in their assembly of the small component clutch,
valued at £40 to £72, for I could see the component had a useful
future if expanded in value, with the objective of forming a system
of auto-motorised control for fire and killer smoke expulsion from
premises, particularly where people needed an essential safety exit. I
made arrangements to close their negative financial system and
purchase the partnership to develop my programme to a proper
budget and company.

When I left Arrow Abrasives, my situation was obviously very
clean. It was important to ensure my bankers clearly understood my
commercial position with the name Simpson as separate from my
private position with the name Camp Simpson. I opened the
commercial bank account of Electro Motive Ltd. under the name of
H.A. Simpson at Lloyds TSB on 28 July 1995.

Now I shall explain with the 'slender arm of the restless wind' the
horrific true story, the 'Black Horse Southern Block'. To me the
history is far worse than the descent of the Government's tripartite
effort, ending with nationalisation, of the mortgage bank Northern
Rock.

There is one huge difference. Northern Rock has had much
publicity with political intervention, whereas the Lloyds 'Black Horse
Southern Block' kept everything in dark secret silence even to this
day. There was also the irresponsible unauthorised meeting on 31
March 2004 that caused my unauthorised fellow director to confirm
his immediate termination with only a misty possible bank guarantee
connection.

When I had previously authorised a company overdraft, confirmed, the agreed status, as usual, included directors' guarantees. He
had already a failed partnership account with Lloyds in Dorset, while
I was organising purchase of the partnership.

In 2001 he had decided without warning to give notice to leave, to be a consultant to gain more power. The situation was settled by talking it over until an agreement was reached. I did however feel extremely doubtful of his honest intent for the future development of the company in accordance to my policy of running to strictly budget terms including a legal agreement to cover company drawings, and technical and intellectual knowledge. I had said 'no relatives while I am in charge', to avoid interference; this is normal in most efficient companies that are not initially a family affair.

I decided to approach my bankers to safeguard the company account should I be away at any time. We confirmed the procedure in the concluded letter of 21 August 2002. On 31 March 2004, the manager in control of Electro Motive Ltd decided to interview my unauthorised fellow director.

Because of the meeting on 31 March 2004, when I had been absent for only a day, this unauthorised fellow director had handed in his notice to my company office at Old Ditcham Farm Unit, Petersfield. The bank manager, a rather self opinionated person in my opinion, decided he would personally interfere with the company while I was absent. This unwise interference caused the closure of Electro Motive Ltd. For some unknown reason he had cancelled my properly authorised cheques and standing orders including the rent of the assembly premises, all without any notification to my commercial account.

The interfering action that started on 31 March was confirmed by a private Camp Simpson letter to my private address and was never destined to have a possible answer. Thus closed my vibrant, important safety company in 2004 after nearly ten years of private cash investment plus a considerable development progress of budget and hard work, with my bank commercial account opened in 1995 with a valuable product development of increasing value without any valid reason, all with no financial worry at all to the bankers.

The Bank were no doubt laughed at by my unauthorised employee, who really deceived them to set up his competitive business, Paxmatic, controlled by his twin brother, on 31 March 2004, despite Company legal agreement plus the possible MD supply of Colt International, a contract that ceased to be active for Electro Motive on 31 March 2004 as shown by the following disclosure of Paxmatic details displayed today on Google.

> Paxmatic Drives and Controls – Failsafe Drivelock Smoke Vent Drives – Paxmatic Limited designs and manufactures. All our products are also compatible with the Electro Motive Limited range.

So we notice the stealing of the ideas of Electro Motive Ltd, the designs of current equipment, intellectual knowledge and production drawings, despite legal confidential agreement, leaving my very small staff disgusted. This was all in complete disregard of the specific Bank written instructions confirmed in writing to H.A. Simpson, chairman and chief executive of Electro Motive Ltd.

I issued a Compensation Invoice dated 31 March 2004 for £499,000 plus interest to the Bank for irreparable damage done to my future earnings and pension facility, when I was ninety years old, after seventy-five years loyal bank private and commercial service.

The Bank eventually forced me to lay my complaint to the Ombudsman in 2005. Although I provided full information, the Bank supplied only part, to say the Company was in closure action and the Bank guarantees due. After six months the Ombudsman only provided a report concerning the payment of Bank overdraft guarantees.

In 2006 I dispatched a letter showing my non-acceptance of the Ombudsman report with copies to the Bank, the FSA (Financial Services Authority) and the Ombudsman. The FSA's reply ended with this advice:

> I have forwarded a copy of your letter to the area of the FSA that is responsible for supervising the firm. As advised in my email of 16 January 2007, the FSA will not be able to provide you with any feedback on what action it takes, if any, following receipt of your letter. This is because of confidentiality restrictions that are imposed on the FSA under the Financial Services & Markets Act 2000.

To me this means no teeth to do anything to its members in regard to a citizen's right to fair trading.

The Bank continued to keep all things secret about their irresponsible error of judgement and could only issue notes of the Director's Guarantee but I refused to consider the position of the Guarantee, for to me it was cancelled by their disastrous action. I later confirmed that I would prefer to go to Her Majesty's Court of Justice so the Ombudsman's notice was cancelled. Later Lloyds TSB confirmed that the Ombudsman had upheld my complaint with no correction to this day.

In view of the Bank's continual negative compensation position, I was running low on money, so with assistance from a welcome friend, I made application to HM Courts of Justice and obtained as Claimant, for Southampton County Court hearing on 23 November 2007 at a cost of £1530. The Defendant, Lloyds TSB Bank plc, employed Counsel as their legal solicitors via a senior associate Ms A.C. Wright, whilst asking for the case to be struck out owing to the Company closure on 16 November 2005.

The Defendants' Counsel and I did meet beforehand and they laughed at my absence of Counsel and forced the forward No Hearing. We then sat before the District Judge who deliberated on the question of the Company closure leaving the Directors no status to operate. The Judge did however mention my private situation and at this point I was able to speak, saying that the Lloyds TSB Bank letter of 14 April 2004 was a private letter to Mr Camp Simpson, not a commercial letter. When the Judge asked about the Bank reaction, I said the Bank had made it impossible to operate whether Company or privately, that they had forced the Company closure on 16 November 2005 when Electro Motive was enjoying a secure and wonderful future to budget.

On returning from the County Court Hearing, I received some new papers from the Defendant's solicitors relevant to my case, that had been delayed owing to a wrong address. I had therefore to write to the solicitors with copies to the Court and Lloyds TSB Bank to keep them up to date. I had not had to identify myself at the Court, so explained my passport information.

The District Judge decided that the reconvening of the court hearing was not possible as my initiative to do so was not a proper Legal Court Application, so the decision of 23 November would not change.

However, the Bank were hiding behind the false information they had received as a member of the FSA in connection with the FSA controlled authorised budget of Ombudsman and my complaint. The same happened with their false information supplied to Her Majesty's Southampton County Court, received as fact by both judicial bodies.

At present the solution seems as far away as ever, despite my age of ninety-four without a self-earned pension after seventy-five years with Lloyds Bank. Naturally the stress plays hell with my health, so that my life was threatened.

My horrific story does not end there. 'The strengthened arm of the boisterous wind' will take over what the 'slender arm of the restless wind' has achieved, with the need to find a solution for the lack of justice to right the wrongs, now costing double or treble the original invoice submitted on 31 March 2004 long before the closure date effective, within my ninety-fifth year. The obvious error in Lloyds counsel accepted evidence.

Appendices

Chris Parsons Esq.
Senior Officer
Lloyds TSB Credit Operations
Customers Service Recovery, Brighton
City Park, Three City Park
The Droveway
Hove
BN3 7AU

1 March 2009   Your ref: - CSRC/110058 a/c 30 96 61**** 7244
                      My ref:- a/c 30 96 61 00197244 by HACS- PRIVATE
                                a/c 00585619 by HAS- COMMERCIAL
Dear Mr Parsons   a/c Lloyds TSB invoice 31/03/2004+

I have your letter 06/02/2009 and note you say my complaint is only with reference to
account 30 96 61 ****7244, the statement is not true, you have received my true
complaint that concerns the unexplained small recent file I sent to you dated
23/01/2009, with the details of complaint that have been in Lloyds TSB Bank
Managers files for some time, as you know and are aware

The only problem concerning your previous letter 01/12/08 plus statements, it is
wrong in more ways than one, as you know, from your Business Manager 30
96 61, apart from the Bank manager's reckless irresponsible risky
unauthorised meeting' against the agreed Bank Business Manager's policy
that caused such Bank's disastrous results, leading to the requirement of
compensation. (Bank letter 21/08/2002 ref:AK014/ms, you have)

30 96 61 also made many other mistakes with the private account direct
debits, thus it was often necessary for me to request the list to amend, also on one
occasion the Bank returned a private cheque, with a rough written note to say I did not
have a private account for the cheque, I replied with note known, at 30 96 61 .Also an
expensive direct debit kept on being paid after expiration, resulting in Macmillan
Publishers chasing me over a large repayment after many months

One serious error, which you also fail to observe, is that all the copy statements you
sent to me with your letter 01/12/08 are labelled limit £22,500.00, with Renewal date
15/06/2002, which of course is not true, but concerns nearly 100 statements since
2002. Also should be noted the statements should have had at least two up grades in
2004 made by 30 96 61 in response to HAS/HACS requirements

Also you fail to recognise the date of my 30 96 61 cancellation of the private account
with cancellation of D/D list, naturally afterwards cancelled the income as necessary to
the private account, because of the Lloyds TSB Bank non payment of my
compensation after me writing to the Chief Executive Officer of Lloyds TSB Group.

Thereafter 30 96 61 Bank assembled charges, often repeated, to keep the private
account going, for themselves, against common sense. See Bankers code and
deliberations of OFT. Information reveals Lloyds TSB Bank refunds in 2007
amounted to £36,000,000.00.

My ref: a/c 30 96 61 00197244 by HACS-Private
a/c 00585619 by HAS- COMMERCIAL a/c
Lloyds TSB invoice 31/03/04+

Date 1 March 2009

From my information received by you with letter 23/01/2009 ref: above it is obviously clear the major Lloyds TSB Bank error was the non conformance of the Bank policy agreed between Lloyds TSB Bank and Simpson as known and confirmed by Bank letter above dated 21/08/2002 ref: AK014/ms Thus the. completely not authorised meeting 31/03/2004, caused the Bank closure of Electro Motive Ltd and the emergence of the competitive Paxmatic steal of Electro Motive information via 30 96 61 as known, thus the complete error of judgement by Bank 30 91 61 was the result of fictitious intake of clever despite caused your Bank action

My complete offer of my last letter for co-operation to solve, is still open to you, if you are capable of representing Lloyds TSB Bank otherwise I must apply elsewhere with the information within a week or so

Thank you, Sir I await your reply please, for the invoice amount has increased to over £4,000,000.00 due to my reckoning, including the obvious dangerous health factor

Yours truly

Harry A Camp Simpson aka Harry A Simpson

Please use my references when you write

DIN Deutsches Institut fur Normung e. V.

DIN

2007-06-04

Dear Mr Simpson,

We are very pleased to welcome you as a participant in the standards committee headed by DIN, the German- Institute for Standardization.

We are looking forward to your active involvement and your expertise which will make a vital contribution to maintaining the high quality of standardization.

The influence and benefits of standardization today are both significant and manifold:

- Standards are conducive to rationalization, quality assurance, environmental protection, as well as security and communication.

- Standards open up new markets for businesses, and help ensure contractual certainty.

- International standards play a fundamental role in removing barriers to trade.

- Standards have a more positive effect to the economy than do patents and licences.

You have decided to become part of the standardization success story and help it continue. We wish you every success, and look forward to working with you.

Yours sincerely

Kietat

Dr.-Ing. Peter Kiehl

P.S. Please read the enclosed information carefully.

Hausanschrift in
Berlin-Mine
BurggrafenstraQe 6
10787 Berlin

Bankverbindungen:
Ore seiner Bank AG,
BLZ100800 00,
Konto-Nr 921 676500.
IBAN: _ . .
0E88 10080000 0921676500,
S.W.I.F.T.-Code (B1C):

Deutsche Bank AG,   PostbankAG,
BLZ 100 700 00,   BLZ1001O010,
Konto-Nr 130368400 Konto-Nr. 38456-101
UST.-HM°.: .... UmsatzsteuerNr..
DE 136 622 143   27e40/50470

Mitgliedder Interr
Organisation <Qr N
(ISO) und des Eur
Komitees fur Nom.-..a√

DIN Deutsches Institut fur Normung e. V.

DIN

Protection of personal data

The standards committees and other areas of DIN, the German Institute for Standardization handle personal data. The data involved, name, first name, title, position, company, address, member status in standards committee etc. fulfil the criteria of § 3, clause 1 of the German Federal Data Protection law (BDSG).

Personal data are protected in accordance with § 28, clause 1, no.2 of the German Federal Data Protection Law (BDSG):

'The collection, storage, modification or transfer of personal data or their use as a means of fulfilling one's own business purposes shall be admissible in so far as this is necessary to safeguard justified interests of the controller of the filing system and there is no reason to assume that the data subject as an overriding legitimate interest in his data being excluded from processing or use."

For DIN "own business purposes" include the following:

- written correspondence
- distribution of proceedings of meetings and other relevant documents
- information on positioning the results of standards work in relevant sectors.

Your personal data will be stored by DIN in electronic form, and used for business and advertising purposes by DIN and its subsidiary and associated companies. You may withdraw permission for your data to be used for advertising or market research purposes at any time.

If the personal data stored by DIN include your e-mail address, this will not be used for advertising purposes by DIN or its subsidiary and associated companies without your express permission.

If you wish to be informed by e-mail by DIN and its associates about new publications, products or services, please use the registration form at www.myBeuth.de or the confidentiality declaration for DIN Livelink.